P9-CFD-569

Classical

Feng Shui

for

Romance, Sex & Relationships

About the Author

Master Denise Liotta Dennis is one of fewer than one hundred genuine Feng Shui Masters in America today. She has studied with four noted Feng Shui Masters from China, Malaysia, and Australia, including Grand Master Yap Cheng Hai, and she belongs to his four-hundred-year-old Wu Chang Pai Feng Shui Mastery lineage. Born to an entrepreneurial family, Denise possesses more than thirty years of business ownership experience and is among a rare breed of Feng Shui consultants. Denise divides her time between Scottsdale, Arizona, and her hometown of Houston, Texas.

To Write to the Author

If you wish to contact the author or would like more information about this book, please write to the author in care of Llewellyn Worldwide, and we will forward your request. Both the author and the publisher appreciate hearing from you and learning of your enjoyment of this book and how it has helped you. Llewellyn Worldwide cannot guarantee that every letter written to the author can be answered, but all will be forwarded. Please write to:

Master Denise Liotta Dennis
℅ Llewellyn Worldwide
2143 Wooddale Drive
Woodbury, MN 55125-2989

Please enclose a self-addressed stamped envelope for reply,
or $1.00 to cover costs. If outside the USA, enclose
an international postal reply coupon.

Many of Llewellyn's authors have websites with additional information and resources. For more information, please visit our website at www.llewellyn.com.

Classical
Feng Shui
for
Romance, Sex
& Relationships

Design Your Living Space for
Love, Harmony & Prosperity

MASTER DENISE LIOTTA DENNIS

Llewellyn Publications
Woodbury, Minnesota

FIRST EDITION
First Printing, 2015

Book design by Bob Gaul
Cover art: iStockphoto.com/18898488/©MeiKIS
            iStockphoto.com/10729688/©knape
Cover design by Ellen Lawson
All interior art © Llewellyn art department except Figure 9: Chinese Luo Pan/
            Compass © *Guide to the Feng Shui Compass* by Stephen Skinner,
            published 2010 by Golden Hoard Press/Llewellyn Publications.
Editing by Laura Graves

Llewellyn Publications is a registered trademark of Llewellyn Worldwide Ltd.

Library of Congress Cataloging-in-Publication Data
Liotta Dennis, Denise, 1954–
Classical feng shui for romance, sex, & relationships: design your living space for
love, harmony & prosperity/Master Denise Liotta Dennis.—First Edition.
    pages cm
Includes bibliographical references and index.
ISBN 978-0-7387-4188-8
1. Feng shui. 2. Love—Miscellanea. 3. Interpersonal relations—Miscellanea.
4. Wealth—Miscellanea. I. Title.
BF1779.F4L57555 2015 133.3'337—dc23

                    2014035550

Llewellyn Publications
A Division of Llewellyn Worldwide Ltd.
2143 Wooddale Drive
Woodbury, MN 55125-2989
www.llewellyn.com

Printed in the United States of America

*This book is dedicated with love and affection
to my son, Mark Ashley Weightman*

Contents

Acknowledgments   *xi*

Introduction   *1*

Part I: Feng Shui Basics

One: Feng Shui, Sex, and Relationships   7

Two: The Art, Science, and Basics of
Classical Feng Shui   15

Three: Adultery, Affairs, and Divorce:
Feng Shui to Avoid   33

Part II: Eight Mansions

Four: Using Eight Mansions for
Remarkable Relationships   55

Five: Life-Gua Zodiac Personalities   65

Part III: Flying Stars

Six: Using Flying Stars to Understand
Relationships   157

Seven: Feng Shui Secrets to Enhance
Romantic Love and Relationships   173

Eight: Period 8 Charts: How to Extract
Love, Prosperity, and Harmony   183

Nine: Period 7 Charts: How to Extract
Love, Prosperity, and Harmony   233

Glossary of Terms   281

Appendix   301

Bibliography   303

Feng Shui Resources   305

Index   309

Acknowledgments

Without relationships, life wouldn't be worth living. Even with our accomplishments and successes, life doesn't have the same significance without the admiration, support, and glowing approval of our loved ones. Nothing is, in fact, accomplished alone—every endeavor needs the support, encouragement, constructive criticism, and objective observation of others.

I am grateful for all the relationships of my life, particularly those that have taught (or forced) me to improve myself. Without my Feng Shui teachers, I would not have elected this path nor felt compelled to write books on my favorite subject. I have a deep appreciation for all four of them but most of all to my primary teacher and mentor, Grandmaster Yap Cheng Hai (Kuala Lumpur, Malaysia). Without his willingness to pass on his extensive knowledge and wisdom, it would have been lost. Therefore, it is with great care that I honor this relationship by teaching; in this way the information is not forgotten and that many generations to come will benefit from it.

I'd like to acknowledge my extraordinary family and thank them for their love and support, including my son, Mark Weightman, to whom this book is dedicated; much love to his family, especially to his three gorgeous children—Makenzy, Kaitlyn, and Grayson. To my beloved sister, Linda Dennis, a friend, true sister, fellow writer, and a wickedly witty cohort, and to my favorite nephew, Madison Dennis Smith. All of my Texas and Louisiana relatives are also much loved and appreciated especially my lifetime buddy and cousin Kaki Scott. Tremendous thanks to all my clients who, for the past two decades, have been a continual source of knowledge and inspiration.

It is with enormous pride that I acknowledge my beloved core students who are now Feng Shui Masters; they are powerful, beautiful, and smart: Katherine Gould, Jennifer Bonetto, Peg Burton, Kelsey Groetken, Marianne Kulekowskis, and Nathalie Ekobo. I have equal admiration for my soon-to-be Masters: Kristy Coup, Peggy Lanese, and Barbara Harwell. I also wish to recognize my colleagues around the world whose association I value greatly; these Feng Shui Masters' consulting and teachings are a tribute to the world: Jennifer Bartle-Smith, Australia; Maria Santilario, Spain; Bridgette O'Sullivan, Ireland; Cynthia Murray, Colorado; Jayne Goodrick; England; Di Grobler and Christine McNair, South Africa; Angle de Para, Florida; Scheherazade "Sherry" Merchant, India; Nathalie Mourier and Helen Weber, France; and Birgit Fischer, Petra Coll-Exposito, Nicole Zoremba, and Eva-Maria Spöetta, Germany.

And finally, I'd like to extend gratitude to my literary agent, Kristina Holmes, and Llewellyn Publications for their continued confidence and support; thank you for taking a chance on me!

Denise Liotta Dennis
Feng Shui Master
Scottsdale, AZ

Introduction

Classical Feng Shui for Romance, Sex & Relationships is a book for both skeptics and those looking to Feng Shui with great enthusiasm to attract love, marriage, or happiness. While Feng Shui addresses prosperity, health, and relationships, personal relationships are often what's largely in our hearts and on our minds. This book's primary focus is on attracting love, romance, or your soul mate, and it will also help you improve relationships with your spouse, children, coworkers, friends, siblings, and clients. Feng Shui enthusiasts, you will be thrilled to find a superior collection of techniques to accomplish your goals of love, most of which have never been published. And to the skeptics reading, you will be presented with methods you've never heard of; give them try and see for yourself!

My own experience in first discovering Feng Shui in the mid-nineties was the amazingly broad areas of life that Feng Shui was designed to address and improve. I was intrigued by the importance the Chinese placed on harmony between people. While this is important to most cultures around the world, they went about solving the mystery of why some people seem to thrive in every area of life and others are plunged into despair. These ancient discoveries can be used in the modern world to achieve our heart's desire; then and now, family happiness is usually at the top of the list.

All Classical Feng Shui methods, systems, and techniques to create/ augment excellent relationships are presented in the book. However, don't worry about mastering any of them; the recommendations to change your life are clearly described in a simple step-by-step, room-by-room approach in chapters 8 and 9 (no changes for the southern hemisphere). This is where all the Feng Shui methods come together in the book. Just grab a compass, and you're on your way to a sweeter life!

The book goes as follows—first, we'll start with a brief discussion on the spirituality of sex and the Taoist view of sexual energy. Next, the science, art, and basic tools of Feng Shui are described. More importantly I will give you the purpose of each of these famous precepts such as the Ba Gua, Five Elements, the Luo Shu, Yin-Yang, and so forth. In chapter 3, I'll identify all the sites you'll either want to avoid or correct as they may lead to divorce, affairs, bankruptcy, disharmony, or adultery. Whatever your current status—married or single—these sites can destroy your peace.

In the next chapter, you'll learn the simple, yet profound Eight Mansions system. Here you'll discover your personal Life Gua Number; this is highly significant in forming remarkable relationships by using directional energy. In chapter 5, you will learn a more expanded version of the Life Gua Personalities, first introduced in my book *Classical Feng Shui for Wealth and Abundance* which is a revolutionary and original facet of the Eight Mansions system. The newest, even more expanded version of the Life Guas portrayals has never been seen in any Feng Shui book; I've named them the Life Gua Zodiac Personalities. I think you will find it compelling as it will give you insights into yourself and your past/present relationships.

Next, we will take the complex and advanced system of Flying Stars and break it down in easy to understand, bite-size pieces. This extraordinary system is one that will transform your living space into a haven for superior energy; it too is based on directions. In chapter 7, you'll learn a variety of secret formulas used by Feng Shui masters to attract and sustain incredible relationships such as Three Harmony Doorways, the Peach Blossom technique to attract romance, and how to activate special energy charts such as the Pearl and Parent Strings and Combination of Ten.

Everything comes together in chapters 8 and 9 where I give very specific and detailed recommendations for your home that will lead to the most dramatic results if diligently implemented. Your home's unique energy and the room-by-room suggestions on how to activate it for harmony, prosperity, and romance will be located in either chapter 8 or 9; the chapter you'll refer to will depend on your move-in date and the home's facing direction. The rest is reference material that can be used to find applicable information for the homes of your family and friends. No Feng Shui book has ever attempted to put together all systems for the non-professional to put into action—but I think if you have this book, you're up for it! *Classical Feng Shui for Romance, Sex & Relationships* is a comprehensive guide to improve the energy of your living space today and can serve as an excellent reference for many years to come.

May love, prosperity, and harmony always find you.

Denise Liotta Dennis
Feng Shui Master
Scottsdale, AZ

Part I
Feng Shui Basics

One

Feng Shui, Sex, and Relationships

Thou art to me a delicious torment.

Ralph Waldo Emerson

Just imagine Emerson's "delicious torment" if he could have logged onto websites such as Perfectmatch, Match.com, eHarmony, AmericanSingles, and hundreds of other dating sites. Never before has there been so much available contact between complete strangers in the pursuit of love.

Love is our deepest need. It is not death, illness, or poverty that strikes fear into our hearts, but being alone in the world with no one to love, share, or appreciate our lives. No matter how accomplished we are, everyone longs or reaches out for love.

Classical Feng Shui does not use love magic to put a spell on your intended lover, no indeed. Everything discussed in this book will introduce you to the most potent Feng Shui formulas to enhance *all* relationships, including romantic ones. Feng Shui will help you in every possible type of interaction with others—lawsuits, romance, business, betrayals, back-stabbing, gossip, family, teachers, friends, support in the workplace, mentors, connecting with the community, and your children. This book is filled with Feng Shui methods to enhance romantic relationships *and* numerous techniques to improve other areas of your life such as prosperity and harmony.

Feng Shui in Brief

Classical Feng Shui is an ancient science and art that addresses three main categories of life—prosperity, relationships, and health—what I fondly refer to as the *human experience*. Feng Shui considers the energy that is exterior and interior of your site, both will absolutely affect your opportunities regarding these three categories. This energy is the unseen influence in our lives. The ancients developed a cache of techniques to evaluate energy and enhance the human experience. *All* methods of Classical Feng Shui involve the use of directional energy, so make friends with a compass (a simple hiking compass or an app on a smartphone will suffice). You will need it to successfully implement the potent recommendations in this book.

Feng Shui is a science designed to improve the quality of your life by evaluating the landscape, the structure itself, and important rooms in the home such as the master bedroom, home office, kitchen, and the door you use to enter your space. Determining how the energy flows both inside and outside of your home is paramount. Therefore it is vital to gather very specific data about your homesite, as all will vary greatly. There are several key pieces of information that are of the upmost importance—the flow of energy, the direction of the structure, the home's orientation, when you moved in, any water on or near the site, mountains in view, and magnetic energy fields.

Feng Shui's primary objective is to determine if the energy of the structure is supporting people in health, relationships, and prosperity. If the energy is good and positive, it can bring wonderful relationships, business opportunities, promotions at work, marriage, or a successful business.

If the home has negative energy and does not offer support, divorce, scandals, poverty, bankruptcy, affairs, and a host of other bad events can manifest. While much of the book will deal with the romantic aspect of relationships, we will discuss relationships in general as well.

Using Classical Feng Shui to enhance romance and maximize your love potential will *not* involve the use of crystals, candles, essential oils, pictures of love birds, chandeliers, and other invented schemes that some Feng Shui books describe and recommend. Instead, you will discover the ancient secrets used by Feng Shui Masters for thousands of years to improve relationships of all types. No matter if you lived then or now—relationships are integral to our existence. Love and sex are such powerful forces that humans have devoted much time and effort trying to understand, use, and unlock their astounding energy.

The Spirituality of Sex: Tantra

Love is the "glue" of the universe, and we know deep down inside that this phenomenal frequency is the key to life. Sexual energy is the most powerful on the planet, and yet we barely understand that it is raw, creative energy at its best! Many ancient cultures knew that the act of love or sex contained within it the possibility of expanding consciousness. In ancient India this was known as tantra. Chinese Taoists also had their version; both methods were designed to merge with the divine part of ourselves.[1]

Americans find the concept difficult to understand, as we tend to be very reserved regarding sex, perhaps a vestige from our nation's Puritan beginnings. While Tantric sex is not for everyone, it does show the immense power and potential of sexual energy, and it's worth visiting briefly. So what is Tantric sex? In "What is Tantra?" Niyaso Carter explains:

---

1. Taoism (modernly spelled Daoism) is a philosophical and religious tradition that emphasizes living in harmony with the Tao. *Tao* means "way," "path," or "principle," and can also be found in Chinese philosophies and religions other than Taoism. In Taoism, however, *Tao* denotes something that is both the source and the driving force behind everything that exists.

Since the famous singer Sting appeared on the television show *Oprah* and declared that learning Tantric sex has enabled him to make love for hours and hours without stopping, lots of people are curious about Tantric sex. Tantric sex is sex imbued with love that allows us to merge with the divine. Sexuality was honored as a potent form of life force energy that could be used for spiritual advancement. Many of their sexual practices involved much discipline, patience, and diligence. Tantric masters taught their students how to use sexual energy and sexual expression consciously, with great awareness, as an opener to love, to life, to God, and all existence.

Taoist Views on Sexual Energy

Taoists also unlocked secrets of the human body and understood its energy a little differently. The famous Taoist master Mantak Chia is a leading expert on techniques using sexual energy for maintaining health and healing the organs in the body. He states that when humans are formed, the sexual organ cells store part of the primordial force energy. Also, he claims that the heart stores the original spirit of the primordial force. The following is from an article entitled "Immortal Self's Nine Secrets of Taoist Inner Alchemy":

> Some may find it interesting to hear that spiritual development can go hand in hand with a loving, respectful sexual relationship as well as for solo cultivation practice. And further, that the sexual energy generated in the process is a critical element for spiritual development. One learns to cultivate, control, conserve, refine and store sexual energy in the body in the basic practices. From there, there are more refined inner alchemy practices that enable Universal Tao practitioners to grow and attain their Immortal Spirit Body.

Through inner alchemy processes, one refines immaterial (sexual energy essence and healthy positive energy) generated from material (physical body) and sources of Earth, nature, planets, and the universe. It takes time, patience and commitment. Therefore, Taoists value a healthy, happy, emotionally balanced life and longevity to support feeling good and to be willing to persevere with this higher inner alchemy process!

It's very interesting that both Tantric practices and Taoism have enjoyed a worldwide resurgence around the world. The staying power of these teachings speaks for itself and they undeniably offer valuable insights. Without question, of all relationships, romantic and sexual ones confuse us the most. The intimate connections with one another—while having the staggering potential to be rich—are the most difficult to comprehend.

Relationships in Modern Society

All in all, the Chinese place a great deal of importance on relationships, family life, and their partners. As my teacher, Grandmaster Yap Cheng Hai (first made famous by Lillian Too in her books in the 1990s) explained, they believe that a man's real "wealth" is his wife; this is because she inspires him to succeed *and* his children come from her.

Traditionally, divorce was looked down on in China as it disrupts harmony in the house; there is a famous saying, "Be married until your hair turns white." Modern-day China is much different, of course, but their values about family and home are mostly unchanged. Feng Shui masters of old developed these relationship techniques just like those to enhance wealth and secure health—by observation and documentation.

Observing what happened to people's love lives, family ties, business partnerships, and work relationships gave them insight into how the internal and external environment played its part. Forget that these brilliant observations were made hundreds or even thousands of years ago; humans are still concerned with the same basic things—romantic love, good business relationships, a good reputation, close community ties, successful and filial children, and family love and support. We are, however, in the most interesting time for male and female relationships. Today, in American society (and most parts of the world as well), there are just as many singles as married people; very different from just twenty years ago. Married people are still perceived to be more stable and certainly more socially acceptable than "singletons." Divorce rates have increased, yet people don't give up on love; they are still romantic at heart, looking for their soul mates and perfect spouses.

Since the West's advent of sexual freedom beginning in the 1960s, the roles of men and woman have become a quagmire of confusion; it's been equally difficult for both sexes. But the fundamentals remain—men want respect and appreciation from the women they love/pursue and women want to be cherished and cared for by the men they love/accept. According to some recent statistics on single adults in the United States from the U.S. Census Bureau; they report that in 2011, there were 102 million unmarried people 18 years or older. There were 17 million unmarried residents 65 or older. They also report that as of 2010, 45 percent of households nationwide were unmarried.

The Yin and Yang Roles in Relationships

There is yin and yang energy in everything, including relationships, and sometimes it has nothing to do with a male or female body. Even in same-sex relationships, one partner will have more male or female energy than the other; or else there would be no attraction. Couples will naturally fall into the role in which they are most comfortable. There is no right or wrong, only what people are best suited to express and accept in each other. Being cognizant of our prevailing energy will assist us in selecting the opposite in a partner/spouse so that the relationship will be rewarding and long-lasting. This is simply the yin and yang of it; the exquisite pull of opposite poles which creates the "attraction." Without question, the ideal scenario is when both partners are very balanced in their energy, creating an equal partnership sustained by love and respect. Actually, as my metaphysician friend explains, there are four things that must exist in order for love to be born and to grow: trust, loyalty, consistency, and safety. Without these important aspects, the lust—often mistaken for love—will eventually fizzle out, leaving us unfulfilled and plotting an exit.

In their very popular *Getting to "I Do,"* Dr. Patricia Allen and Sandra Harmon present some extremely enlightening information on how gender roles in marriages and relationships play out. Equally compelling is John Gray's *Venus on Fire, Mars on Ice,* which reveals scientific data on how hormone levels affect the quality of our relationships. Dr. Gray discusses the ways in which men rebuild their supply of testosterone through activity, and how women need to talk in order to ensure sufficient amounts of oxytocin, the "feel good" hormone.

If you are single, in addition to keeping informed with good books on relationship advice, you will need your environment to support your efforts and goals with excellent Feng Shui. You will find all the information necessary to ensure this in chapters 8 and 9. Personally, I've read more than a hundred books on relationships and have narrowed that list down to what I think are the best books on the subject; refer to the recommended reading section at the back of the book for a list of—in my opinion—some of the most powerful, informative, and eye-opening relationship books.

––––––––

Without question, relationships have changed in America and in almost all societies around the world as well. We are most certainly challenged to interact differently with one another, and this is particularly true concerning romantic relationships. The ancient Chinese devoted a great deal of time and research in an effort to understand how our living spaces would affect the dynamics between people. Let's explore some of the earliest inklings of how energy and the interior and exterior of our structures could be assessed for their ability to enhance the human experience.

Two

··························

The Art, Science, and Basics of Classical Feng Shui

··························

A journey of a thousand miles begins with a single step.
Lao Tzu

If you have several books on Feng Shui, you may already be familiar with the Ba Gua and other basic tools and principles of this fascinating subject. In that case, feel free to skip or skim this chapter. However if this is your first book, you'll want to read over what is actually behind the potent Feng Shui formulas and what drove it to its huge popularity in modern times.

Feng Shui is called both an art and science, but which is it? It's a science—it has deep roots in astronomy, mathematics, and earth's magnetic energy. The art of it is in knowing when and where to apply its numerous techniques to enhance, correct, or evaluate your site and living space. This richly complex praxis took thousands of years to fully develop into what we see today.

However, Feng Shui is part of a multifaceted body of knowledge known as Chinese metaphysics of which there are five major categories of study. What all five categories share in common are the energy tools: Ba Gua, Five Element theory, the Yin-Yang principle, and so forth. While these energy tools are mentioned in every Feng Shui book, most readers are not clear what to do with them. Well, you don't do anything *with* them, per se; they are the basis and foundation of all systems, techniques, and methods devised. Of course, if you elect to professionally practice Feng Shui, you must have extensive knowledge of them. Let's start with the five arts and then address the energy tools one by one.

———

Classical Feng Shui is one of the five main art-sciences of Chinese metaphysics. Rooted in the I Ching, these philosophical tenets—mountain, medicine, divination, destiny, and physiognomy—are the root of the Chinese culture developed over five thousand years. Being able to master just one of these studies is considered a significant life accomplishment.

The Five Metaphysical Arts (Wu Shu)

Mountain (Shan or Xian Xue): This category encompasses philosophy, including the teachings of the fourth-century BC philosophers Lao Zi and Zhuang Zi, Taoism, martial arts, Qi Gong, Tai Chi Chuan, meditation, healing, and diet. This category also includes the study of alchemy—the science of prolonging life through specific rituals and exercises, which are deeply rooted in Taoism.

Medicine (Yi): The Chinese follow an integrated, holistic, and curative approach to medicine: acupuncture, herbal prescriptions, and massage fall into this category.

Divination (Po): The Chinese are acknowledged for their intuitive skills and abilities to read and interpret symbols. The divination techniques of Da Liu Ren, Tai Yi Mystical Numbers, Qi Men, and Mei Hua Xin Yi (Plum Blossom oracle) employ numbers to predict everything from wars to missing persons to the details of one's past and future.

Destiny (Ming): Most forms of Chinese augury seek to interpret fate and determine the timing of life events; the ancient sages devoted much time and research to this study. The most popular methods of Chinese fortune-telling include Zi Wei Dou Shu (Purple Star Astrology) and Ba Zi (literally means "eight characters" but is also commonly known as the Four Pillars of Destiny), both of which examine a person's destiny and potential based on their date and time of birth. A complimentary form of Ming is the science of divination (Bu Shi), which is analogous to the mathematics of probability.

Physiognomy (Xiang Xue): Grandmaster Yap Cheng Hai refers to this category as *Sow,* and it involves making predictions based on the image, form, and features of the landscape, the human face and palms, architecture, and gravesites. Feng Shui is the fortune-telling of a building by rendering an accurate observation of the structure's appearance, shape, direction, and other surrounding environmental features.

The Nature of Chi

The Purpose: Energy (chi) permeates our Universe; Feng Shui evaluates the quality of energy at property sites and in living spaces.

Chi simply means "energy"; the ancient Chinese were one of the first cultures to discover that humans and our entire universe are comprised of pure energy. Modern-day science confirms this. Also spelled *qi* (both spellings are pronounced *chee*), it is the life-force energy of the universe, heaven, earth, and man. Sometimes it is also referred to as the *cosmic breath*, which is present in every living and nonliving entity; it can be auspicious, inauspicious, or benign. Chi is the life-force energy that pervades mankind's existence; it is the unseen force that moves through the human body and the environment. Feng Shui's main objective is to attract and harness auspicious energy to support people. It is energy that determines the shape and form of the landscape as well as the vitality of all living things. The famous Tai Chi symbol which resembles two interlocking fish demonstrates the polarity of energy—yin (female) or yang (male).

Figure 1: The famous Tai Chi
symbol representing polarity.

While the Chinese had this secret knowledge for thousands of years, it was unknown to most of the world including the Western and European cultures. Until we witnessed with our own eyes the power of a skilled martial arts black belt focus his energy and crack a stack of bricks, we were clueless as to the secrets of energy. The Western world was next introduced to acupuncture, another science dealing with the energy of the human body that identified hundreds of meridian points. Finally, Feng Shui makes its way to us—a science that involves evaluating and improving the energy of a site and living spaces.

The Eight Guas or Trigrams
The Purpose: Feng Shui uses the Guas (Trigrams) to represent the eight directions

The Guas, also known as trigrams, date back to Chinese antiquity. These important symbols give a macro, inclusive perspective of our universe, energy, and direction. Each of the eight Guas is comprised of three lines, either solid or broken. The broken lines indicate yin (female) energy while the solid lines represent yang (male) energy. The three lines also represent the cosmology of heaven, earth, and man. The famous Ba Gua includes all eight trigrams; *ba* means eight, and *gua* means the result of divination.

The eight Guas, in addition to representing the eight directions, have several layers of information that becomes useful in assessing the energy of land, homes, or buildings. The Chinese related this information to everyday life so that there is a Gua representing the father, mother, eldest son, eldest daughter, and so forth. In the end, each Gua represents yin or yang energy, relates to a family member, an element, a body part or possible related illness, a season, number, personality type, direction, and natural and human phenomena. Additionally, they have numerous interpretations and slight distinctions that can be overwhelming for the Feng Shui novice. All the same, these implications and interpretations have great significance in Feng Shui and other Chinese metaphysical studies. The eight Guas are Kan, Gen, Chen, Xun, Li, Kun, Dui, and Chien representing north, northeast, east, southeast, south, southwest, west, and northwest respectively.

The Eight Trigrams (Guas)

Chien Gua

The "Creative" and Heaven
Family Member: Father
Element: *Big* Metal
Represents the Northwest
Color: Gold, Silver, White
Body Part: Head, Lungs
Luo Shu Number: 6

Kun Gua

The "Receptive"
Family Member: Mother
Element: Earth
Represents the Southwest
Color: Brown, Yellow
Body Part: Stomach, Abdomen
Luo Shu Number: 2

Chen Gua

"Arousing" and Thunder
Family Member: Oldest Son
Element: *Big* Wood
Represents the East
Color: Jade Green
Body Part: Liver, Feet
Luo Shu Number: 3

Xun Gua

"Gentle" and the Wind
Family Member: Oldest Daughter
Element: *Small* Wood
Represents the Southeast
Color: Green
Body Part: Liver, Thighs, Buttocks
Luo Shu Number: 4

Kan Gua

The "Abysmal" and Water
Family Member: Middle Son
Element: Water
Represents the North
Color: Black, Blue
Body Part: Kidneys, Blood
Luo Shu Number: 1

Li Gua

"Clinging" and Fire
Family Member: Middle Daughter
Element: Fire
Represents the South
Color: Red, Purple, Orange, Pink
Body Part: Heart, Eyes
Luo Shu Number: 9

Gen Gua

"Stillness" and Earth
Family Member: Youngest Son
Element: *Mountain* Earth
Represents the Northeast
Color: Brown, Yellow
Body Part: Bones, Hands/Fingers
Luo Shu Number: 8

Dui Gua

"Joyful" and the Marsh
Family Member: Youngest Daughter
Element: *Small* Metal
Represents the West
Color: Gold, Silver, White
Body Part: Mouth, Throat, Lungs
Luo Shu Number: 7

Figure 2: The Eight Guas representing the eight directions.

Tien-Di-Ren
(The Three Types of Luck/Opportunities)

The Purpose: Excellent Feng Shui covers roughly
65 to 80 percent of your overall luck and opportunities

The three types of luck (opportunities), known as Tien-Di-Ren, are Heaven Luck, Earth Luck, and Man Luck. Each one of these categories will champion you in a very different way. This aspect of Feng Shui is called the Cosmic Trinity; in other words all three areas will influence your life and living space.

Heaven Luck (Tien)—This category of luck is often referred to as destiny or karma. The Chinese believe that what goes around comes around; that past deeds—for good or evil—will visit you again in this life. They also contend that this area of luck is fixed and may not be influenced; it counts as a third of your overall luck and opportunities in life.

Earth Luck (Di)—This category is the dominion of Feng Shui. If your home site and living space has auspicious and harmonious energy, you will reap the rewards. Additionally, life will support your efforts, goals, relationships, health, and prosperity if this aspect is taken care of. With earth luck you have total control, and it can exceed the normal third associated with it if you have superior energy at home and work; Grandmaster Yap purports that it can be raised to two-thirds.

Man Luck (Ren)—This category of luck is another area you have total control over. This is created by your own efforts and the choices you make in life. This may include your education, morals, hard work, beliefs, and your ability to seize and exploit good opportunities that might come your way. This area accounts for approximately a third of your overall luck.

The He Tu and Luo Shu

The Purpose: Feng Shui uses these numerical diagrams to unlock the secrets of universal energy

These two very distinct mathematical diagrams representing universal energy are so ancient and intrinsic in the Chinese culture that its people are often referred to as the He-Luo culture. Together they form the foundation of Chinese philosophy and are the genesis of Classical Feng Shui. These famous diagrams are frequently mentioned in ancient Chinese literature and are shrouded by legend and mystery. There are a series of lines connected with black and white dots in both diagrams. Most scholars believe the He Tu chronicles the cycle of birth, while the Luo Shu represents the process of death: yin and yang.

Ancient lore surrounding the He Tu began with the reign of the shaman king Fu Xi, who was born in the 29 BCE. He witnessed a mythical dragon-horse bearing strange, unusually patterned markings on its back emerge from the mighty Yellow River. This design became known as the He Tu (pronounced "hur too"). As Fu Xi examined these markings (see illustration), valuable information pertaining to cosmic laws of the universe was revealed. The dots (black are yin and white are yang) of the He Tu illustrate several concepts; including direction, the five elements of Feng Shui, and the flow of chi.

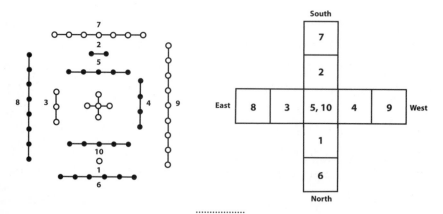

Figure 3: The He Tu diagram pertaining to cosmic energy dating back to the 28 BCE.

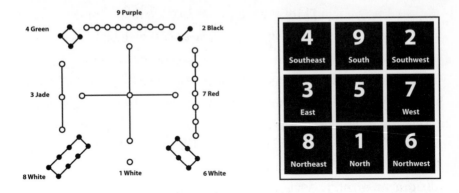

Figure 4: The Luo Shu representing movement of energy dates back to 2100 BCE.

Following Fu Xi's discoveries, succeeding scholars meticulously preserved and passed down the mysteries of the He Tu. Even today, it is found in written texts and ancient scrolls which pervade Eastern ideologies, including traditional Chinese medicine and some of the initial principles of Feng Shui. The five element theory (Water, Wood, Fire, Earth, and Metal) has its basis in the He Tu; these elements identify, interpret, and predict natural phenomena. Later arriving on the scene would be the Guas or trigrams. Therefore, the theories and principles of the He Tu gave birth to the first Ba Gua known as the Early Heaven Ba Gua (Xien Tien Ba Gua).

The Luo Shu is also surrounded by legend and myth; Emperor Yu of the Xia Dynasty, while sitting next to the River Lo, saw a giant turtle emerge in or around 2100 BCE. It too had a pattern and series of black and white dots on its back. The Luo Shu is a nine square grid containing nine numbers; each of the nine numbers represents a trigram, body organ, family member, direction, or element; it is either male or female energy. Interestingly, no matter which way you add the numbers in the grid, they total 15, and indeed it is often referred to as the Magic Square of 15. This arrangement of numbers became part of the Later Heaven Ba Gua (LHB). The Luo Shu is used extensively in all methods and applications of Classical Feng Shui.

The Luo Shu and He Tu are coded maps that represent the cosmology of heaven and earth; they are energy tools which are used to assess buildings, living spaces, and land sites. These ancient oracles are considered the backbone of Chinese metaphysics; unlocking their mysteries takes many years of study, contemplation, and a learned teacher.

The Five Elements: Wu Xing

The Purpose: Feng Shui
allocates energy into five categories

As with most brilliant discoveries, nature served as the inspiration. In ancient China, they paid close attention to the predicable cycles of energy—Fire burns Wood, and Metal comes from Earth. By associating this information with the human body and everyday life and events, the Five Element theory was created. They knew energy was part of everything, so placing pervasive energy into five categories offered a viable solution in assessing their interaction with one another. These five categories or five phases of energy are known as Wu Xing. The five elements are Metal (*jin*; literally "gold"), Wood (mu), Water (shui), Fire (huo), and Earth (tu). Each element is a representation of matter and energy as it coalesces from one form to the next. The Five Element theory simply elucidates the relationship among different types of energy; it is understood as both figurative and literal for Feng Shui applications.

The premise of the Five Elements is used in virtually every study of Chinese metaphysics—Feng Shui, astrology, traditional Chinese medicine, and martial arts. If you wish to master Feng Shui, you must master the Five Elements. The Five Elements have three cycles—productive, weakening, and controlling.

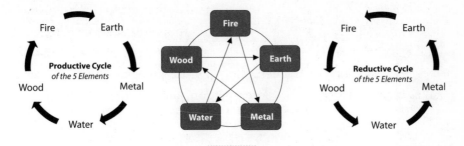

**Figure 5: The Three Cycles of the Five Elements:
Productive, Controlling, Reductive.**

The Productive Cycle: This important cycle produces or gives birth to something. Wood feeds Fire. Fire produces ash and creates Earth. Earth gives birth to Metal. Metal melts to a fluid and becomes Water, which in turn produces Wood.

The Controlling Cycle: This process can conquer, control, or destroy. Water extinguishes Fire, Fire melts Metal, and Metal cuts Wood. Wood, in the form of plants or tree roots, controls Earth by breaking it apart or keeping it together. Earth is big enough to hold Water—without Earth, Water would have no boundary.

The Reductive Cycle: This process is the reverse of the productive cycle, because what we give birth to weakens us. Wood stokes Fire; therefore Fire weakens Wood. Fire generates ash and creates Earth; therefore Earth weakens Fire. Earth produces Metal; therefore Metal weakens Earth. Metal melts to a fluid and produces Water; therefore Water weakens Metal. Water produces wood; therefore, Wood weakens Water.

Element	Color	Shape	Physical Objects	Direction	Properties	Number
Wood	Greens	Tall and rectangular	Trees, plants, furniture, bamboo, tall objects	**East** **Southeast**	Grows upwards, tall and outwards	**3, 4**
Fire	Red, purple	Pointed and triangular	Stoves, fireplaces, grills, TVs, computers, lamps, electrical towers	South	Heat, radiates and spreads in every direction	9
Earth	Brown, terra-cotta	Square	Mountains, granite, stone, boulders, rocks	**Southwest** **Northeast**	Attractive, dense, stable, centered	**2, 5, 8**
Metal	Silver, Gold	Round and spherical	Swords, knives, coins, bronze, gold, silver	**Northwest** **West**	Piercing, pointed and sharp	**6, 7**
Water	Blue, black	Wavy	Ocean, lakes, ponds, pools, fountains	**North**	Unfettered, free, runs to low ground	1

Figure 6: The Five Element chart.

The Two Ba Guas

The Purpose: The Two Ba Guas are the mother to all Feng Shui formulas/techniques

Likely the second most recognized image after the Tai Chi symbol is the Ba Gua; however most are not aware that there are two. The Ba Gua literally appears in all Feng Shui books; it is an octagonal map that depicts the eight trigrams. The two Ba Guas are the Early Heaven Ba Gua (*Fu Xi* or *Xien Tien Ba Gua*) and Later Heaven Ba Gua (*Ho Tien* or *Wen Wang Ba Gua*). Both are used in the practice of Classical Feng Shui as all formulas, methods, and techniques are born from the two arrangements of the Guas.

Figure 7: The first arrangement of the Guas
known as Early Heaven Ba Gua (EHB).

The Early Heaven Ba Gua (EHB), which dates back approximately six thousand years, depicts the polarities in nature. It reflects an ideal world of harmony in which chi is in a constant, perfect state of polarization. The eight Guas, or trigrams, create a conceptual model that marks the changes in energy. The Early Heaven Ba Gua, representing a "perfect" world, can be commonly seen over doorways to repel negative energy; it is used extensively in Westernized styles of Feng Shui. It has more profound implications and uses in Classical Feng Shui as it is the basis of complex formulas, primarily water/road formulas.

The Later Heaven Ba Gua (LHB) was the brilliant work of King Wen, a Chou Dynasty ruler who elaborated on Fu Xi's earlier diagrams. This arrangement was done to represent the cyclical forces of nature. The Later Heaven Ba Gua describes the patterns of environmental changes. Unlike Earlier Heaven Ba Gua, the LHB is dynamic, not static; it represents the ever-changing structure of the universe and the circular nature of life. Many Feng Shui applications stem from the understanding of the Later Heaven Ba Gua. For instance, the Luo Shu is the numerical representation of the Later Heaven Ba Gua.

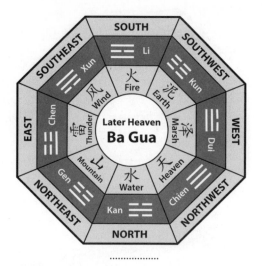

**Figure 8: The second arrangement of the Guas
known as Later Heaven Ba Gua (LHB).**

The Chinese Luo Pan

The Purpose: Feng Shui measures "directional" energy via a compass

The ancient Chinese were the first to discover the magnetic compass, having this valuable tool well before Europeans. The lore surrounding its discovery sounds like something out of a movie: the warrior Goddess of the Nine Heavens presented Huangdi, the Yellow Emperor, first ruler of a united China, with a compass to find his way out of the fog to defeat his enemies. Other stories tell of Huangdi's unique invention, a compass cart that led to victory. Either way, the Luo Pan became and is *the* quintessential tool of the Feng Shui master.

Figure 9: A Chinese Luo Pan compass.

Throughout its illustrious and long history, the Luo Pan has been re-designed and refined many times over so that it would align with the latest discoveries relating to landforms, techniques, and directional energy. There are two standard types of Luo Pans—San He and San Yuan—designed to include formulas of these two main disciplines/branches of Feng Shui. The third standard Luo Pan is the Chung He, which combines the most important information of the San He and San Yuan types.

The purpose of the Luo Pan is the same as a conventional compass—to indicate direction. However, the Luo Pan contains some very important differences. A typical compass may display four or eight directions, but a Luo Pan divides up the 360 degrees into 24 sectors, derived by dividing the

45 degrees of the eight directions into three 15-degree increments (3 x 8 = 24). This is very fundamental in Classical Feng Shui, and this ring on the Luo Pan is known as the 24 mountain ring (not actual mountains, only a term). The Luo Pan is an impressive and beautiful instrument, a true work of art well worth the several hundred dollars it commands. Here are the three types:

San Yuan Luo Pan: Used in the Flying Stars and the Xuan Kong systems, the San Yuan Luo Pan is readily indentified by the 64 hexagrams of the I Ching ring. It has only one 24 mountain ring. The first ring of this Luo Pan is always the Later Heaven Ba Gua arrangement of trigrams.

San He Luo Pan: The San He Luo Pan, used for San He formulas and schools, is easily identified by its *three* 24 mountain rings. These rings are used to measure direction, mountains, and water as each of these elements has distinctly different energy; however, these rings also relate to the *three harmonies* associated with this school.

Chung He Luo Pan: Also spelled or referred to as Zong He, Zhung He, or Chong He. This Luo Pan is an amalgamation of the San He and San Yuan compasses. This is a great instrument for practitioners who enjoy using both systems. Though some rings have been eliminated for size considerations, all essential rings are in place.

This extraordinary instrument is often called the "universe on a plate" by Feng Shui masters and practitioners. For more information on the Luo Pan and its history, refer to Stephen Skinner's *Guide to the Feng Shui Compass*, the most comprehensive book ever written on the subject.

Western versus Classical Feng Shui

Most Americans and those in Europe, Australia, New Zealand, Canada, and Mexico are more familiar with a style of Feng Shui that was first introduced to the U.S. around thirty years ago. While it barely resembled traditional Feng Shui practiced for thousand of years in China, it became wildly popular. One of the main differences is the use of the compass or Luo Pan; all classical, authentic Feng Shui practice is based on direction. The other main distinction is that Classical Feng Shui encompasses numerous systems, techniques, and formulas that the simplified, Western interpretations (including Black Hat Sect Feng Shui) do not possess.

Classical Feng Shui is a living science born out of the astute observations of sages, scholars, and shamans of old China—knowledge so powerful it has survived more than four thousand years! Savvy business people and institutions such as Donald Trump, Sir Richard Branson, Bill Gates, Oprah Winfrey, Wells Fargo, and Chase Bank use the principles to build and sustain wealth and harmony. For more information, refer to *Classical Feng Shui for Wealth and Abundance* for a detailed history and critique.

————

It took thousands of years to fully develop Feng Shui formulas and techniques, the Chinese compass, and the numerous tools to determine the quality of energy and how it would affect human lives using the principles of the Tao, astronomy, mathematics, and earth's magnetic energy. The energy tools of Feng Shui are mysterious but not; modern science has discovered our world is totally composed of energy with quantum and mechanical physics some of the more intriguing aspects.[2] Now let's take a look at some of the techniques that may indicate failure in relationships and how to cure them.

———

2. Quantum mechanics provides a mathematical description of much of the dual particle-like and wave-like behavior and interactions of energy and matter.

Three

....

Adultery, Affairs, and Divorce: Feng Shui to Avoid

....

Love itself is calm; turbulence arrives from individuals.

Chinese Proverb

It is an unfortunate fact that divorce in the United States is at an all-time high, especially in the warmer part of the country with Nevada holding the record high. Adultery and affairs have become commonplace as well. In John Gottman's *Why Marriages Succeed or Fail*, Dr. Gottman headed the University of Washington's "Love Lab," in which he studied thousands of married couples by watching a recording of them interacting with each other. He was able to tell within minutes who would stay married and who would divorce.[3] He had an accuracy rate of 95 percent if he watched the video for an hour and 90 percent if he watched for only fifteen minutes.

---

3. http://www.relationshipcounseling.us/gottman-relationship-counseling.html

The study was covered in Malcom Gladwell's book *Blink*, where he explains that this ability of rapid cognition is referred to as "thin slicing," a phrase coined by Nalini Ambady and Robert Rosenthal. He shows how each of us has the ability to do this, and if we dissect the process or second-guess it, we dilute the accuracy. This is why speed-dating has become so popular. People who have participated in speed dating say that within a few seconds to a minute they can answer the important question: "Do I want to see this person again?" There are literately millions of pieces of data that go into that split-second decision.

Divorce Worldwide

There are many factors that will indicate affairs and divorce in a household, and Classical Feng Shui has many methods of evaluating the potentials of such scenarios. We will discuss them all one by one a little later in this chapter; you will be amazed at the accuracy and the comprehensive details they reveal. How are we faring with wedded bliss in America? In an intriguing article entitled "What's the Real Status of Divorce in America?" are the statistics:

> Nearly everyone in America has heard the statistic: roughly half of marriages end in divorce. In the year 2000 alone, 957,200 divorces were granted in the United States. The odds seem stacked against couples considering marriage. In fact, marriage rates are declining in nearly every state. But what is the real story behind divorce in America? Are the odds of a marriage failing really 50/50? Studies suggest that many factors contribute to the success or failure of a marriage, including geography, age, religion, race, income and education level, and family history of divorce. Study the truth behind the numbers, and you may find your own marriage has a higher chance of success. Another strange, but accurate, predictor of divorce rates is warm weather. More than

60 percent of the total U.S. population lives in the northern half of the country, yet less than half of all divorces occur there.[4]

I would add that in addition to the many factors mentioned above, bad Feng Shui can be another major contributor of adultery and divorce. Ironically, "Bible belt" states (southeastern and south-central states) have some of the highest divorce rates of all. Looking at divorce worldwide, Sweden has the highest, followed by the United States, and India has the lowest rate. The main causes for divorce worldwide are adultery, extramarital liaisons, infidelity, and domestic violence, followed by addiction: gambling, alcoholism, and drugs.

The External Environment and Its Influence on Relationships

Detrimental Land Forms

How is it possible that the environment near and around your site, natural or human-made, can affect your relationships? It is because energy is all around us and some formations will support us while others do not. By simply observing where people lived, the ancient Chinese made astute conclusions about how it would affect them. And not only that, in which category of life—health, wealth, or relationships—it would influence; many sites will affect all three important categories. The following are either formations or techniques in which a Feng Shui master will examine your site for unlucky romance such as adultery, affairs, and divorce, or the ending of business relationships.

These formations almost always affect your wealth as well. Later in the book, we will discuss the many excellent methods and techniques used by a Feng Shui master to attract and enhance relationships. It would be good to reflect back and remember if you or a friend lived in homes where

---

4. http://www.legalzoom.com/legal-articles/article13573.html

disastrous relationships occurred. It is good to be aware of these but focusing on the possible negative scenarios is not; going through a divorce or surviving an affair does not necessarily mean you have any of the following formations. Also, sometimes a divorce is needed by one or the other partner for numerous reasons. If you have divorced in your current home, do not automatically assume that your Feng Shui is bad; in general, it could have very good energy. In chapters 8 and 9, you will be alerted to the possible formations that may apply to your home's facing direction.

Eight Roads of Destruction
Indicating Divorce, Money Loss, Abandonment

This is one of the worst formations that involve a door direction and water exits. This could be virtual water as well, specifically a road. It is also known as "Eight Roads to Hell" which aptly denotes what it can bring to the householders. It only involves 15-degree increments for the door direction and the water or road. The real danger is how the chi "exits" the site, and then disaster can ensue. One example of an Eight Roads of Destruction is when a door is south (between 157 and 172 degrees) and the road or water is coming from or exiting the southeast (between 127 and 142 degrees).

MASTER'S TIP

The door or the road (or water) needs to be changed as these formations can wreck a family. This formula only involves specific 15-degree increments for both the road and the door. Tilting the door a few degrees is usually the way a Feng Shui expert will take care of it. Re-angling the door a few degrees forces the door to receive energy differently, thus eliminating the Eight Roads formation.

Peach Blossom Sha Road Formations
Indicating Affairs and Fatal Attractions

The Peach Blossom Sha Road formation is a technique evaluating the home for bad relationships, primarily romantic ones. The formula includes twelve possible door facings with four "offending" roads (incoming water even if it is virtual water like a road or driveway) that will cause a variety of very negative events regarding relationships. A Peach Blossom Sha Road may be present if there is too much real water in that sector such as a pool, waterfall, river, lake, or stream. These features can be constructed or natural, but either way they may cause problems for the family. The Peach Blossom "roads" are confined to 15-degree increments only, and not the entire 45 degrees of that direction. Here is an example of a Peach Blossom Sha Road formation: the door faces south (172.6 to 187.5 degrees) and the road (virtual water) or real water (pool, pond, fountain, etc.) comes from the east (82.6 to 97.5 degrees).

These formations will need to be corrected, as they can bring on any or several of the following results when there is a road or too much water in certain directions or locations:

- Turns the family upside down

- Soils the reputation of the house

- Scandals that are made public

- The female runs away

- Sexual problems

- Sex maniacs

- Disloyalty

- Incest

- Exile

It is interesting that in the news nowadays there is so much scandalous behavior involving politicians "sexting," posting lewd pictures of themselves on the Internet, or sexually harassing women. Without a doubt they will likely have a Peach Blossom formation: those "scandals made public."

One of my clients in The Woodlands, a community in Houston, Texas, had this formation. When I saw the house in 2008, she was separated from her husband of almost thirty years. He was having a steamy affair with a woman almost twenty years younger who was also a family friend. When I pointed out that the house had a Peach Blossom Sha Road formation, she told me that her husband had just confessed last week that this was *not* the only affair he'd had; in fact he had been having affairs since the year they moved in. Recently, she had met a man she was very interested in, so we altered her Feng Shui to counter the formation. My client had enough heartache and was done with this "affair" energy! As strange as it may sound, these formations and energies have the power to influence our behavior.

MASTER'S TIP

The door or the road (or water) needs to be changed. This formula only involves specific 15-degree increments for both the road and the door. Tilting the door a few degrees is usually the way a Feng Shui expert will take care of it; re-angling the door forces it to receive chi differently. Door tilts are hugely popular in southeast Asia, and they take care of the problem very effectively.

T-Juncture or T-Road Formations
Indicates Fighting, Discord, and Divorce

A T-juncture or T-road formation is when there is a road that is directly aligned with your front door or, perhaps even the garage door. In Feng Shui, this is considered one of the most toxic formations, causing a host of negative events for the householders. While energy is good, too much will have the opposite, desired effect. This intense, direct energy is called sha or "killing" chi; in almost all cases, it will lead to discord, money loss, divorce, accidents, and other mishaps depending on how fast and close the road is to your site.

MASTER'S TIP

Block off a T-juncture with a stucco wall, a solid gate near the front door, boulders, or dense landscaping. Whatever you choose should be enough to stop a car. If you are shopping for a new home, pass on these residences; even when cured they can cause issues.

A Home Built on Top of a Mountain
Indicates Losing a Partner and Affairs

If you buy or build a home sited on top of a mountain, the energy cannot be retained, and the indication is a lack of support in most areas of your life. Without sufficient retaining walls, these homes bring disastrous luck in relationships and money. You could lose a business partner, a spouse, or experience discord with your children, family, or clients. While a generous plateau is much better, it still may discourage energy from properly accumulating. If you have a beautiful mountain property, nestle the back of your home near the mountain; do not place it on top. Having the back of your home supported by the mountain can be wonderfully auspicious. Unsupported mountainous sites can bring bankruptcy through an extended, bitter divorce, affairs, and the loss of a partner/spouse.

MASTER'S TIP

Create a wall around the property so that the energy can be retained. If you plan to build on a mountain, create good support on all sides. Better yet, build so that the mountain can be used as backing.

Goat Blade Water
Indicates Adultery, Gambling, and Drug Abuse

A Goat Blade Water formation (also known as a Frightened Goat) is very similar to the Peach Blossom Sha Road; both can bring a host of negative events that can drive couples apart. There are eight possible door facings with eight offending roads or incoming water (even if it is virtual like a road or driveway) that will cause a variety of very negative results regarding relationships. For example, if the home faces west between 277.6 to 292.5 degrees and there is water or a road coming from the southwest between 232.6 to 247.5 degrees, the house has a Goat Blade Water formation.

Just like the Peach Blossom Sha Road formation, the danger is too much real water (natural or constructed) in that sector such as a pool, waterfall, river, lake, or stream. These features may cause problems for the couple or family. The "roads" that are the offending Goat Blade Water formation are confined to 15-degree increments, and you must have a trained, keen eye to determine if you in fact have one.

This will need to be corrected as they can bring on any of the following results when there is a road or too much water in certain directions or locations:

- Divorce

- Adultery

- Gambling

- Alcohol abuse

- Family break-ups

- Overindulgence in sex

- Illegal activities leading to failure in business

MASTER'S TIP

Try to block off from view the offending road or re-locate the water. Door tilts are also effective if this energy has manifested in a very negative way in your life.

Homes Surrounded by Too Many Roads
Indicates Affairs, Money Loss, and Divorce

Roads are fast-moving purveyors of energy and they act much like raging rivers. It is extremely inauspicious to be too close or have too many roads surrounding your site. Numerous roads near a home can make it vulnerable and unstable—think about the stories in the news where someone is describing a car crashing into their bedroom or living room where they barely escaped with their life. Roads near the back of the property can be the worst, as can virtual "roads" such as ditches or huge, open drains located in cities where heavy and frequent rains cause flooding. I had a client in Arizona who had two such open drains large enough for a car to drive on. The other two sides of her property were real roads, one in front and one on the right-hand side. This is a sad example of a site that feels like a moat; water—real and virtual—on all four sides! These sites are very unstable and indicate affairs, divorce, illness, and all types of misfortunes.

MASTER'S TIP

Create a strong backing at the rear of the property. Also, insulate the site on the left- and right-hand sides from the roads. Consider moving if you have experienced very bad luck from the beginning.

Eight Killing Mountain Forces
Indicating Divorce, Love Triangles, and Murder

The Eight Killing Mountain Forces *(Pa Sha Hwang Chuen)* is a very serious formation; the energy of the mountain and door are in conflict, causing a host of negative events for the householders. These formations involve specific 15-degree increments for both the door direction and the mountain. Even if you live in an area of the world without mountains, tall buildings must be considered as well. Here is an example of the formation: if your door faces south (172.6 to 187.5 degrees) and you have a real mountain or tall building in the northwest (307.6 to 322.5 degrees), you may have an Eight Killings.

The Eight Killings is more dangerous in certain years, depending on where your mountain or tall building is located. They can cause enormously bad luck such as failures in romance and marriage, blood-related accidents, serious injury, disasters, bloody and violent murders, and loss of wealth. A client in Awatukee, Arizona (an area near Phoenix known for its beautiful hills and mountains) was going through a divorce; he had just moved out, and his ex-wife was still living in their house. The house itself was a total nightmare; not only did it have the Eight Killings formation but also a T-juncture, three real roads surrounding the huge site, *and* a Peach Blossom Sha! The house was two months into foreclosure; my client said the bad luck started less than a year after moving in. The house was worth over a million dollars when they moved in four years prior. It was stunningly beautiful but energetically quite devastating, as it was poorly placed in its environment.

When I asked the ex-wife to leave the house lest her life spiral into total disaster, she declined—she was living there rent-free until the bank claimed the house. I explained that the next year the Eight Killings was going to be more potent than ever and that she should reconsider. I checked on her months later and she was still in the house; as a result of staying there, the divorce had gained a negative momentum that became like a "war of the roses," and it lasted three painful years. We did eventually find the woman a great house, and a year after living there she met a wonderful, slightly older gentleman who adores her. The tortuous events she endured could have been avoided if she would have escaped this home when I suggested. Master Yap says "sometimes you have to run away from the bad luck!"

MASTER'S TIP

It takes a great deal of practice and skill to determine whether you have this formation because it hinges on such small increments and involves any exterior door. Since it is impossible to move a mountain or a building, a Feng Shui master or practitioner will usually change the degree of the door in question to avoid the "crush of the dragon."[5] If you have not experienced any of the above mentioned bad luck, it is unlikely that you have this formation. Implementing the recommendations in either chapter 8 or 9 will ensure the most supportive energy for your home without contacting a professional.

Water Improperly Placed
Indicating Affairs, Drugs, Divorce, Gambling, and Alcoholism

Water is one of the most powerful elements on the planet; ancient Feng Shui scholars discovered when it was properly located or placed it would bring you extremely auspicious events and opportunities. When it is not located well, according to Feng Shui principles, it can cause illness, bankruptcy, affairs, gambling, alcoholism, scandals, loss of reputation, divorce, and drug abuse. It is an old wives' tale that if water is placed on the left-hand side of your front door, the man of the house will stray. However, we will discuss throughout this book how a river, lake, canal, pond, fountain, or swimming pool can affect your relationships.

MASTER'S TIP

In chapters 8 and 9, you will find the exact locations of where you should place water features according to the facing direction of your home; these placements will bring benevolent, prosperous, and harmonious energy to your site and living space.

---

5. In Feng Shui, the term Dragon is used to indicate a mountain.

Split-Level Homes
Indicates Families Splitting Up and Falling Apart

A split-level designed home or business can devastate your romantic, family, or business relationships. A traditional, two-story home is not a split-level home. A genuine split-level building has multiple levels going in several directions, and this design is the real culprit. These designs were very popular in the mid '70s, but Americans fell out of love with this style of home long ago.

They are still part of the landscape however in older homes and neighborhoods—especially where land is limited or the region is hilly or mountainous. However, there are signs (not exactly constituting a revival) that the split-level is gaining new respect by architects. The reasons range from nostalgia for splits as the midcentury modern style increases in popularity to the resettlement of more people from sprawling suburbs back to the split-level-filled inner-ring neighborhoods, with their easier commutes to cities. Both trends see architects reconfiguring split-level designs for today's lifestyles, which is unfortunate from a Feng Shui perspective, as these homes cause the occupants problems. These designs do not allow chi to be distributed evenly, resulting in scattered, unstable energy for the occupants. Typically the results of these types of structures are family breakups, business partners splitting, disjointed thinking, migraine headaches, and things falling apart in your life.

MASTER'S TIP

Avoid buying a home with disjointed energy that has too many levels splitting off into several different directions. There is no real cure for this as the house is already constructed; if you have experienced very bad luck in such a house, consider moving. If you are unable to move, be very diligent about implementing the recommendations in either chapter 8 or 9 about activating superior energy in your home; this will counteract some of the negative energy of a split-level design.

The Interior Environment

Front Doors Located on the Side of the House

Indicates Divorce, Disharmony, Money Loss

When I first moved to Arizona, I lived in a community where about half the homes had a front door located on the side of the house at an angle. My neighbors across the street were a lovely young couple who had been married about ten years and lived in the home for about five years. Their home had one of these side doors. About a year after I was there, they divorced and sold the house. These homes where the front door is located on the side are terrible for money and relationships. Placing the doors this way is popular, as the garage is taking front and center. When the front door does not face the road it it is on, it cannot intake chi properly and its occupants will struggle. Pass on these properties.

MASTER'S TIP

If you are able to open a door that faces the road, do so. If not and you are experiencing difficult relationships and struggles with money, consider moving. If you do not wish to relocate, make sure you implement the recommendations found in chapters 8 and 9 for your home's facing direction to significantly improve the Feng Shui.

Toilet Locations

Indicates Failed Romance,
Bad Relationships, and Things Turning Nasty

Where your toilets are located within the house is very important when it comes to relationships. Your personal relationship sector is determined by your date of birth and gender using the Eight Mansions system in chapter 4 to figure out your Life Gua Number. I had a beautiful, young realtor client who wanted a relationship, and she hired me to take a look at her home in the Phoenix area. Her master bathroom toilet was located in her personal relationship area. I asked her if relationships ever turned out badly. She said the last man she was engaged to, ran off with more than $100,000; since they shared a bank account, no "crime" was committed. I asked her to stop using just the toilet in her master and instead use the guest bathroom (she could still use the master bath's shower/tub, sink, and closet). About three months later, she met a wonderful man who was also a successful dentist; he became her husband two years later. Today, they are still in love and have a beautiful little boy.

MASTER'S TIP

Toilets will affect your relationships—good or bad—so pay close attention to the section on the Eight Mansions to find your personal relationship area known as the Yen Nien (coded as +70). Toilets should not be located here, and if they are, try to use another one in the house if you can. Conversely, when toilets are located in your bad sectors (especially your –70), relationships are enhanced.

Kitchen and Stove Locations
Indicates "Burning Up" Relationships,
Burned-out Love Affairs, and Abuse

The location of your kitchen and more importantly the stove will affect your relationships. If the stove is badly placed it will "burn up" your relationships. It can cause divorce, failure to conceive, and/or inhibit your ability to find a spouse. If a stove is placed on your personal relationship area within the kitchen, it may be very difficult to sustain a romantic relationship. A badly placed stove will affect the family unit, business partners, friends, extended family members and clients.

MASTER'S TIP

Stoves (fire) will affect your relationships—good or bad—so pay close attention to the section on the Eight Mansions to find

*your personal relationship area known as the Yen Nien (+70). A
stove, the most important fire in the home, should not be located
here. If so, you may struggle to maintain good, smooth relationships in all areas of your life.*

Mirrors in the Bedroom
Indicates Fighting/Bickering,
Extra-Marital Affairs, and Love Triangles

The rule for mirrors in a master bedroom is—while lying on the bed—you
should not be able to see yourself. This means mirrors on the ceiling, while
very sexy, will violate this basic principle. The ever-popular mirrored-closet
doors are also very bad. Improperly placed mirrors can bring extra-marital
affairs, fighting, conflict, love triangles, and divorce. Mirrors placed behind
the bed are not as serious or harmful, but are not ideal either. Dressing mirrors that do not reflect the martial bed or full-length ones behind a door
are fine. Mirrors hung high so that you cannot see yourself while lying in
bed are fine too. While mirrors located in master bedrooms can cause strife
and affairs, they can disturb the chi and thus sleep patterns when located
in other bedrooms. Conflict with family members is a possibility as well.

MASTER'S TIP

*Cover closet doors that have mirrors (usually nearly floor to ceiling
and at least eight feet wide) with drapes, wallpaper, or better yet,
replace them with wooden doors if you own the home. If you use
drapes to cover the mirrors, you only need to cover them at night.
Remove or cover mirrors on the ceiling, and re-hang mirrors in
the bedroom in locations where you cannot see the bed.*

Exposed Overhead Beams
Indicates Separation or Divorce

Beams that are located over the bed and run vertical can cause the couple to split. They are bad for health without a doubt as this is killing or sha energy, and when they "divide" the bed in half, then they can divide the couple. The lower the ceiling and the closer the beams are, the more serious.

MASTER'S TIP

The only real remedy for this is to completely cover the beams with plaster or sheet rock.[6] Classical Feng Shui does not rely on bamboo flutes in these scenarios as a cure. The beams are still there and can still cause great harm. If no matter where you place the bed you are under them, make them disappear by covering them up. If you do not own the home, try covering the area where your bed is located with fabric using thumb tacks.

Televisions and Computers in the Bedroom
Indicates Couples Separating and Restlessness

Televisions can reflect objects just like a mirror and should not be placed directly across from the martial bed. This placement can cause fights and arguments over petty things. Your love life will also improve if you do not have a television in the master bedroom. In addition to having a reflective quality like mirrors, a television emits electromagnetic energy that is disturbing to human chi. The closer you are to televisions, and the bigger they are, the more you can experience negative results. This can cause restlessness and insomnia. Computers also have the same affect on our energy fields and are best left out of the master bedroom.

---

6. Drywall (also known as sheet rock, plasterboard, wallboard, gypsum board, or gyprock) is a panel made of gypsum plaster pressed between two thick sheets of paper. It is used to make interior walls and ceilings. Drywall construction became prevalent as a speedier alternative to traditional lath and plaster.

Leave the work and careers out of the bedroom and focus on each other. Master bedrooms should be reserved for sleeping and sex only—find other areas for your home office and exercise equipment.

MASTER'S TIP

Remove televisions and computers from the master bedroom. If you enclose the television in an armoire with doors to block it from view and unplug it before sleeping, you will not be affected negatively.

Water Features in the Marital Bedroom
Indicates Affairs and Sex Scandals

Water features should not be placed in a master bedroom, as it will disturb your energy and may cause affairs. Water is primarily used to enhance wealth and harmony in a home, but when water is improperly placed, it will ignite sex scandals, affairs, incest, alcoholism, drug abuse, and other undesirable results. Aquariums, wall fountains, desk fountains, or waterfalls in the bedroom can generally bring scandals and affairs and should be avoided.

MASTER'S TIP

Remove all water features from the master bedroom; they should be placed in areas of the home to enhance wealth and harmony. For more information on where to properly place water for your home's facing direction, refer to chapters 8 and 9.

Additional Bedroom Feng Shui

Beds should not be placed against a wall sharing a toilet or fireplace; while not detrimental to a relationship, it is not ideal. Do not place your bed directly under a toilet from the floor above. Newly married couples should purchase a new mattress to begin the marriage.

The furniture in the master bedroom should be proportional to the size, and the room should be free of excess clutter. Make sure that you have a solid headboard; the open type design is not as auspicious. The lack of headboard will harm your relationships and they will not be as stable. Children need a solid headboard to make them feel more secure; the lack of one may cause them to misbehave or act out.

It's important to create a peaceful environment. The bedroom should have a nice balance of yin and yang energy. For example, windows should have blinds or drapes (or both) so that at night the room can become yin. During the day, the yang energy of the sun can infiltrate the room. But exposed windows at night are too yang for restorative sleep. If the room is not yin enough (dark, quiet, soothing, and a cool temperature), it is difficult to get into the deep REM sleep stage that helps us stay young-looking.[7]

Fireplaces in bedrooms are romantic but must be placed well according to the home's energy. Loud wall patterns or yang colors (reds, oranges, and purples) should be used sparingly. When placing the bed, the Eight Mansions and Flying Star system discussed in chapters 8 and 9 should be implemented.

MASTER'S TIP

Since the master bedroom is one of the most important rooms in the house, in order to extract excellent relationship-luck, great consideration should be undertaken to use all of the suggestions presented in this book. This is an opportunity not to be missed; spare no expense in creating a bedroom that supports prosperity, harmony, and relationships!

---

7. This stage is known as a slow-wave, or delta sleep. If aroused from sleep during this stage, a person may feel disoriented for a few minutes. During the deep stages of REM sleep, the body repairs and regenerates tissues, builds bone and muscle, and appears to strengthen the immune system. As we age, we sleep more lightly and get less deep sleep. Aging is also associated with shorter time spans of sleep, although studies show the amount of sleep needed doesn't appear to diminish with age. REM (Rapid Eye Movement) indicates deep, dream sleep state.

The scenarios and formations discussed in this chapter can seriously wreak havoc on your relationships, so be diligent about curing and mitigating the energy by using the Master's Tips. Some are very quick fixes, and others require a bit more work but are certainly worth the effort to ensure you will not have a situation that harms your life or the harmony of your household. We'll now move on to the Eight Mansions system, which contains powerful techniques to improve and understand your current relationships or attract more desirable ones.

Part II
Eight Mansions

Four
·····················

Using Eight Mansions for Remarkable Relationships

·····················

There is wisdom of the head, and wisdom of the heart.
Charles Dickens

The primary objective of Feng Shui is to determine whether the energy will support people in their homes and offices or not; the two main systems to do this are the Eight Mansions and Flying Stars. First we'll examine each system separately and then put it all together for you in chapters 8 and 9.

Positive energy will bring dazzling prospects for love and romance, business opportunities, health, promotions at work, flourishing investments, and wealth-luck. Negative energy will be apparent when householders suffer from disease, poor health, a crippling divorce, bad relationships, accidents, disastrous events, and bankruptcy.

This chapter is devoted to enhancing your relationships by using the very popular system of Eight Mansions. You will be astonished and delighted at how a few simple changes can alter your life for the better. Eight Mansions dates back to the Tang Dynasty, and is not part of the Eight Life

Aspirations found in Western styles of Feng Shui touting a wealth corner, marriage sector, fame area, and so forth. Indeed, Eight Mansions is the real deal, a genuine system that can deliver powerful results! You will see in this chapter, that there's no "universal" marriage or romance area that fits everyone. You'll have your own *personal* relationship direction to activate that allows you to attract love, romance, sex, and more harmonious relationships.

Eight Mansions (*Ba Zhai* in Chinese) is direct and simple. When applied correctly, many people have solved or overcome serious problems concerning family, career, relationships, marriage, health, and children. This was simply done by applying the principles of Eight Mansion using good directions and reorienting specific rooms in their homes. After you have determined your Life Gua Number, you will be able to drastically improve the Feng Shui of your home and office.

According to this Feng Shui system, based on your birthday and gender, you will be influenced in positive and negative ways by the eight directions: four will support you and four won't. The lucky directions will augment wealth and money-luck, health, good relationships, and stability; the other four can set into motion divorce, bankruptcy, betrayals, lawsuits, terminal illness, and so forth. The idea is to use and activate your good directions and diminish the negative ones. Before you can begin using this great system, you will need to determine your personal Life Gua Number.

To find your personal Life Gua Number, refer to the Eight Mansions chart; make sure you are in the right column as there is one for males and one for females. There is a specific calculation behind this number, but I've included the quick reference chart for ease.[8] If you were born prior to February 4 in any given year, use the previous year to get your Life Gua Number. For example, if you were born January 28, 1970, use the year 1970 to get the correct Life Gua Number.

---

8. For the Eight Mansions formula, refer to *Classical Feng Shui for Wealth and Abundance*.

1933 to 1959				1960 to 1986				1987 to 2013			
Animal	Year	Male	Female	Animal	Year	Male	Female	Animal	Year	Male	Female
Rooster	1933	4	2	Rat	1960	4	2	Rabbit	1987	4	2
Dog	1934	3	3	Ox	1961	3	3	Dragon	1988	3	3
Pig	1935	2	4	Tiger	1962	2	4	Snake	1989	2	4
Rat	1936	1	8	Rabbit	1963	1	8	Horse	1990	1	8
Ox	1937	9	6	Dragon	1964	9	6	Goat	1991	9	6
Tiger	1938	8	7	Snake	1965	8	7	Monkey	1992	8	7
Rabbit	1939	7	8	Horse	1966	7	8	Rooster	1993	7	8
Dragon	1940	6	9	Goat	1967	6	9	Dog	1994	6	9
Snake	1941	2	1	Monkey	1968	2	1	Pig	1995	2	1
Horse	1942	4	2	Rooster	1969	4	2	Rat	1996	4	2
Goat	1943	3	3	Dog	1970	3	3	Ox	1997	3	3
Monkey	1944	2	4	Pig	1971	2	4	Tiger	1998	2	4
Rooster	1945	1	8	Rat	1972	1	8	Rabbit	1999	1	8
Dog	1946	9	6	Ox	1973	9	6	Dragon	2000	9	6
Pig	1947	8	7	Tiger	1974	8	7	Snake	2001	8	7
Rat	1948	7	8	Rabbit	1975	7	8	Horse	2002	7	8
Ox	1949	6	9	Dragon	1976	6	9	Goat	2003	6	9
Tiger	1950	2	1	Snake	1977	2	1	Monkey	2004	2	1
Rabbit	1951	4	2	Horse	1978	4	2	Rooster	2005	4	2
Dragon	1952	3	3	Goat	1979	3	3	Dog	2006	3	3
Snake	1953	2	4	Monkey	1980	2	4	Pig	2007	2	4
Horse	1954	1	8	Rooster	1981	1	8	Rat	2008	1	8
Goat	1955	9	6	Dog	1982	9	6	Ox	2009	9	6
Monkey	1956	8	7	Pig	1983	8	7	Tiger	2010	8	7
Rooster	1957	7	8	Rat	1984	7	8	Rabbit	2011	7	8
Dog	1958	6	9	Ox	1985	6	9	Dragon	2012	6	9
Pig	1959	2	1	Tiger	1986	2	1	Snake	2013	2	1

Figure 10: The Eight Mansion Chart.

		East Life Group				West Life Group			
		1	3	4	9	2	6	7	8
Code:	Indications:								
+90	Wealth	SE	S	N	E	NE	W	NW	SW
+80	Health	E	N	S	SE	W	NE	SW	NW
+70	Relationships	S	SE	E	N	NW	SW	NE	W
+60	Stability	N	E	SE	S	SW	NW	W	NE
-60	Setbacks	W	SW	NW	NE	E	SE	N	S
-70	Lawsuits/Affairs	NE	NW	SW	W	SE	E	S	N
-80	Bad Health	NW	NE	W	SW	S	N	SE	E
-90	Total Disaster	SW	W	NE	NW	N	S	E	SE

Figure 11: The Eight Mansion Directions.

Now that you have your personal Life Gua Number, this chart will give you all the pertinent information to start improving your Feng Shui.

Now let's examine the chart, it has a good deal of information on it. First, based on your Life Gua Number, you will be part of the East Life Group or the West Life Group. Those who are a 1, 3, 4, or 9 Guas are part of the East group, and those who are a 2, 6, 7, or 8 belong to the West group. As opposites attract, it's not unusual for couples to belong to different groups.

Next, notice the Code column; this is the clever creation of my teacher Grandmaster Yap Cheng Hai to refer to your good and bad directions without using the Chinese words associated with them. For example your best direction will be +90 which indicates prosperity or wealth-luck. The +80 will help you to secure good health. The +70 direction is your personal direction to enhance romance, relationships, harmony, and so forth. Once you have located your personal Life Gua Number on the chart, just follow down that column to see all good and bad directions and a brief description of what they'll indicate if you use them.

The Gua number is highly significant. Not only can you derive the directions that support you, but it will also gives you important clues about your personality (more about this in the next chapter) and key relationships. It's also used to determine the capability of spouses, the relationship between parents and children, and the dynamic between siblings, work mates, and business partners.

The Four Best Directions

Sheng Chi (+90)—Wealth: *Sheng Chi* means "generating breath" or energy that gives life. This is the number one direction to stimulate wealth. Often referred to as *millionaire chi*, this direction is one that is good for business opportunities, promotions at work, descendants, and wealth-luck. Your Sheng Chi direction will also establish positions of authority and powerful connections.

Tien Yi (+80)—Health: *Tien Yi* means "heavenly doctor," and this is the best direction to ensure good health. This direction also has been known to bring unexpected wealth, as if from the heavens. Using this direction can bring long life, close friends, excellent social standing, and the power of speech.

Yen Nien (+70)—Relationships: This direction is all about personal relationships, love of family, romantic partners, networking, and family harmony in general. If this direction is used it can bring well-off, famous, and rich descendants. If you want to have children quickly, place your bed to this direction. The Yen Nien direction also connotes health and longevity; it is often misspelled Nien Yen.

Fu Wei (+60)—Stability: This direction is a mirror of your own energy, and can bring stability. It indicates moderate wealth and happiness; it is a good alternative if you cannot use your best directions. The Fu Wei direction suggests a middle-class family with good harmony. If you want older children to move out of the house, place their headboards in this direction.

The Four Worst Directions

Wo Hai (-60)—Setbacks: If this direction is used, it will attract all sorts of aggravating obstacles, persistent set-backs, and losing money in investments. It can bring small disasters, but not overwhelming ones; nothing goes smoothly. For example, you may win your court case, but not receive the monetary settlement.

Wu Gwei (-70)—Lawsuits, Affairs, and Betrayals: This direction is referred to as the "five ghosts," and it primarily indicates lawsuits and litigation. If you use this direction, it can bring lots of trouble in romance, rebellious children, drug use, petty people, robberies, illicit affairs, hot-tempered people, betrayals, lack of support from employees, gossip, and being undermined.

Liu Sha (-80)—Bad Health, Backstabbing, and Accidents: Known as the "six killing" direction; using this direction will attract injury, loss of wealth, backstabbing, affairs, awful money-luck, harm to you and the family, betrayals in business, accidents of all sorts, and serious illness such as cancer. The Liu Sha direction can have you become *unrecognized* in the world.

Chueh Ming (-90)—Total Disaster and Major Losses: Activating this direction can bring grievous harm that may include bankruptcy, a death in the family, divorce, horrific failure in business, accidents, and no descendants. It brings total disaster and major losses and should be avoided.

Now that you have your Life Gua Number and have located your best and worst directions, you will be able to improve the Feng Shui of your home and business environments considerably, maximizing the potential of the rooms in which you live and work. The following recommendations concern features such as doors, toilets, stove/knobs, bedroom locations, and bed directions. The stove knob direction is important because it ignites fire and stoves are the most important fire feature in a house.

The following is great information but need not be committed to memory; the Eight Mansions' principles are automatically factored in for you in the recommendations for your home in chapters 8 and 9. Here are some important ways you can use Eight Mansions in your living space in order to enhance relationship-luck:

Doors: You must have a good door that brings you great relationship-luck. If you have a door facing one of your four good directions, use it. Be sure to take a compass direction of the interior garage door if this is the door you primarily use. Doors are very important in Feng Shui; they get the highest priority. Your house and front door ideally would face and receive energy from your +70. The door you enter from 90 percent of the time must be one of your four good directions (+60, +70, +80, or +90). If not, use another door to enter. For example, if your front door is excellent, and your interior garage door is not—mix it up. Use your garage door only 20 percent of the time and your front door 80 percent of the time. This one change alone will immediately alter your luck—that's how powerful doors are!

Bedrooms and Bed Direction: Bedrooms are such an important part of our lives, and the energy should be conducive for harmonious living. Since the master bedroom is crucial, particular attention should be paid to this room as it will determine the luck of the patriarch, head of household, or breadwinner (of any gender). This room governs the finances, harmony, and the family's well-being. It will determine the relationship luck, personal and business. The woman of the house's luck is also affected by the master bedroom location and arrangement. Feng Shui places great emphasis on not only the location of the bedroom but the bed direction as well. The sleeping direction is of vital significance for both married and single people. This area of the house is an opportunity not to be missed to enhance your life.

If your master bedroom is located in a good sector of the house for you, this is a good start to excellent relationships. Obviously, you can choose any area of the house in a custom-designed home. However, since direction is more powerful than location, make sure your bed is to a good direction. If you wish to attract a good partner or enjoy good relationships—it is best to sleep to your +70 (Yen Nien) direction. In order to activate the correct bed direction, you will need to place your headboard to that direction. Move your bed to the relationship direction; even if it means you have to angle it to do so. Your bedroom should ideally be *located* in the +70 sector of the house. The bed direction/headboard would be to your +70 direction as well.

Toilet Placement: The toilets of the house should not be located in any of your good sectors. Toilets are best placed in your -90, -80, -70 or -60 locations. You should *not* have a toilet located in your +70 sector of the house; relationships will be very difficult and may turn out "crappy." Many have the mistaken idea that the toilet will "flush" away something—money or good relationships. This is not accurate; the reason toilets should *not* be located in your good sectors is the *nature* and *use* of the toilet.

The Stove: A good location of the stove is another powerful way to use the Eight Mansions system. It is said that "fire" has the ability to burn up your bad luck. So it should be located on any of your negative areas, especially in your -70 or -80 area if you want to increase relationship and romance-luck. By doing this, you'll be burning up your bad luck. However, you will not have a good result if your stove is located in your +70, as relationships and romance can burn out quickly. The knobs of the stove should be to one of your good directions, particularly your +70. Knobs are typically located in the front or right-hand side.

Office and Desk: The location of a home office becomes really important if you have a home-based business or if you spend a great deal of time there. At minimum, you will need to face, while sitting at your desk, a good direction (+60, +70, +80, or +90). Face your +70 direction if possible, as it will support romance, family, employee, and client relationships. If you face your -70, you will activate lawsuits, betrayals, and possibly bad romance.

Advanced Eight Mansions

The Eight Mansions system has two levels; basic Eight Mansions and Advanced Eight Mansions (AEM). Basic Eight Mansions is used to determine your Life Gua Number, good/bad directions, and personality type. (More on the personality profiles in the next chapter.)

Advanced Eight Mansions is used when a couple consisting of people of different Life Groups lives together, necessitating the need for one living space to support both people. It allows certain 15-degree increments of "bad" directions to be used and activated. In general, this is how it works: Basic Eight Mansions dictates that south is a bad direction for anyone who is West Life Group (2, 6, 7, or 8), but in AEM, the first and third 15-degrees of south can be used. Which means you can face your bed direction or desk or use doors facing these increments. If you are East Life Group (1, 3, 4, or 9), west is one of your bad directions. However, in AEM you can use the first and third 15-degree increments. Keeping this in mind, the entire 45 degrees of north unfortunately cannot be used by anyone part of the West Life Group (2, 6, 7, or 8)—not one single degree.

Couples who are part of different life groups need special considerations to make it work for both people. These differences have already been factored in the recommendations located in chapters 8 and 9, so pay close attention to suggested directions according to your Life Gua. This is really important where you may share the same space—the marital bed. In this case, choose a direction that is good for all Guas. Don't worry if you see me recommending what appears to be a "bad" direction; remember that in Advanced Eight Mansions certain fifteen-degree increments are allowed. Conversely, you may see that I'm not recommending using one of your "good" directions. The reason for this is that the "stars" are not good in that particular direction; if used you will likely get mixed results depending on how bad the stars are. By following the recommendations, you get the best of both worlds—great Eight Mansions and Flying Stars!

––––––––

The Eight Mansions system has various aspects; this chapter addressed the best ways to use your good and bad directions based on your Life Gua Number. That number is derived from your birth date and gender. Certainly, it is excellent to have your home face your best direction (Sheng Chi, +90), or perhaps to attract better relationships, a door that is in the direction of your Yen Nien (+70). In this system, fire (stoves) can burn up your bad luck/directions (-90, -80, -70, or -60), bringing good relationships, money, and health-luck. Now, let's examine the personality traits of all eight Life Guas and the relationships between them.

Five

·····················

Life-Gua Zodiac
Personalities

·····················

Love is like a war; easy to begin, hard to end.
Ancient Chinese Proverb

In this chapter we will fully explore several important and key aspects of
Eight Mansions involving the eight Life Guas (some masters call this
the *Ming Gua*). Now that you know your personal Life Gua Number,
you have information on which directions support you and which bring
trouble. Also, based on your Life Gua, you're assigned certain personality
traits, energy, and certain characteristics. This facet is *not* used for directional luck; rather it provides insight into ourselves and the Life Guas
with which we are most compatible.

The personality narratives work very similar to astrology; each Life
Gua will have an element (Water, Wood, Fire, Earth, or Metal) and this
energy will influence the person's behavior, habits, physical looks, health
issues, attraction to specific occupations, thinking process, and sexual
desires—both negative and positive in all these areas. I call these portrayals

the Life Gua Personalities, and I'm the originator of this particular extraction from the Eight Mansions system (first introduced in *Classical Feng Shui for Wealth and Abundance*). Although the Life Gua Personalities cannot be found in the ancient classical texts, the information on Guas can. The idea started when Master Yap gave us quick, verbal descriptions of each of the Life Guas in class one day. We were greatly entertained by this and I began sharing the descriptions when consulting with my clients, giving them key information about their spouses, children, coworkers, business partners, bosses, and family members. I also started including it in my training classes and public lectures; people loved it. After many years of doing this verbally and informally, I decided to expand on Master Yap's three-word description of the Life Guas and pen it, based on the extensive information available on the Guas and their elements. Do keep in mind that they are general and not meant to be definitive. That said, I've found that they are very accurate, after consulting with thousands of clients.

Even though the Life Gua gives great insights into our personalities, I noticed that not all Life Guas were created equal. For example, while the 1 Life Guas in general are very intelligent, secretive, freedom-loving, and highly sensuous, they can be very different depending on the animal year in which they were born. For example a 1 Gua born in a Snake year is very different from a 1 Gua born in a Horse year. So I decided to once again expand the Life Gua Personalities by matching them with the Chinese zodiac animal years of birth, giving an even more specific picture of the personality traits and proclivities.

In the following descriptions you'll see the good…and bad. Keep in mind that everyone is capable of exhibiting their negative, dark side at any given time. All energy, including that of us, has yin and yang aspects—this is our nature. Our awareness level largely depends on which of the qualities we primarily show to the world. We all have times we are not "on" and may slip into our negative selves. Try not to be offended or focus on the negative aspects of your personality descriptions, as you may already have evolved past most of it.

Life-Gua Zodiac Personalities
Life Guas Combined with Animal Years of Birth

Below you will find all eight Life Guas combined with the twelve Chinese zodiac animal signs; there are 96 possible combinations, but some Life Guas never match up with certain animal years. For example, those born in the years of the Ox, Dragon, Goat, or Dog will only be a 3, 6, or 9 Gua. Other combinations will be exclusive to one gender. I've named this expanded version of the Life Gua personalities the Life Gua Zodiac Personalities. You will need your Life Gua Number and the animal year in which you were born to find your personality description; both may be found using the Eight Mansions chart in chapter 4. Keep in mind the new year according to the Chinese solar calendar begins on February 4 in any given year about 99.9 percent of the time. On rare occasions, it begins on February 3 or 5. If you were born on February 3, 4, or 5, refer to the chart in the appendix to see when the new year actually began for your birth year. For everyone else, refer to your year of birth to locate your Life Gua.

Also note that in the following descriptives, the elements of the animals are not based on element of the year, (e.g., the year of the Water Snake). Rather, the element of the animals are based on the 24 Mountain directions (and part of the stems and branches theory).[9] For example, the Pig is Water, the Dragon is Earth, and the Monkey is Metal energy, and so forth. Using the element of each year would produce hundreds of combinations, so I opted for a simple, concise approach when combining them with the Life Guas. There are two elements listed for each Life Gua Zodiac Personality; the first one represents the Gua's energy and the second is the animal's energy. For example, the 1 Gua is Water and the Rat is also Water; this makes the 1 Gua-Rat people a double Water sign.

---

9. The 24 Mountain directions are 15-degree increments representing all possible facings for buildings. There are twelve animal parts of these directions as well; each is assigned an element. See more on the 24 Mountain directions in chapter 6 on Flying Stars.

The 1 Guas
1 Gua as a Rat
Men Only!
Sensuous, High Strung, Survivors
Elements: Yang Water and Yang Water
Years Occurring: 1936, 1972, 2008, 2044
No female 1 Guas are ever born in the year of the Rat.

Famous 1 Gua Rat Men: Vidal Sassoon, Buddy Holly, Engelbert
Humperdinck, Glen Campbell, Kris Kristofferson, Albert Finney,
Wilt Chamberlain, Silvio Berlusconi, Robert Redford, Burt Reyn-
olds, Bobby Darin, David Carradine, Jim Henson, John McCain,
Bruce Dern, Yves Saint-Laurent, Louis Gossett Jr., Ben Affleck,
Jude Law, Dwayne Johnson, Marlon Wayans, Eminem, Brad Pais-
ley, Dane Cook, Josh Duhamel, Scott Peterson, Antonio Sabato Jr.,
Notorious B.I.G, Billie Joe Armstrong, Shaquille O'Neal.

Personality and Romance: The 1 Gua men who are born in the year of
the Rat are in a double Water sign making them extremely emotional, sensuous, and high strung. These men are highly intelligent,
imaginative, and very charming. The Water-Water combination
also enhances their natural intuitive abilities in sizing people up;
when provoked the 1 Gua Rat can become very aggressive. With
the appearance of being cool and dignified, deep down these men
tend to be insecure and react very well to praise rather than criticism. The rat is one of the oldest survivors on the planet; their
energy adapts, endures, and overcomes almost any challenge presented. They love being free, mobile, and the excitement of travel. 1
Gua Rats tend to be very loyal in relationships and need a partner
who can handle their deep sexuality, moodiness, high energy, and
intensity. If they have love affairs, they are still loyal to their wives
and family and would not abandon them—these temptations are
never affairs of the heart, per se, just dalliances.

The Best Stuff: When 1 Gua Rats are fully exhibiting their best qualities, they are very intelligent, forthright, disciplined, systematic, meticulous, charismatic, charming, cool, dignified, hardworking, industrious, charming, eloquent, sociable, and shrewd.

The Worst Stuff: When 1 Gua Rats move into the darker side of their nature, they can be manipulative, cruel, dictatorial, rigid, selfish, obstinate, critical, over-ambitious, ruthless, intolerant, scheming, and stubborn.

Career: Some of the best professions for the 1 Gua Rats where they may attain wealth, fame, or fulfillment are as writers, advisors, counselors, lawyers, politicians, designers, managers, directors, entrepreneurs, researchers, historians, and race car drivers, or in the finance, communications, entertainment, and publishing industries.

Best Matches: Anyone part of the East Life Group (1, 3, 4, or 9 Life Guas); excellent matches are 4 Guas born in the year of the Monkey or Rat; 3 or 9 Guas born in the Dragon. In the West Life Group, the 2 or 8 Guas may try to control or pressure you; however, the 6 and 7 Guas work well. Avoid any Life Gua born in the year of the Horse as this is considered a direct clash with your energy.

1 Gua as an Ox
There are no 1 Guas, male or female, ever born in the year of the Ox; it will only produce a 3, 6, or 9 Gua.

1 Gua as a Tiger
Women Only!
Leaders, Risk-Takers, Raw Energy
Elements: Yang Water and Yang Wood
Years Occurring: 1914, 1950, 1986, 2022
No male 1 Guas are ever born in the year of the Tiger.

Famous 1 Gua Tiger Women: Dorothy Lamour, Karen Carpenter, Cybill Shepherd, Natalie Cole, Joan Lunden, Susan Anton, Arianna Huffington, Princess Anne, Deniece Williams, Cristina Ferrare, Patti Austin, Christina Onassis, Dianna Agron, Leighton Meester, Camilla Belle, Amber Heard, Lea Michele, Ellie Goulding, Megan Fox, Amanda Bynes, Lindsay Lohan, Lady Gaga, Mary-Kate and Ashley Olsen.

Personality and Romance: The 1 Gua born in the year of the Tiger is a mix of Water and Wood, making their energy progressive, powerful, and commanding, and they're usually the smartest people in the room. These women are gutsy and are natural leaders due to their highly developed intelligence. They exhibit and have a natural, primal and raw energy that is almost palatable. The 1 Gua Tigers are huge risk-takers, spontaneously using their charm and independent nature to influence people in any setting to always come out on top. Despite their powerful energy, they can be very vulnerable and often become victims of their own outrageous, unchecked passions. They can get bored with their partners quite easily and may move from lover to lover—all in the pursuit of finding true love. In general, they are very talented at making money; they also may squander it. In relationships, 1 Gua Tiger women never bore their partners; they are intensely passionate and are protective of their mates, employees, children, and anyone in their care.

The Best Stuff: When the 1 Gua Tigers are fully exhibiting their best qualities, they are powerful, passionate, daring, stimulating, sincere, affectionate, humanitarian, and generous.

The Worst Stuff: When the 1 Gua Tigers move to the darker side of their nature, they can be restless, reckless, impatient, secretive, quick-tempered, moody, obstinate, and selfish.

Career: Some of the best professions for 1 Gua Tigers where they may attain wealth, fame, or fulfillment are in advertising, art, commercial aviation, travel, design, politics, travel journalism, exploration, business leadership, sales, freight, shipping, fishing, and firefighting.

Best Matches: Anyone part of the East Life Group (1, 3, 4, or 9 Life Guas); excellent matches are 4 Guas born in the year of the Tiger or Horse; 3 or 9 Guas born in the year of the Dog. In the West Life Group, the 2 or 8 Guas may try to control or pressure you; however, the 6 and 7 Guas work well. Avoid any Life Gua born in the year of the Monkey, as this is considered a direct clash with your energy.

1 Gua as a Rabbit
Men Only!
Highly Sexual, Refined, Very Clever
Elements: Yang Water and Yin Wood
Year Begins February 4
Years Occurring: 1927, 1963, 1999, 2035
No female 1 Guas are ever born in the year of the Rabbit.

Famous 1 Gua Rabbit Men: Clint Walker, Harry Belafonte, Tom Bosley, Bob Fosse, Jerry Stiller, Doc Severinsen, Robert Shaw, Neil Simon, Pope Benedict XVI, Peter Falk, Roger Moore, Sidney Poitier, George C. Scott, Brad Pitt, Michael Jordan, Bret Michaels, John Stamos, Seal, George Michael, Dermot Mulroney, Kevin Sorbo, Marc Jacobs, Conan O'Brien, David Thewlis, Mike Myers, Charles Barkley, James Hetfield, Donnie Yen, Johnny Depp, Jet Li, Quentin Tarantino, Benjamin Bratt.

Personality and Romance: The 1 Gua men who are born in the year of the Rabbit are a mix of Water and Wood elements, giving them lightning-quick intelligence accentuated by acute cleverness. Highly social, they are classy and refined men that are well-mannered with high style. The 1 Gua Rabbits are low-profile, extremely tactful, accommodating, always correct, and well-groomed. They are known for their good judgment and tend to be very shrewd about people and their character. These men are very concerned with how they are perceived and must have the right address, the right woman, and the right kind of car; image is very important. They tend to be insecure by nature and are not risk-takers at all—prone to being on the cautious side of investments, relationships, and feelings. 1 Gua Rabbits are naturally sensuous and highly sexual. These men are proficient at holding on to their money, ideas, and concepts; they are also skillful at hiding secrets.

The Best Stuff: When the 1 Gua Rabbits are fully exhibiting their best qualities, they are gracious, kind, sensitive, soft-spoken, amiable, elegant, reserved, cautious, artistic, thorough, tender, self-assured, astute, compassionate, and flexible.

The Worst Stuff: When the 1 Gua Rabbits move to the darker side of their nature, they can be moody, detached, superficial, self-indulgent, opportunistic, and lazy.

Career: Some of the best professions for the 1 Gua Rabbits where they may attain wealth, fame, or fulfillment are in design, cultivation, education, medicine, culture, judiciary, public relations, life coaching, advising, shipping, communications, entertainment, the sex industry, or as a diplomat.

Best Matches: Anyone part of the East Life Group (1, 3, 4, or 9 Life Guas); excellent matches are 4 Guas born in the year of the Pig or Rabbit; 3 or 9 Guas born in the year of the Goat. In the West Life Group, the 2 or 8 Guas may try to control or pressure you; however the 6 and 7 Guas work well. Avoid any Life Gua born in the year of the Rooster, as this is considered a direct clash with your energy.

1 Gua as a Dragon

There are no 1 Guas ever born in the year of the Dragon; it will only produce a 3, 6, or 9 Gua.

1 Gua as a Snake

Women Only!
Seductive, High-Strung, Intelligent
Elements: Yang Water and Yin Fire
Year Begins February 4
Years Occurring: 1905, 1941, 1977, 2013, 2049
No 1 Gua males are ever born in the year of the Snake.

Famous 1 Gua Snake Women: Joan Crawford, Greta Garbo, Julie Christie, Linda McCartney, Helen Reddy, Martha Stewart, Sally Kirkland, Juliet Mills, Vikki Carr, Ann Margret, Faye Dunaway, Nora Ephron, Sophia Rossi, Sarah Michelle Gellar, Maggie Gyllenhaal, Gaby Espino, Jaime Pressly, Katheryn Winnick, Irina Voronina, Melanie Jayne Lynskey, Brittany Murphy, Liv Tyler.

Personality and Romance: The 1 Gua women who were born in the year of the Snake are a mix of Water and Fire, both are volatile types of energy that make this personality almost impossible to pin down. Usually blessed with beauty, allure, dignity, and charm, they have lovely manners and are rarely short of admirers. These women are masters at the waiting game and will take their time finding the right job, the right house, and the right spouse. 1 Gua Snakes are extremely intelligent, high-strung, and know how to get what they want from people using their incredible seductive skills. It's unwise to make an enemy of this personality, as they will get their revenge. They tend to be highly sexual, sensuous, and emotional in nature. They are adept in using their internal energy for powerful results in all areas of their life.

The Best Stuff: When 1 Gua Snakes are fully exhibiting their best qualities, they are deep thinkers, wise, mystical, graceful, soft-spoken, sensual, creative, secretive, prudent, shrewd, ambitious, elegant, cautious, responsible, calm, strong, constant, and purposeful.

The Worst Stuff: When 1 Gua Snakes move to the darker side of their nature, they can be loners, bad communicators, possessive, moody, emotional, hedonistic, self-doubting, distrustful, and mendacious.

Career: Some of the best professions for 1 Gua Snakes to attain wealth, fame, or fulfillment, are as scientists, analysts, astrologers, politicians, lawyers, archaeologists, entrepeneurs, philosophers or diplomats, or in banking, freight, entertainment, fire fighting, and in the publishing industry.

Best Matches: Anyone part of the East Life Group (1, 3, 4, or 9 Life Guas); excellent matches are 4 Guas born in the year of Snake or Rooster; 3 or 9 Guas born in the year of the Ox. In the West Life Group, 2 or 8 Guas may try to control or pressure you, but 6 and 7 Guas work well. Avoid any Life Gua born in the year of the Pig, as this is considered a direct clash with your energy.

1 Gua as a Horse
Men Only!
Confident, Proud, Intelligent
Elements: Yang Water and Yang Fire
Year Begins February 4
Years Occurring: 1918, 1954, 1990, 2026
There are no female 1 Guas ever born in the year of the Horse.

Famous 1 Gua Horse Men: Nelson Mandela, Eddy Arnold, Billy Graham, Leonard Bernstein, Mike Wallace, Howard Cosell, Sam Walton, William Holden, Denzel Washington, John Travolta, Jackie Chan, Ron Howard, Dennis Quaid, Ray Liotta, James Cameron,

Jermaine Jackson, Elvis Costello, Adam Ant, David Lee Roth, Chris Noth, Yanni, Al Roker, Stone Phillips, Dennis Haysbert, Bruce Hornsby, Jerry Seinfeld, James Belushi, Ang Lee, Dev Patel.

Personality and Romance: The 1 Gua born in the year of the Horse is a mix of Water and Fire—unpredictable energies that can be powerful but unstable. The 1 Gua Horse characteristics are that of strength and persistence. These people are highly intelligent, high-speed, and analytical thinkers, but they also have rich emotional and varied inner landscapes. These men have tremendous inner confidence, love to be the center of attention, and are stimulated by the next challenge. 1 Gua Horses are proud and independent but long for a life partner who can match their deeply sensuous nature. They prefer to live in harmony with a good mate who can bring stability and allow them to exhibit their full power and spirit. 1 Gua Horse men tend to fall hard and fast in relationships but get a great deal mellower late in life.

The Best Stuff: When 1 Gua Horses are fully exhibiting their best qualities, they are cheerful, popular, quick-witted, changeable, earthy, perceptive, talkative, agile (mentally and physically), magnetic, astute, flexible, open-minded, and intelligent.

The Worst Stuff: When 1 Gua Horses move to the darker side of their nature, they can be moody, fickle, anxious, rude, gullible, stubborn, and lack perseverance and emotional stability.

Career: Some of the best professions for 1 Gua Horses where they may attain wealth, fame, or fulfillment are in journalism, language instruction, public performance, aviation, library science, politics, sports, construction, geography, finance, banking, communications, entertainment, diplomacy, and as executives.

Best Matches: Anyone part of the East Life Group (1, 3, 4, or 9 Life Guas); excellent matches are 4 Guas born in the year of the Tiger or Horse; 3 or 9 Guas born in the year of the Dog. In the West

Life Group, 2 or 8 Guas may try to control or pressure you; however 6 and 7 Guas work well. Avoid any Life Gua born in the year of the Rat, as this is considered a direct clash with your energy.

1 Gua as a Goat

There are no 1 Guas ever born in the year of the Goat; it will only produce a 3, 6, or 9 Gua.

1 Gua as a Monkey
Women Only!
Quick, Highly Intelligent, Sexual
Element: Yang Water and Yang Metal
Year Begins February 4
Years Occurring: 1896, 1932, 1968, 2004, 2040
There are no male 1 Guas ever born in the year of the Monkey.

Famous 1 Gua Monkey Women: Wallis Simpson (Duchess of Windsor), Elizabeth Taylor, Debbie Reynolds, Loretta Lynn, Patsy Cline, Ellen Burstyn, Catherine Bell, Vanessa Marcil, Stephanie Seymour, Yasmine Bleeth, Helena Christensen, Lucy Lawless, Gillian Anderson, Patricia Arquette, Ricki Lake, Naomi Watts, Lucy Liu, Ashley Judd, Rachael Ray, Celine Dion, Lisa Marie Presley, Debra Messing, Traci Lords.

Personality and Romance: The 1 Gua born in the year of the Monkey is Water and Metal energy, making it mercurial in nature. These women's personalities can be moody, quick, highly intelligent, and at certain times of their life, promiscuous, as they can get easily bored with their lovers. 1 Gua Monkeys are always hatching new ideas, concepts, or inventing new systems. They are playful and may be hard to pin down in relationships, and they won't settle down quickly. However, with an excellent partner, they will commit to that person in every way. 1 Gua Monkey ladies can be secretive, having arcane aspects to their lives or possibly whole other lives.

The Best Stuff: When 1 Gua Monkeys are fully exhibiting their best qualities, they are inventive, motivators, improvisers, quick-witted, inquisitive, flexible, innovative, problem solvers, self-assured, sociable, polite, dignified, competitive, objective, factual, and intellectual.

The Worst Stuff: When the 1 Gua Monkeys move to the darker side of their nature, they can be egotistical, vain, selfish, cunning, jealous, and suspicious.

Career: Some of the best professions for 1 Gua Monkeys where they may attain wealth, fame, or fulfillment are in media, banking, science, engineering, the stock market, film directing, jewelry, public relations, surveying, sports, construction, geography, communications, entertainment, the sex industry, or publishing.

Best Matches: Anyone part of the East Life Group (1, 3, 4, or 9 Life Guas); excellent matches are 4 Guas born in the year of the Monkey or Rat; 3 and 9 Guas born in the year of the Dragon. In the West Life Group, the 2 or 8 Guas may try to control or pressure you but 6 and 7 Guas work well. Avoid any Life Gua born in the year of the Tiger as this is considered a direct clash with your energy.

1 Gua as a Rooster
Men Only!
Creative, Trustworthy, Very Social
Element: Yang Water and Yin Metal
Year Begins February 4
Years Occurring: 1909, 1945, 1981, 2017, 2053
No female 1 Guas are ever born in the year of the Rooster.

Famous 1 Gua Rooster Men: James Mason, Burl Ives, Benny Goodman, Steve Martin, Bob Seger, Bob Marley, Henry Winkler, Eric Clapton, Bubba Smith, Neil Young, John Lithgow, John Fogerty, Barry Bostwick, Van Morrison, Pete Townshend, Michael Nouri, Richard

Thomas, José Feliciano, Phil Jackson, John Heard, Davy Jones, Joseph Gordon-Levitt, Josh Groban, Ben Barnes, Jay Sean.

Personality and Romance: The 1 Gua born in the year of the Rooster is also a mix of Metal and Water energy, but this mix is grounded. 1 Gua Roosters have the strength of persistence and formidable personal power. They tend to be very social and are loyal and trustworthy with family, friends, and business associates. Since these men tend to "tell it like it is," the best life partner for the 1 Gua Roosters is one that understands that underneath their "crowing" and gruffness lies a heart of gold. These personalities are more transparent and less secretive than most 1 Guas. 1 Gua Roosters are excellent at ferreting people out, and they have very sharp opinions. Filled with a sensuous nature, sex and loyalty are paramount to these sensitive, social creatures.

The Best Stuff: When 1 Gua Roosters are fully exhibiting their best qualities, they are neat, meticulous, organized, self-assured, decisive, conservative, alert, zealous, practical, scientific, responsible, and perfectionists.

The Worst Stuff: When the 1 Gua Roosters move to the darker side of their nature, they can be secretive, moody, overzealous, critical, puritanical, egotistical, abrasive, and opinionated.

Career: Some of the best professions for 1 Gua Roosters where they may attain wealth, fame, or fulfillment are as an author, restaurateur, athlete, journalist, dentist, surgeon, soldier, fireman, entertainer, news anchor, politician, banker, or diplomat, or in communications or the military.

Best Matches: Anyone part of the East Life Group (1, 3, 4, or 9 Life Guas); excellent matches are 4 Guas born in the year of the Snake or Rooster; 3 or 9 Guas born in year of the Ox. In the West Life Group, 2 or 8 Guas may try to control or pressure you; however 6 and 7 Guas work well. Avoid any Life Gua born in the year of the Rabbit as this is considered a direct clash with your energy.

1 Gua as a Dog

There are no 1 Guas ever born in the year of the Dog; it will only produce a 3, 6, or 9 Life Gua.

1 Gua as a Pig

Women Only!
Generous, Sexual, Intelligent
Elements: Yang Water and Yin Water
Years Occurring: 1923, 1959, 1995, 2031
No male 1 Guas are ever born in the year of the Pig.

Famous 1 Gua Pig Women: Rhonda Fleming, Maria Callas, Lorrie Morgan, Marie Osmond, Rebecca De Mornay, Rosanna Arquette, Sheena Easton, Sean Young, Emma Thompson, Patricia Clarkson, Kelly Emberg, Nancy Grace, Irene Cara, Mackenzie Phillips, Marcia Gay Harden, Sarah Ferguson (Duchess of York), Aphrodite Jones, Jordyn Wieber, Kendall Jenner, Gabrielle Douglas, Missy Franklin.

Personality and Romance: 1 Guas born in the year of the Pig are double Water, making them very emotional, sensuous, and intelligent. These women are very generous and are keenly perceptive. 1 Gua Pigs are affectionate, highly sexual, and make great partners. They possess an inner power that makes them reliable and wise in times of crisis. Those born under these energies are great accumulators of wealth, energy, or wisdom (think of it as the pig's "pot belly"). They are studious, diligent, and compassionate. The double Water of 1 Gua Pig females also makes them very anxious, nervous, and a bit high strung. These ladies love their freedom, and even in a solid marriage need lots of space; keeping tight reins will lead to rebellion, remoteness, or an exit.

The Best Stuff: When 1 Gua Pigs are fully exhibiting their best qualities, they are honest, sturdy, sociable, peace-loving, patient, loyal, hard-working, trusting, sincere, calm, understanding, thoughtful, scrupulous, passionate, and intelligent.

The Worst Stuff: When 1 Gua Pigs move to the darker side of their nature, they can be naïve, secretive, over-reliant, self-indulgent, gullible, moody, fatalistic, excessively emotional, and materialistic.

Career: Some of the best professions for 1 Gua Pigs where they may attain wealth, fame, or fulfillment are in medicine, entertainment, catering, veterinary medicine, interior decoration, science, banking, horticulture, fishing, firefighting, the sex industry, or publishing.

Best Matches: Anyone part of the East Life Group (1, 3, 4, or 9 Life Guas); excellent matches are 4 Gua born in the year of the Pig or Rabbit; 3 or 9 Guas born in the year of the Goat. In the West Life Group, 2 or 8 Guas may try to control or pressure you; however the 6 and 7 Guas work well. Avoid any Life Gua born in the year of the Snake as this is considered a direct clash with your energy.

The 2 Guas
2 Gua as a Rat
Women Only!
Calm, Intelligent, Intuitive
Elements: Yin Earth and Yang Water
Year Begins February 4
Years Occurring: 1924, 1960, 1996, 2032
No male 2 Guas are ever born in the year of the Rat.

Famous 2 Gua Rat Women: Gloria Vanderbilt, Ruby Dee, Lauren Bacall, Eva Marie Saint, Kelly LeBrock, Kathy Griffin, Dorothy Stratten, Carol Alt, Emma Samms, Roma Downey, Meg Tilly, Robin Roberts, Jennifer Grey, Kristin Scott Thomas, Sarah Brightman, Daryl Hannah, Julianne Moore, Valerie Bertinelli, Greta Scacchi, Amy Grant, Abigail Breslin, Sasha Pieterse, Kyla Ross, Zendaya.

Personality and Romance: The 2 Gua born in the year of the Rat is a mix of Earth and Water energy, bringing a bit more emotion to their normal, calm nature. 2 Gua Rats are very intuitive, observant people with sharp accuracy. These women are attracted to the healing arts such as psychiatry in which they can use their energy and communicative skills. They make talented doctors with a compassionate, charming bedside manner that is reassuring to those in their care. The 2 Gua Rats are survivors, comfortable in dark spaces. They have relaxed demeanors but can be rigid as well. Since their energy is very yin, 2 Gua Rats can suffer from depression if not kept in check. Focusing on their creative side and love of travel will keep their energy high and expressed in productive outlets.

The Best Stuff: When 2 Gua Rats are fully exhibiting their best qualities, they are forthright, disciplined, systematic, meticulous, charismatic, hardworking, industrious, charming, eloquent, sociable, and shrewd.

The Worst Stuff: When 2 Gua Rats move to the darker side of their nature, they can be manipulative, cruel, dictatorial, rigid, selfish, obstinate, critical, depressed, over-ambitious, ruthless, intolerant, and scheming.

Career: Some of the best professions for 2 Gua Rats where they may attain wealth, fame or fulfillment, are as writers, broadcasters, advisors, lawyers, politicians, designers, engineers, entrepreneurs, race car drivers, or musicians, or in publishing, real estate, construction, hotels, architecture, or OB-GYN.

Best Matches: Anyone part of the West Life Group (2, 6, 7, or 8 Life Guas); excellent matches would be 8 Guas born in the year of the Monkey or Rat; 6 and 9 Guas born in the year of the Dragon. The 3 or 4 Guas may try to control or pressure you. Avoid any Life Gua born in the year of the Horse, as this is considered a direct clash with your energy.

2 Gua as an Ox

There are no 2 Guas ever born in the year of the Ox; it will only produce a 3, 6, or 9 Life Gua.

2 Gua as a Tiger

Men Only!
Primal Energy, Protective, Passionate
Elements: Yin Earth and Yang Wood
Year Begins February 4
Years Occurring: 1914, 1926, 1950, 1962, 1986, 1998, 2022, 2034
No female 2 Guas are ever born in the year of the Tiger.

Famous 2 Gua Tiger Men: Joe DiMaggio, Jack LaLanne, Andy Griffith, Chuck Berry, Hugh Hefner, Fidel Castro, Tony Bennett, Jerry Lewis, David Cassidy, Stevie Wonder, Huey Lewis, Bruce Boxleitner, Gabriel Byrne, Peter Frampton, William Hurt, Jay Leno, Ed Harris, Teddy Pendergrass, Bill Murray, Sir Richard Branson, Dr. Phil McGraw, Axl Rose, William H. Macy, Jon Bon Jovi, Tom Cruise, Tommy Lee, Ralph Fiennes, Garth Brooks, M.C. Hammer, Clint Black, Usain Bolt, Shia LaBeouf, Robert Pattinson.

Personality and Romance: The 2 Gua Tiger is a mix of Earth and Wood energy making them intense, but with a calm, self-assured, and primal energy. Like the powerful cat always aware of his natural environment, they are deeply sensitive and intuitive. They have a great deal of influence in any setting—personal or business—and they are natural, instinctive leaders. 2 Gua Tigers are huge risk-takers, spontaneous, independent, and they thrive by being on top! As they tend to be very passionate in relationships, they never bore their partners. Their natural, nurturing energy makes them very protective of what "belongs" to them.

The Best Stuff: When 2 Gua Tigers are fully exhibiting their best qualities, they are nurturing, unpredictable, colorful, powerful, passionate, daring, vigorous, stimulating, sincere, affectionate, humanitarian, and generous.

The Worst Stuff: When 2 Gua Tigers move to the darker side of their nature, they can be rebellious, impulsive, restless, reckless, impatient, quick-tempered, obstinate, and selfish.

Career: Some of the best professions for 2 Gua Tigers where they may attain wealth, fame, or fulfillment are in advertising, acting, aviation, comedy, design, politics, the military, exploration, property, real estate, consultancy, architecture, human resources, OB-GYN, or as business executives.

Best Matches: Anyone part of the West Life Group (2, 6, 7, or 8 Life Guas); excellent matches are 8 Guas born in the year of the Tiger or Horse or 6 or 9 Guas born in the year of the Dog. In the East Life Group, the 3 or 4 Guas may try to control or pressure you. Avoid any Life Gua born in the year of the Monkey as this is considered a direct clash with your energy.

2 Gua as a Rabbit
Women Only!
Quick, Sexual, Intuitive
Elements: Yin Earth and Yin Wood
Year Begins February 4
Years Occurring: 1915, 1951, 1987, 2023
No 2 Gua males are ever born in the year of the Rabbit.

Famous 2 Gua Rabbit Women: Ingrid Bergman, Billie Holiday, Beverly D'Angelo, Lynda Carter, Jane Seymour, Anjelica Huston, Olivia Hussey, Crystal Gayle, Jean Smart, JoJo Starbuck, Melissa Manchester, Suze Orman, Kathryn Bigelow, Queen Noor, Morgan Brittany,

Cheryl Ladd, Blake Lively, Ashley Greene, Hilary Duff, Rosie Huntington-Whiteley, Ellen Page, Joss Stone, Maria Sharapova.

Personality and Romance: 2 Gua Rabbits are always on the alert and are very sensitive, soft, and vulnerable. They tend to be honest, calm-natured, dependable, highly intelligent, clever, and their minds move lightning quick. 2 Gua Rabbits are generally insecure, and are not risk-takers at all. However, they are highly social, refined, and classy women with superior manners and great style. 2 Gua Rabbits are ladies who are naturally sensuous and highly sexual. They may have unrealistic expectations such as the "Cinderella complex," and need a partner who will not take advantage of them, as disappointment could lead to depression. Since their energy is really yin, at times they may be moody and detached.

The Best Stuff: When 2 Gua Rabbits are fully exhibiting their best qualities, they are gracious, kind, sensitive, soft-spoken, amiable, elegant, nurturing, reserved, cautious, artistic, thorough, tender, self-assured, astute, compassionate, and flexible.

The Worst Stuff: When the 2 Gua-Rabbits move to the darker side of their nature, they can be moody, detached, superficial, depressed, self-indulgent, opportunistic, and lazy.

Career: Some of the best professions for 2 Gua Rabbits where they may attain wealth, fame, or fulfillment are in cultivation, medicine, justice, politics, public relations, literature, law, advising, property, real estate, construction, consultancy, architecture, interior design, recruitment, or OB-GYN.

Best Matches: Anyone part of the West Life Group (2, 6, 7, or 8 Life Guas); excellent matches would be 8 Guas born in the year of the Pig or Rabbit, or 6 or 9 Guas born in the year of the Goat. In the East Life Group, the 3 or 4 Guas may try to control or pressure you. Avoid any Life Gua born in the year of the Rooster, as this is considered a direct clash with your energy.

2 Gua as a Dragon

There are no 2 Guas ever born in the year of the Dragon; it will only produce a 3, 6, or 9 Life Gua.

2 Gua as a Snake

Men Only!

Seductive, Possessive, Intuitive

Elements: Yin Earth and Yin Fire

Year Begins February 4

Years Occurring: 1917, 1941, 1953, 1977, 1989, 2013, 2025, 2050

No female 2 Guas are ever born in the year of the Snake.

Famous 2 Gua Snake Men: John F. Kennedy, Dean Martin, Desi Arnaz, Franco Nero, Ryan O'Neal, Michael Bolton, Bob Dylan, Paul Simon, Nick Nolte, Jesse Jackson, Pierce Brosnan, John Malkovich, Hulk Hogan, Alex Van Halen, Keith Hernandez, Bill Pullman, Tim Allen, John Mayer, Kanye West, Jonathan Rhys Meyers, Travis Alexander, Tom Hardy, John Cena, Ludacris, Joe Jonas, Daniel Radcliffe, Chris Brown, David Henrie, Prince George Alexander Louis.

Personality and Romance: The 2 Guas born in the year of the Snake have an interesting combination: very Earthy energy mixed with Fire. Men born under these signs are grounded, sensitive, intelligent, and are masters at the waiting game. They also know how to get what they want from people, making them consummate seducers. 2 Gua Snake men are often soft-spoken or use seductive speech; shrewd, cautious, calm-natured, and responsible. They can be possessive in relationships and of their possessions. Generally distrusting of everyone, they use their intuitive abilities to weed out the bad characters. One of their best qualities is how they reserve and use their internal energy for powerful results.

The Best Stuff: When 2 Gua Snakes are fully exhibiting their best qualities, they are deep thinkers, wise, mystic, graceful, soft-spoken, sensual, creative, prudent, shrewd, ambitious, elegant, cautious, responsible, calm, strong, constant, nurturing, and purposeful.

The Worst Stuff: When 2 Gua Snakes move to the darker side of their nature, they can be lonely, poor communicators, possessive, depressed, hedonistic, self-doubting, distrustful, and mendacious.

Career: Some of the best professions for 2 Gua Snakes where they may attain wealth, fame, or fulfillment are as scientists, investigators, jewelers, magicians, politicians, lawyers, astrologers, archaeologists, entrepreneurs, spelunkers, psychologists, philosophers, architects, interior designers, or in human resources.

Best Matches: Anyone part of the West Life Group (2, 6, 7, or 8 Life Guas); excellent matches would be 8 Guas born in the year of the Snake or Rooster, or 6 and 9 Guas born in the year of the Ox. In the East Life Group, the 3 or 4 Guas may try to control or pressure you. Avoid any Life Gua born in the year of the Pig, as this is considered a direct clash with your energy.

2 Gua as a Horse

Women Only!

Persistent, Confident, Magnetic

Elements: Yin Earth and Yang Fire

Year Begins February 4

Years Occurring: 1906, 1942, 1978, 2014, 2050

No male 2 Guas are ever born in the year of the Horse.

Famous 2 Gua Horse Women: Mary Astor, Josephine Baker, Jean Shrimpton, Carole King, Sandra Dee, Penny Marshall, Annette Funicello, Linda Evans, Barbra Streisand, Aretha Franklin, Carole King, Geneviève Bujold, Rachel McAdams, Katie Holmes,

Katherine Heigl, Maria Menounos, Ginnifer Goodwin, Nicole Scherzinger, Stana Katic, Zoe Saldana, Karina Smirnoff.

Personality and Romance: The 2 Gua women born in the year of the Horse bring a powerful combination of Earth and Fire energy making them both grounded and exciting to be around! They thrive on being the center of attention, have incredible inner confidence, and are always looking to be stimulated by the next big thing or challenge. The 2 Gua Horses are very proud, calm, dependable, and supportive of everyone in their inner circle. However, they need their independence even when they choose a life partner. They prefer to live in harmony with a good mate where they can feel safe to live to their full potential. While they may fall hard and fast in relationships, they do mellow out as they age. If they are not fully able to influence their life and living environment, they tend toward depression and melancholy episodes.

The Best Stuff: When 2 Gua Horses are fully exhibiting their best qualities, they are nurturing, cheerful, popular, quick-witted, changeable, earthy, perceptive, talkative, agile both mentally and physically, magnetic, intelligent, astute, flexible, and open-minded.

The Worst Stuff: When 2 Gua Horses move to the darker side of their nature, they can be stubborn, fickle, anxious, rude, depressed, gullible, and lack stability and perseverance.

Career: Some of the best professions for 2 Gua Horses, where they may attain wealth, fame or fulfillment, are as a publicist, journalist, translator, performer, librarian, archaeologist, entrepreneur, or psychologist, or in politics, sports, real estate, construction, architecture, interior design, human resources, or OB-GYN.

Best Matches: Anyone part of the West Life Group (2, 6, 7, or 8 Life Guas); excellent matches would be 8 Guas born in the year of the Tiger or Horse; 6 or 9 Guas born in the year of the Dog. In the

East Life Group, the 3 or 4 Guas may try to control or pressure
you. Avoid any Life Gua born in the year of the Rat as this is considered a direct clash with your energy.

2 Gua as a Goat

There are no 2 Guas ever born in the year of the Goat; it will only produce 3, 6, or 9 Life Guas.

2 Gua as a Monkey

Men Only!
Sexual, Lightning Quick, Intuitive
Elements: Yin Earth and Yang Metal
Year Begins February 4
Years Occurring: 1908, 1944, 1968, 1980, 2016, 2040, 2052
No female 2 Guas are ever born in the year of the Monkey.

Famous 2 Gua Monkey Men: Nelson Rockefeller, Louis L'Amour,
James Stewart, Ian Fleming, Alistair Cooke, Joe Cocker, Sam
Elliott, Robert Kardashian, Michael Douglas, George Lucas, Barry
White, Sir Richard Branson, Kenny Chesney, Hugh Jackman, Will
Smith, Daniel Craig, Marc Anthony, Edward Burns, Eric Bana,
Ryan Gosling, Channing Tatum.

Personality and Romance: 2 Guas born in the year of the Monkey are
a mix of Earth and Metal and are quick as lightning! Inside, however they are calm, steady, dependable, and altogether persistent.
They are fond of creating concepts that give a new spin on old ideas
and paradigms. 2 Gua Monkeys make caring and talented health
professionals as their nurturing nature coupled with their natural
intuition are a winning combination. These men feel comfortable in
dark spaces such as caves or may have a "man-cave" in their home
in which they can retreat. In relationships, they will not settle on
a partner quickly and may give the appearance of being playful,

promiscuous, or cavalier. When they do find an excellent mate for life, they will commit 100 percent and be very devoted.

The Best stuff: When the 2 Gua Monkeys are fully exhibiting their best qualities, they are quick-witted, inventive, motivators, improvisers, inquisitive, nurturing, flexible, innovative, problem-solvers, self-assured, sociable, polite, dignified, competitive, objective, factual, and intellectual.

The Worst Stuff: When the 2 Gua Monkeys move to the darker side of their nature, they can be moody, egotistical, vain, selfish, cunning, depressed, jealous, and suspicious.

Career: Some of the best professions for the 2 Gua Monkeys where they may attain wealth, fame or fulfillment are in accounting and banking, science, engineering, stock market trading, film directing, jewelry, media, public relations, design, real estate, construction, consultancy, architecture, interior design, or OB-GYN.

Best Matches: Anyone part of the West Life Group (2, 6, 7, or 8 Life Guas); *excellent* matches would be 8 Guas born in the year of the Monkey or Rat, or 6 or 9 Guas born in the year of the Dragon. The 3 or 4 Guas may try to control or pressure you. Avoid any Life Gua born in the year of the Tiger as this is considered a direct clash with your energy.

2 Gua as a Rooster
Women Only!
Honest, Opinionated, Nurturing
Elements: Yin Earth and Yin Metal
Year Begins February 4
Years Occurring: 1897, 1933, 1969, 2005, 2041
No male 2 Guas are ever born in the year of the Rooster.

Famous 2 Gua Rooster Women: Amelia Earhart, Grand Duchess Tatiana Nikolaevna of Russia, Jayne Mansfield, Yoko Ono, Joan Collins, Carol Burnett, Joan Rivers, Jennifer Lopez, Catherine Zeta-Jones, Gwen Stefani, Pauley Perrette, Jennifer Aniston, Lara Spencer, Rachel Hunter, Renée Zellweger, Rachel Hunter, Cate Blanchett, Anne Heche, Alana "Honey Boo Boo" Thompson.

Personality and Romance: The 2 Guas who were born in the year of the Rooster are Earth and Metal energy. They have a strong, independent, calm and confident nature. One minute they enjoy being the center of attention, the next they want to retreat as they can be intensely private. They are naturally intuitive, loyal, trustworthy, and social. Since they tend to be painfully honest with strong, often abrasive opinions, their partners and friends cannot be overly sensitive. However, under their gruffness and sharp opinions lie hearts of gold. These women can be very clear thinkers with logical, grounded, and earthy energy. Their character is nurturing and (if they choose) makes them talented healers or physicians. When exhibiting the dark side of their nature, they tend toward moodiness or depression, but this may be overcome with a purposeful life.

The Best Stuff: When 2 Gua Roosters are fully exhibiting their best qualities, they are neat, meticulous, organized, self-assured, decisive, conservative, nurturing, critical, perfectionists, alert, zealous, practical, scientific, and responsible.

The Worst Stuff: When 2 Gua Roosters move to the darker side of their nature, they can be overzealous and critical, puritanical, depressed, egotistical, reclusive, abrasive, and opinionated.

Career: Some of the best professions for 2 Gua Roosters where they may attain wealth, fame, or fulfillment are as a restaurateur, public relations officer, athlete, journalist, travel writer, dentist, surgeon, politician, writer, or entertainer, or in real estate, construction, architecture, interior design, or sales.

Best Matches: Anyone part of the West Life Group (2, 6, 7, or 8 Life Guas); excellent matches would be 8 Guas born in the year of the Snake or Rooster; 6 or 9 Guas born in the year of the Ox. A 3 or 4 Gua may try to control or pressure you. Avoid any Life Gua born in the year of the Rabbit as this is considered a direct clash with your energy.

2 Gua as a Dog
There are no 2 Guas ever born in the year of the Dog; it only produces a 3, 6, or 9 Gua.

2 Gua as a Pig
Men Only!
Inner Power, Affectionate, Intuitive
Elements: Yin Earth and Yin Water
Years Occurring: 1923, 1935, 1959, 1971, 1995, 2007, 2031, 2043
No female 2 Guas are ever born in the year of the Pig.

Famous 2 Gua Pig Men: Hank Williams, Henry Kissinger, Woody Allen, Sonny Bono, Luciano Pavarotti, Bryan Adams, Val Kilmer, Simon Cowell, Kenneth "Babyface" Edmonds, John McEnroe, Kyle MacLachlan, Magic Johnson, Tupac Shakur, Mark Wahlberg, Josh Lucas, Ricky Martin, Chris Tucker, Paul Bettany.

Personality and Romance: The 2 Guas born in the year of the Pig are a mix of Water and Earth that can create inner tension. These men are honest and affectionate with a tolerant and peaceful side to their nature. The 2 Gua Pigs are naturally grounded, confident, and dependable, with a calm demeanor making them everyone's friend. However, only those in the intimate inner circle will hear their true thoughts and feelings. They are highly intelligent and perceptive men who are also in possession of a great inner power; this makes them invaluable in a time of crisis. They enjoy nurturing and can make excellent doctors or practitioners of alternative healing arts such as chiropracty, massage therapy, and acupuncture. In relationships they are loving and affectionate, yet allowing a great deal of freedom, which they too must have to feel trapped. However, a little time spent in introspection will set things back in balance; some alone time is important for these men.

The Best Stuff: When 2 Gua Pigs are fully exhibiting their best qualities, they are honest, gallant, sturdy, sociable, peace-loving, patient, loyal, hard-working, nurturing, natural healers, trusting, sincere, calm, understanding, thoughtful, scrupulous, passionate, and intelligent.

The Worst Stuff: When 2 Gua Pigs move to the darker side of their nature, they can be reclusive, depressed, naïve, over-reliant, self-indulgent, gullible, fatalistic, and materialistic.

Career: Some of the best professions for 2 Gua Pigs where they may attain wealth, fame, or fulfillment are as an entertainer, doctor, veterinarian, interior decorator, scientist, horticulturist, or artist, or in transportation, retail, medicine, real estate, construction, consultancy, architecture, or OB-GYN.

Best Matches: Anyone part of the West Life Group (2, 6, 7, or 8 Life Guas); excellent matches would be 8 Guas born in the year of the Pig or Rabbit, or 6 or 9 Guas born in the year of the Ox. The 3 or 4 Guas may try to control or pressure you. Avoid any Life Gua born in the year of the Snake as this is considered a direct clash with your energy.

The 3 Guas

Please note that the 3 Guas only occur in the years of the Ox, Dragon, Goat, and Dog. All other animal years do not produce a 3 Gua.

3 Gua as a Rat

There are no 3 Guas ever born in the year of the Rat.

3 Gua as an Ox

Men and Women!

Enterprising, Steady, Outspoken

Elements: Yang Wood and Yin Earth

Years Occurring for Males and Females: 1925, 1961, 1997, 2033

Famous 3 Gua Ox Men and Women: Margaret Thatcher, Rock Hudson, Tony Curtis, Angela Lansbury, Robert F. Kennedy, Princess Diana, George Clooney, Melissa Etheridge, Eddie Murphy, Enya, Nadia Comaneci, Mariel Hemingway, Laurence Fishburne, k.d. lang, Heather Locklear, Barack Obama, Dennis Rodman, Bonnie Hunt, Billy Ray Cyrus, Jeremy Northam.

Personality and Romance: 3 Guas born in the year of the Ox are a mix of Wood and Earth energy causing a bit of inner turmoil; with the right outlet however, it is mitigated. With a dependable and steady nature, these men and women work hard with a methodical, focused determination. 3 Gua Oxen prefer to develop life-long relationships to casual ones. They will take their time finding the perfect partner in life as change is out of the comfort zone for them. These people are full of energy that is often punctuated with bursts of nervousness. Tending towards outspokenness, they often surprise or shock those around them. Because 3 Gua Oxen are prone to spreading their energy a little thin and committing to too much, they are often overwhelmed. When they move to the darker side of their nature, they can become demanding and rigid.

The Best Stuff: When 3 Gua Oxen are fully exhibiting their best qualities, they are dependable, calm, methodical, patient, organized, hardworking, ambitious, conventional, steady, modest, logical, resolute, and tenacious.

The worst stuff: When 3 Gua Oxen move to the darker side of their nature, they can be outspoken, stubborn, narrow-minded, brash, materialistic, nervous, rigid, demanding.

Career: Some of the best professions for 3 Gua Oxen where they may attain wealth, fame or fulfillment are in manufacturing, pharmaceuticals, engineering, artistry, politics, philosophy, entertainment, publishing, fashion, transportation, and music, and as technicians, broadcast announcers, and chefs.

Best Matches: Those part of the East Life Group (1, 3, 4, or 9 Life Guas); excellent matches are 3 or 9 Guas born in Ox years. 6 or 7 Guas may try to control or pressure you. Avoid any Life Gua born in the year of the Goat as this is considered a direct clash with your energy.

3 Gua as a Tiger
There are no 3 Guas ever born in the year of the Tiger.

3 Gua as a Rabbit
There are no 3 Guas ever born in the year of the Rabbit.

3 Gua as a Dragon
Men and Women!
Powerful, Steady, Outspoken
Elements: Yang Wood and Yang Earth
Year Begins February 4
Years Occurring for Males and Females: 1916, 1952, 1988, 2024
This is the only Gua that in certain years will be the same for males and females.

Famous 3 Gua Dragon Men and Women: Betty Grable, Kirk Douglas, George Strait, Grace Jones, Liam Neeson, Patrick Swayze, Isabella Rossellini, Steven Seagal, Christopher Reeve, Beverly Johnson, Dan Aykroyd, Susan Dey, Mr. T, Sharon Osbourne, Mickey Rourke, Marilu Henner, Jeff Goldblum, Roseanne Barr, David Hasselhoff, John Goodman, Bob Costas, John Tesh, Emma Stone, Julianne Hough, Rihanna, Rupert Grint, Vanessa Hudgens, Candice Swanepoel, Nikki Reed, Haley Joel Osment, Michael Cera, Adele, Sergio Aguero, Petra Ecclestone Stunt.

Personality and Romance: The 3 Guas born in the year of the Dragon have a mix of Wood and Earth giving them power and confidence, yet they are grounded as well. In Chinese culture, the mythical dragon is the most powerful and revered creature, and it is considered one of the most auspicious signs under which one can be born. The 3 Guas can exude power as well as progressive and enterprising energy—the mix is indeed intense. These people have lots of vigor, fiery passion, and decisive and zealous ambition. 3 Gua Dragons feel most alive when they are inventing new things, starting new businesses, or off on new adventures as their energy is very open-minded and modern, no matter their age. When they have their creative juices flowing they exhibit their best qualities of being loyal, dignified, and generous. In relationships they are charming and draw in their chosen partner/s with their charisma. They easily find lovers, but it's harder for them to settle down—even in love they like a challenge. When and if they marry, they will need lots of space.

The Best Stuff: When 3 Gua Dragons are fully exhibiting their best qualities, they are magnanimous, vigorous, strong, self-assured, proud, noble, direct, dignified, zealous, fiery, passionate, decisive, pioneering, ambitious, generous, and loyal.

The Worst Stuff: When 3 Gua Dragons move to the darker side of their nature, they can be arrogant, imperious, tyrannical, demanding, eccentric, grandiloquent and extremely bombastic, prejudiced, dogmatic, overbearing, outspoken, violent, impetuous, and brash.

Career: Some of the best professions for 3 Gua Dragons where they may attain wealth, fame, or fulfillment are as a journalist, inventor, computer analyst, lawyer, engineer, architect, broker, clergy person, involved in the arts, entrepreneur, actor, estate manager, philosopher, entertainer, and in the arts and pharmaceuticals.

Best Matches: Those part of the East Life Group (1, 3, 4, or 9
Life Guas); excellent matches are 9 Guas born in the year of the
Dragon. 6 or 7 Guas may try to control or pressure you. Avoid any
Life Gua born in the year of the Dog as this is considered a direct
clash with your energy.

3 Gua as a Snake
There are no 3 Guas ever born in the year of the Snake.

3 Gua as a Horse
There are no 3 Guas ever born in the year of the Horse.

3 Gua as a Goat
Men and Women!
Generous, Steady, Outspoken
Elements: Yang Wood and Yin Earth
Years Occurring for Males and Females: 1907, 1943, 1979, 2015, 2051
This is the only Gua that in certain years will be the same for males and females.

Famous 3 Gua Goat Men and Women: John Wayne, Katharine Hep-
burn, Jim Morrison, Janis Joplin, Mick Jagger, Robert De Niro,
Julio Iglesias, George Benson, Chevy Chase, Penny Marshall, Mal-
colm McDowell, John Kerry, Geraldo Rivera, Lynn Redgrave, Jim
Croce, Joe Namath, Jennifer Love-Hewitt, Kourtney Kardashian,
Kate Hudson, Heath Ledger, Norah Jones, Rose Byrne, Adam
Levine, Coco Austin, Jason Momoa, Pink.

Personality and Romance: The 3 Guas born in the year of the Goat
are a mix of Wood and Earth energy, causing some internal unrest
that with a purposeful and focused life is eased. 3 Gua Goats are
extremely reliable and steadfast; even under undue pressure they
remain calm. They have nurturing personalities, and are generous
and sensitive to the world around them. Intensely private people,

it takes some time and effort to know them. Having projects and creating new ventures is most rewarding to them. They have lots of nervous energy and need an outlet, but often have too many irons in the fire. This can leave them feeling overwhelmed, exhausted, and unfulfilled. Regarding romantic love, they can be insecure or shy. They do not like to be overpowered in relationships and too many "rules" will make them feel repressed. While 3 Gua Goats are at times brash and outspoken, they have kind and gentle hearts.

The Best Stuff: When 3 Gua Goats are fully exhibiting their best qualities, they are righteous, sincere, sympathetic, mild-mannered, shy, artistic, organized, creative, gentle, compassionate, understanding, mothering, determined, peaceful, generous, and seeking security.

The Worst Stuff: When 3 Gua Goats move to the darker side of their nature, they can be outspoken, brash, moody, indecisive, overly passive, anxious, pessimistic, over-sensitive, and whiny.

Career: Some of the best professions for 3 Gua Goats where they may attain wealth, fame, or fulfillment are in pediatrics, acting, interior design, floral design, music, entrepreneurship, estate management, philosophy, entertainment, culinary arts, medicine, print media, agriculture, textiles, and transportation.

Best Matches: Those part of the East Life Group (1, 3, 4, or 9 Life Guas); excellent matches are 9 Guas born in a Goat year. 6 or 7 Guas may try to control or pressure you. Avoid any Life Gua born in the year of the Dog as this is considered a direct clash with your energy.

3 Gua as a Monkey
There are no 3 Guas ever born in the year of the Monkey.

3 Gua as a Rooster
There are no 3 Guas ever born in the year of the Rooster.

3 Gua as a Dog

Men and Women!

Enterprising, Loyal, Restless

Elements: Yang Wood and Yang Earth

Years Occurring for Males and Females: 1898, 1934, 1970, 2006, 2042

This is the only Gua that in certain years will be the same for males and females.

Famous 3 Gua Dog Men and Women: George Gershwin, Golda Meir, Louis Armstrong, Enzo Ferrari, Irene Dunne, Elvis Presley, Sophia Loren, Bridgett Bardot, Maggie Smith, Pat Boone, Giorgio Armani, Carl Sagan, Gloria Steinem, Mariah Carey, Matt Damon, Leah Remini, Naomi Campbell, Heather Graham, Queen Latifah, Uma Thurman, Vince Vaughn, Rachel Weisz, Claudia Schiffer, River Phoenix, Giada De Laurentiis, Shemar Moore, DMX.

Personality and Romance: The 3 Guas born in the year of the Dog have a mix of Wood and Earth energy, which may cause some inner tension or feeling restless. They are loyal and ready to fight for the underdog or leap into action when needed. 3 Gua Dogs are very enterprising and resourceful; whatever they give their attention to is sure to thrive. They are diligent about completing things. Blessed with lots of vigor, energy, and vitality, they are in their element with inventions, new ventures, or being involved in the latest thing. They have trouble trusting others, and partners are often frightened off by the Dog's insecure, worrisome, and anxious nature. 3 Gua Dogs tend to be faithful and loyal; they do not enjoy the excitement of the chase nor do they take pleasure in jealous scenes.

The Best Stuff: When 3 Gua Dogs are fully exhibiting their best qualities, they are honest, intelligent, straightforward, loyal, attractive, organized, surprising, amiable, unpretentious, sociable, openminded, idealistic, moralistic, practical, affectionate, and have a sense of justice and fair play.

The Worst Stuff: When 3 Gua Dogs move to the darker side of their nature, they can be dogged, cynical, lazy, cold, brash, judgmental, pessimistic, outspoken, excessively worried, stubborn, and quarrelsome.

Career: Some of the best professions for 3 Gua Dogs where they may attain wealth, fame, or fulfillment are as a scientist, professor, politician, nurse, judge, lawyer, entrepreneur, philosopher, chef, doctor or nurse, in publishing, bookselling, fashion, technical work, music, and transportation.

Best Matches: Anyone part of the East Life Group (1, 3, 4, or 9 Life Guas); excellent matches are 9 Guas born in the year of the Dog. 6 or 7 Guas may try to control or pressure you. Avoid any Life Gua born in the year of the Dragon as this is considered a direct clash with your energy.

3 Gua as a Pig
There are no 3 Guas ever born in the year of the Pig.

The 4 Guas
4 Gua as a Rat
Men Only!
Gentle, Charming, Witty
Elements: Yin Wood and Yang Water
Years Occurring: 1888, 1924, 1960, 1996, 2032
There are no 4 Gua females ever born in the year of the Rat.

Famous 4 Gua Rat Men: Dale Carnegie, Harpo Marx, George H. W. Bush, Ed Koch, Marlon Brando, Marcello Mastroianni, Henry Mancini, Truman Capote, Sean Penn, David Duchovny, John F. Kennedy Jr., Hugh Grant, Antonio Banderas, Jean-Claude Van Damme, Colin Firth, RuPaul (Andre Charles), James Spader, Prince Andrew, Stanley Tucci, Kenneth Branagh, Stefano Casiraghi.

Personality and Romance: The 4 Gua men born in the year of the Rat are a harmonious mix of Wood and Water energy; this creates sharp minded wit and irresistible charm! To the world, they have a cool and dignified persona, but deep down they are insecure. 4 Gua Rats thrive on praise, recognition, and popularity. They resent being ordered around or made to feel small. If they are cornered or feel trapped, they can become aggressive; stay on their good side as their true nature is gentle. These men have very progressive energy and ideas; they often become famous in writing, acting, or as entrepreneurs. In dealing with these men, you must use diplomacy as they can be overly sensitive to any type of criticism. They are loyal in relationships finding it hard to break away and go forward. A good partner needs to be able to keep up with this high-energy personality. When 4 Gua Rats step into their negative side, they can be obstinate, ruthless, rigid, and selfish. However, they are genuinely romantic and sentimental in relationships.

The Best Stuff: When 4 Gua Rats are fully exhibiting their best qualities, they are forthright, disciplined, systematic, meticulous, gentle, charismatic, hardworking, industrious, charming, eloquent, sociable, and shrewd.

The Worst Stuff: When 4 Gua Rats move to the darker side of their nature, they can be indecisive, manipulative, cruel, dictatorial, critical, over-ambitious, wishy-washy, intolerant, and scheming.

Career: Some of the best professions for 4 Gua Rats where they may attain wealth, fame, or fulfillment are as writers, advisors, lawyers, politicians, designers, engineers, directors, entrepreneurs, researchers, historians, chefs, and auto racers, or in estate management, philosophy, pharmaceuticals, and publishing.

Best Matches: Those part of the East Life Group (1, 3, 4, or 9 Life Guas); excellent matches are 1 Guas born in the year of the Monkey or Rat, or 3 or 9 Guas born in the year of the Dragon. The 6 or 7 Guas may try to control or pressure you. Avoid any Life Gua born in the year of the Horse, as this is considered a direct clash with your energy.

4 Gua as an Ox
There are no 4 Guas ever born in the year of the Ox.

4 Gua as a Tiger
Women Only!
Intense, Protective, Sex Appeal
Elements: Yin Wood and Yang Wood
Years Occurring: 1926, 1962, 1998, 2034
There are no 4 Gua males ever born in the year of the Tiger.

Famous 4 Gua Tiger Women: Marilyn Monroe, Queen Elizabeth II, Demi Moore, Jodie Foster, Sheryl Crow, Paula Abdul, Kelly Preston, Felicity Huffman, Taylor Dayne, Dina Lohan, Star Jones, Genie Francis, Kristy McNichol, Gina Gershon, Laura San Giacomo.

Personality and Romance: The 4 Guas born in the year of the Tiger have pure Wood energy, making these women extremely progressive and exciting with lots of potent sex appeal! Old-fashioned Chinese parents did not approve of their sons marrying Tiger women, believing the marrige would be ill-fated because these ladies have such intense, indecisive, and flamboyant energy. While it is true that 4 Gua Tigers are all about passion and excitement, they are very protective of those who are lucky enough to win their heart. So fiercely passionate, these ladies tend to be their own worst enemies with their do-or-die approach to life and relationships. While they are easily influenced and often blowing with the wind, 4 Gua Tiger women can still make very devoted, protective, and responsible mothers and wives. These ladies are huge risk-takers, spontaneous, direct, honest, and independent—they love being on top.

The Best Stuff: When 4 Gua Tigers are fully exhibiting their best qualities, they are unpredictable, rebellious, colorful, powerful, passionate, daring, impulsive, vigorous, stimulating, sincere, affectionate, humanitarian, and generous.

The Worst Stuff: When 4 Gua Tigers move to the darker side of their nature, they can be restless, reckless, impatient, quick-tempered, indecisive, obstinate, and selfish.

Career: Some of the best professions for 4 Gua Tigers where they may attain wealth, fame, or fulfillment are in advertising, office management, acting, writing, art, aviation, music, politics, exploration, executive roles, entrepreneurship, philosophy, entertainment, culinary arts, pharmaceuticals, and print media.

Best Matches: Those part of the East Life Group (1, 3, 4, or 9 Life Guas); excellent matches are 1 Guas born in the year of the Tiger or Horse, or 3 or 9 Guas born in the year of the Dog. 6 or 7 Guas may try to control or pressure you. Avoid any Life Gua born in the year of the Monkey as this is considered a direct clash with your energy.

4 Gua as a Rabbit
Men Only!
Sexual, Self-Assured, Progressive
Elements: Yin Wood and Yin Wood
Years Occurring: 1915, 1951, 1987, 2023
No 4 Gua females are ever born in the year of the Rabbit.

Famous 4 Gua Rabbit Men: Frank Sinatra, Orson Welles, Anthony Quinn, Luther Vandross, Mark Harmon, Phil Collins, Sting, John Mellencamp, Michael Keaton, Kurt Russell, Peabo Bryson, Stedman Graham, Robin Williams, Lou Ferrigno, Dan Fogelberg, Tony Danza, Stellan Skarsgård, Rob Halford, Treat Williams.

Personality and Romance: 4 Guas born in the year of the Rabbit are pure Wood energy making these men progressive, self-assured, and easy-going. 4 Gua Rabbits are clever, highly intelligent, and their minds can move quickly as lightning. These men are classy, refined, and stylish with wonderful manners. Always aware of how they are perceived, image is very important to 4 Gua Rabbits. They pay a great deal attention to being polished, and they can even be snobs about the status of others and their standing in the world. These men are naturally sensuous and highly sexual; they are not risk takers in love or any other area of their life. Since they may have unrealistic expectations and may be easily influenced by lovers, they need a partner that will not take advantage of them. However, free-loving women need not apply, as these men will only attach themselves to women they consider having the right caliber and status; sexy sirens will not win a husband here.

The Best Stuff: When 4 Gua Rabbits are fully exhibiting their best qualities, they are gracious, kind, sensitive, soft-spoken, amiable, elegant, reserved, cautious, artistic, thorough, tender, self-assured, astute, gentle, compassionate, and flexible.

The Worst Stuff: When 4 Gua Rabbits move to the darker side of their nature, they can be moody, detached, superficial, self-indulgent, indecisive, opportunistic, and lazy.

Career: Some of the best professions for 4 Gua Rabbits where they may attain wealth, fame, or fulfillment are in health care, travel, public relations, design, estate management, farming, publishing, and fashion, and as judges, lawyers, diplomats, explorers, entertainers, technicians, and broadcast announcers.

Best Matches: Those part of the East Life Group (1, 3, 4, or 9 Life Guas); excellent matches are 1 Guas born in the year of the Pig or Rabbit, or 3 or 9 Guas born in the year of the Goat. 6 or 7 Guas may try to control or pressure you. Avoid any Life Gua born in the year of the Rooster as this is considered a direct clash with your energy.

4 Gua as a Dragon

There are no 4 Guas ever born in the year of the Dragon; it only produces a 3, 6, or 9 Life Gua.

4 Gua as a Snake

Women Only!
Seductive, Mystical, Intelligent
Elements: Yin Wood and Yin Fire
Years Occurring: 1917, 1953, 1989, 2025
There are no 4 Gua males ever born in the year of the Snake.

Famous 4 Gua Snake Women: Phyllis Diller, Zsa Zsa Gabor, Lena Horne, Kim Basinger, Bebe Buell, Kathie Lee Gifford, Benazir Bhutto, Cyndi Lauper, Chaka Khan, Kate Capshaw, Mary Steenburgen, Patti Scialfa, Marcia Clark, Oprah Winfrey, Bess Armstrong, Joanna Kerns, Tracy Scoggins, Amy Irving, Kathleen Sullivan, Meredith Vieira, Jordin Sparks, Hayden Panettiere, Chelsie Hightower, Taylor Swift. *Note: Oprah was born January of 1954; the solar new year did not start until February 4, which places her in the year of the Snake, 1953.*

Personality and Romance: 4 Guas born in the year of the Snake are a powerful mix of Wood and Fire energy, making these ladies consummate seducers, even if it's innocently. These women are highly intelligent, deep thinkers, alluring, and very dignified. Often unaware of their potent attraction, they move through life casting a spell with their charm and feminine sexuality everywhere they go. If they pursue an academic or scholastic profession, they will achieve great success and fame. 4 Gua Snake women love exquisite things—homes, jewelry, clothes, jets—all the trappings of a life saturated in luxury and beauty. They are masters of the waiting game, and their patience often pays off with a brilliant marriage that brings them wealth and status. While they are flexible in ideas, they often struggle with making decisions. These women can have movie-star looks and may be obsessed with their appearance. Progressive but not naturally independent, most will seek a partner in life who can bring them stability and status.

The Best Stuff: When 4 Gua Snakes are fully exhibiting their best qualities, they are deep thinkers, wise, mystical, graceful, soft-spoken, sensual, creative, prudent, shrewd, ambitious, elegant, cautious, responsible, calm, strong, constant, and purposeful.

The Worst Stuff: When 4 Gua Snakes move to the darker side of their nature, they can be loners, poor communicators, wishy-washy, possessive, hedonistic, indecisive, self-doubting, distrustful, and mendacious.

Career: Some of the best professions for 4 Gua Snakes where they may attain wealth, fame, or fulfillment are as scientists, analysts, investigators, astrologers, sociologists, archaeologists, psychologists, entrepreneurs, or estate managers, and in medicine, pharmaceuticals, publishing, public relations, the arts, and transportation.

Best Matches: Those part of the East Life Group (1, 3, 4, or 9 Life Guas); *excellent* matches are 1 Guas born in the year of the Snake or Rooster; 3 or 9 born in the year of the Ox. 6 or 7 Guas may try to control or pressure you. Avoid any Life Gua born in the year of the Pig as this is considered a direct clash with your energy.

4 Gua as a Horse
Men Only!
Strong, Proud, Earthy Sensuality
Elements: Yin Wood and Yang Fire
Years Occurring: 1906, 1942, 1978, 2014, 2050
No 4 Gua females are ever born in the year of the Horse.

Famous 4 Gua Horse Men: Bugsy Siegel, Billy Wilder, Jimi Hendrix, Paul McCartney, Harrison Ford, Brian Jones, Isaac Hayes, Brian Wilson, Wayne Newton, Billy Connolly, Jerry Garcia, Larry Flynt, Roger Ebert, Martin Scorsese, Calvin Klein, Ian McShane, Enrique Iglesias, Lou Reed, Ian Somerhalder, Josh Hartnett, Usher, Ashton Kutcher, James Franco, Kobe Bryant.

Personality and Romance: The 4 Gua men born in the year of the Horse are a powerful mix of Wood and Fire; this energy gives them a remarkable drive in life. They also have strength, persistence, inner confidence, and a very proud air. 4 Gua Horses can be very restless, always needing something to do or a project to start. Deeply honest, these men may be quiet, and they value being direct and forthcoming. These men have immense energy, but are not aggressive, though they do come across as being strong and macho. They are attracted to sophisticated women a bit on the glamorous side. When they fall in love, it is usually hard, fast, and forever; 4 Gua Horse men can carry a torch for the same woman for years. They enjoy being the leader in a relationship, and have a wonderful, Earthy sensuality. 4 Gua Horse men tend to be very faithful in a romantic relationship; seldom, if ever, do they stray from their chosen mate.

The Best Stuff: When 4 Gua Horses are fully exhibiting their best qualities, they are cheerful, popular, quick-witted, changeable, earthy, perceptive, talkative, agile both mentally and physically, magnetic, intelligent, astute, flexible, and open-minded.

The Worst Stuff: When 4 Gua Horses move to the darker side of their nature, they can be fickle, anxious, rude, gullible, stubborn, indecisive, and lack stability and perseverance.

Career: Some of the best professions for 4 Gua Horses where they may attain wealth, fame, or fulfillment are in publicity, journalism, library science, aviation, politics, sports, construction, geography, entrepreneurship, philosophy, culinary arts, education, pharmaceuticals, publishing, and fashion.

Best Matches: Those part of the East Life Group (1, 3, 4, or 9 Life Guas); *excellent* matches are 1 Guas born in the year of the Tiger or Horse or 3 or 9 Guas born in the year of the Dog. The 6 or 7 Guas may try to control or pressure you. Avoid any Life Gua born in the year of the Rat as this is considered a direct clash with your energy.

4 Gua as a Goat

There are no 4 Guas ever born in the year of the Ox; it only produces a 3, 6, or 9 Life Gua.

4 Gua as a Monkey

Women Only!
Highly Sexual, Quick-Witted, Modern
Elements: Yin Wood and Yang Metal
Years Occurring: 1908, 1944, 1980, 2016, 2052
No 4 Guas males are ever born in the year of the Monkey.

Famous 4 Gua Monkey Women: Bette Davis, Carole Lombard, Joey Heatherton, Jacqueline Bisset, Diana Ross, Patti LaBelle, Pattie Boyd, Sondra Locke, Gladys Knight, Stockard Channing, Michelle Phillips, Teri Garr, Kim Kardashian, Jessica Simpson, Christina Aguilera, Olivia Munn, Gisele Bündchen, Kristen Bell, Christina Ricci, Venus Williams.

Personality and Romance: The 4 Gua women born in the year of the Monkey are a mix of Metal and Wood energy; this may cause some internal conflict, usually in the form of self-doubt. These women are of high intelligence and have lightning-quick minds. Their energy is very progressive, full of ideas, concepts, and inventing new things. 4 Gua Monkey women love their freedom and may be hard to pin down in relationships; they are playful, slippery, and very quick-witted. These women are generous to a fault, interested in everyone's business, and they definitely have an opinion about everything and everybody. They may be promiscuous at certain times in their lives, as they can get easily bored with their lovers. However, with an excellent partner, they will commit to that person in every way. Their chosen mate must always be aware that if these Monkey women feel confined or "jailed" in the relationship, they will exit in a flash!

The Best Stuff: When 4 Gua Monkeys are fully exhibiting their best qualities, they are inventive, motivating, improvising, quick-witted, inquisitive, flexible, innovative, problem-solving, self-assured, sociable, polite, dignified, competitive, objective, factual, and intellectual.

The Worst Stuff: When 4 Gua Monkeys move to the darker side of their nature, they can be egotistical, vain, selfish, indecisive, cunning, jealous, and suspicious.

Career: Some of the best professions for 4 Gua Monkeys where they may attain wealth, fame, or fulfillment are in banking, science, engineering, stock market trading, film direction, jewelry, media, music, publishing, philosophy, agriculture, entertainment, medicine, or as technicians or entrepeneurs.

Best Matches: Those part of the East Life Group (1, 3, 4, or 9 Life Guas); excellent matches are 1 Guas born in the year of the Monkey or Rat, or 3 or 9 Guas born in the year of the Dragon. The 6 or 7 Guas may try to control or pressure you. Avoid any Life Gua born in the year of the Tiger as this is considered a direct clash with your energy.

4 Gua as a Rooster
Men Only!
Personal Power, Organized, Blunt
Elements: Yin Wood and Yin Metal
Years Occurring: 1933, 1969, 2005, 2041
There are no 4 Gua females ever born in the year of the Rooster.

Famous 4 Gua Rooster Men: Willie Nelson, James Brown, Michael
   Caine, Quincy Jones, Larry King, Gene Wilder, Conway Twitty,
   Lou Rawls, Jay Z, Ice Cube, Triple H, Gerard Butler, Matthew
   McConaughey, Tyler Perry, Jack Black, Zach Galifianakis.

Personality and Romance: 4 Gua men born in the year of the Rooster are
   a mix of Wood and Metal energy; this makes him emotionally complex. These men are very much "roosters," showing off their beautiful
   masculinity every chance they get. Highly social and deep thinkers, 4
   Gua Roosters make excellent leaders, CEOs, or are good in any situation where they may use their potent energy; they are very comfortable
   with power. Under their gruffness lies a heart of gold. In love, Roosters can be skillful and passionate lovers, but they are chiefly in it for
   physical pleasure, not necessarily romance. It is not natural for a 4 Gua
   Rooster man to limit himself to a single partner. Expect that he may
   have many sexual partners without guilt; if he does settle down, he
   will make an excellent provider. After marriage, while on-the-side
   lovers may appear occasionally, 4 Gua Roosters rarely desert their
   partners or family.

The Best Stuff: When 4 Gua Roosters are fully exhibiting their best
   qualities, they are neat, meticulous, organized, self-assured, decisive,
   conservative, critical, perfectionist, alert, zealous, practical, scientific, and responsible.

The Worst Stuff: When 4 Gua Roosters move to the darker side of their nature, they can be overzealous and critical, puritanical, indecisive, egotistical, abrasive, and opinionated.

Career: Some of the best professions for 4 Gua Roosters where they may attain wealth, fame, or fulfillment are in sales, hospitality, journalism, travel writing, dentistry, surgery, fire fighting, the military, culinary arts, education, pharmaceuticals, publishing, music, transportation, or as professional athletes.

Best Matches: Those part of the East Life Group (1, 3, 4, or 9 Life Guas); excellent matches are 1 Guas born in the year of the Snake or Rooster, or 3 or 9 Guas born in the year of the Ox. The 6 or 7 Guas may try to control or pressure you. Avoid any Life Gua born in the year of the Rabbit, as this is considered a direct clash with your energy.

4 Gua as a Dog

There are no 4 Guas ever born in the year of the Ox. It only produces a 3, 6, or 9 Life Gua.

4 Gua as a Pig

Women Only!
Generous, Accumulators, Highly Sexual
Elements: Yin Wood and Yin Water
Years Occurring: 1935, 1971, 2007, 2043
There are no 4 Gua males ever born in the year of the Pig.

Famous 4 Gua Pig Women: Julie Andrews, Loretta Lynn, Diahann Carroll, Jada Pinkett Smith, Christina Applegate, Winona Ryder, Thalía, Denise Richards, Dido, Jenna Elfman, Sandra Oh, Carla Gugino, Amy Poehler, Sanaa Lathan, Shannen Doherty, Selena.

Personality and Romance: 4 Guas born in the year of the Pig are a harmonious mix of Wood and Water, making these ladies highly intelligent and very perceptive people. 4 Gua Pigs make very good friends as they are compassionate, supportive, and devoted. These women are great accumulators of wealth, energy, or wisdom; think of the pot belly of the pig! Whatever work they engage in, they are diligent and generous. In the matters of love, they dream of a knight in shining armor to sweep them off their feet. This fantasy may hurt them at times, but when they let go of it, they make wonderfully affectionate and highly sexual partners to the men who deserve them. 4 Gua Pigs are extremely reliable and wise in times of crisis, and they are always ready to support and serve their friends.

The Best Stuff: When 4 Gua Pigs are fully exhibiting their best qualities, they are honest, gentle, gallant, sturdy, sociable, peace-loving, patient, loyal, hard-working, trusting, sincere, calm, understanding, thoughtful, scrupulous, passionate, and intelligent.

The Worst Stuff: When 4 Gua Pigs move to the darker side of their nature, they can be indecisive, naïve, over-reliant, self-indulgent, wishy-washy, gullible, fatalistic, and materialistic.

Career: Some of the best professions for 4 Gua Pigs where they may attain wealth, fame, or fulfillment are as an entertainer, veterinarian, interior decorator, researcher, scientist, entertainer, technician, or musician, or in retail, hospitality, philosophy, pharmaceuticals, print media, agriculture, or fashion.

Best Matches: Those part of the East Life Group (1, 3, 4, or 9 Life Guas); *excellent* matches are 1 Guas born in the year of the Pig or Rabbit, or 3 or 9 Guas born in the year of the Goat. The 6 or 7 Guas may try to control or pressure you. Avoid any Life Gua born in the year of the Snake as this is considered a direct clash with your energy.

The 6 Guas

6 Gua as a Rat

There are no 6 Guas ever born in the year of the Rat.

6 Gua as an Ox

Men and Women!

Ambitious, Authoritative, Methodical

Elements: Yang Metal and Yin Earth

Years Occurring for Males: 1913, 1949, 1985, 2009, 2021

Years Occurring for Females: 1901, 1937, 1973, 2045

Famous 6 Gua Ox Men and Women: Burt Lancaster, Red Skelton, Gerald R. Ford, Grand Duchess Anastasia Nikolaevna of Russia, Lionel Richie, Richard Gere, Billy Joel, Gene Simmons, Bruce Springsteen, Bruce Jenner, David Foster, Tom Berenger, Jeff Bridges, Rick Springfield, Aishwarya Rai Bachchan, Tyra Banks, Monica Lewinsky, Kate Beckinsale, Heidi Klum, Tori Spelling, Molly Sims, Kristen Wiig, Derek Hough, Reggie Bush, Kris Humphries, Bruno Mars, Cristiano Ronaldo, T-Pain, Michael Phelps.

Personality and Romance: The 6 Guas born in the year of the Ox are a harmonious mix of Metal and Earth energy; this makes these men and women steadfast, dependable, and methodical. 6 Gua Oxen are not particularly romantic, however they can be very passionate and extraordinarily loyal to their partners. These men and women are highly principled and disciplined mixed with steely determination. Neither gender is showy, preferring to develop the intellect rather than dress to "strut their stuff" or as a seductress. 6 Gua Oxen do not like excess, frivolity, or flaunting their wealth. The men can be ruthless and tough; the women can be judgmental, intolerant of idle gossip or silly behavior; they are not naturally social, preferring to stay at home. They feel comfortable with positions of power and authority, making righteous leaders.

The Best Stuff: When 6 Gua Oxen are fully exhibiting their best qualities, they are dependable, calm, methodical, patient, hardworking, ambitious, conventional, steady, modest, logical, resolute, and tenacious.

The Worst Stuff: When 6 Gua Oxen move to the darker side of their nature, they can be stubborn, narrow-minded, judgmental, materialistic, uncompassionate, rigid, and demanding.

Career: Some of the best professions for 6 Gua Oxens where they may attain wealth, fame or fulfillment are in manufacturing, pharmacy, engineering, real estate, interior design, medicine, engineering, IT, goldsmithing, metal mining, excavation, government service, or sports equipment, and as lecturers.

Best Matches: Those part of the West Life Group (2, 6, 7, or 8 Life Guas); excellent matches are 7 Guas born in the year of the Snake or Rooster. 9 Guas may try to control or pressure you except those born in the year of the Ox. Avoid any Life Gua born in the year of the Goat as this is considered a direct clash with your energy.

6 Gua as a Tiger
There are no 6 Guas ever born in the year of the Tiger.

6 Gua as a Rabbit
There are no 6 Guas ever born in the year of the Rabbit.

6 Gua as a Dragon
Men and Women!
Confident, Powerful, Loyal
Elements: Yang Metal and Yang Earth
Years Occurring for Males: 1904, 1940, 1976, 2012, 2044
Years Occurring for Females: 1928, 1964, 2000, 2036

Famous 6 Gua Dragon Men and Women: Dr. Seuss, Robert Oppenheimer, Shirley Temple, Maya Angelou, Rosemary Clooney, Al Pacino, Chuck Norris, Smokey Robinson, Bruce Lee, Frank Zappa, Ringo Starr, John Gotti, Richard Pryor, Martin Sheen, Sandra Bullock, Sarah Palin, Courteney Cox, Elle Macpherson, Melissa Gilbert, Tracy Chapman, Wynonna Judd, Juliette Binoche, Trisha Yearwood, Ville Valo, Ryan Reynolds, Colin Farrell, Alexander Skarsgård, Benedict Cumberbatch, Blake Shelton.

Personality and Romance: 6 Guas born in the year of the Dragon are a harmonious mix of Metal and Earth energy, making these men and women very confident and powerful. They are vibrant and captivating, and you definitely will notice these people whenever they enter a room! 6 Gua Dragons shine in positions of leadership and authority such as senators, governors, entrepreneurs, CEOs, or Supreme Court justices. These men and women play by their own rules, and they also like to "play big"—no acting small or shy in the world for these lucky people. In romantic relationships, the women are very desirable, stunningly sexy with brilliant intelligence—they will have many suitors and admirers. To win this woman's heart, she will have to be properly courted and dazzled before she selects her mate for life. 6 Gua Dragon men have huge egos, are usually highly successful, and they want a partner worth winning—a real trophy before giving up their notoriously unfaithful ways. Both sexes need their independence to some degree; Dragons can have hot tempers and need a tough-skinned mate, but they themselves make loyal life partners.

The Best Stuff: When 6 Gua Dragons are fully exhibiting their best qualities, they are magnanimous, stately, vigorous, strong, self-assured, proud, noble, direct, dignified, zealous, fiery, passionate, decisive, pioneering, ambitious, generous, and loyal.

The Worst Stuff: When 6 Gua Dragons move to the darker side of their nature, they can be arrogant, imperious, tyrannical, demanding, eccentric, grandiloquent, extremely bombastic, prejudiced, dogmatic, over-bearing, violent, over-thinkers, impetuous, and brash.

Career: Some of the best professions for 6 Gua Dragons where they may attain wealth, fame, or fulfillment are as an inventor, lawyer, engineer, architect, broker, philosopher, goldsmith, or lecturer, or in metal mining, excavation, hi-tech goods, the Internet, judging, metal jewelry, and medicine.

Best Matches: Those part of the West Life Group (2, 6, 7, or 8 Life Guas); *excellent* matches are 7 Guas born in the year of the Monkey or Rat. The 9 Guas may try to control or pressure you except those born in the year of the Dragon. Avoid any Life Gua born in the year of the Dog as this is considered a direct clash with your energy.

6 Gua as a Snake
There are no 6 Guas ever born in the year of the Snake.

6 Gua as a Horse
There are no 6 Guas ever born in the year of the Horse.

6 Gua as a Goat
Men and Women!
Cunning, Patient, Creative
Elements: Yang Metal and Yang Earth
Years Occurring for Males: 1931, 1967, 2003, 2039
Years Occurring for Females: 1919, 1955, 1991, 2027

Famous 6 Gua Goat Men and Women: Eva Gabor, Eva Perón, James Dean, Ike Turner, Larry Hagman, William Shatner, Kris Jenner, Reba McEntire, Isabelle Adjani, Whoopi Goldberg, Tanya Roberts, Connie Sellecca, Iman, Debra Winger, Maria Shriver, Vin

Diesel, Jason Statham, Tim McGraw, Jamie Foxx, Kurt Cobain, Criss Angel, Anderson Cooper, Keith Urban, Rufus Sewell, Matt LeBlanc, Vanilla Ice, Liev Schreiber, Jimmy Kimmel, Rhys Ifans, Emma Roberts, Jamie Lynn Spears.

Personality and Romance: The 6 Guas born in the year of the Goat are a harmonious mix of Metal and Earth energy; these men and women are cunning, long-suffering, outwardly innocent, self-disciplined and dignified. The 6 Gua Goats are immensely creative in manipulating things, circumstances, and people for advantageous outcomes. They are cunning and crafty but will give the aura of innocence or detachment; do not make an enemy of these people as they will patiently and seemingly blamelessly *annihilate* you. You will not see this coming as they are famous for avoiding confrontations and arguments; even if they are in positions of authority where their will may be imposed. The 6 Gua Goat women are supremely feminine and deceptively compliant—however she is not a pushover or empty-headed. These women are powerful, ethereally beautiful, and serene. The 6 Gua Goat men desire power and are ambitious, unpredictable, adventurous, and at times, ruthless. In romantic relationships, these men and women are patient and may dream and scheme to find the right life partner. Intensely private people, it takes some time and effort to know them.

The Best Stuff: When 6 Gua Goats are fully exhibiting their best qualities, they are righteous, sincere, sympathetic, mild-mannered, shy, artistic, creative, gentle, compassionate, understanding, mothering, determined, peaceful, generous, and they seek security.

The Worst Stuff: When 6 Gua Goats move to the darker side of their nature, they can be moody, indecisive, over-passive, worriers, pessimistic, over-sensitive, and whiny.

Career: Some of the best professions for 6 Gua Goats where they may attain wealth, fame, or fulfillment are as a pediatrician, interior designer, florist, editor, estate manager, doctor or nurse, chef, engineer, , excavator, web developer, lawyer, metal jeweler, public servant, and working with sports equipment or computers.

Best Matches: Those part of the West Life Group (2, 6, 7, or 8 Life Guas); excellent matches are 7 Guas born in the year of the Pig or Rabbit. 9 Guas may try to control or pressure you, except those born in the year of the Goat. Avoid any Life Gua born in the year of the Ox, as this is considered a direct clash with your energy.

6 Gua as a Monkey
There are no 6 Guas ever born in the year of the Monkey.

6 Gua as a Rooster
There are no 6 Guas ever born in the year of the Rooster.

6 Gua as a Dog
Men and Women!
Loners, Loyal, Anxious
Elements: Yang Metal and Yang Earth
Years Occurring for Males: 1922, 1958, 1994, 2030
Years Occurring for Females: 1910, 1946, 1982, 2018

Famous 6 Gua Dog Men and Women: Mother Teresa, Redd Foxx, Sid Ceaser, Jack Klugman, Carl Reiner, Dolly Parton, Cher, Linda Ronstadt, Suzanne Somers, Susan Sarandon, Sally Field, Diane Keaton, Liza Minnelli, Patti Smith, Susan Lucci, Naomi Judd, Connie Chung, Gilda Radner, Diane von Fürstenberg, Michael Jackson, Prince, Viggo Mortensen, Dr. Drew Pinsky, Alec Baldwin, Gary Oldman, Andrea Bocelli, Ice-T, Tim Robbins, Prince Albert of Monaco, Tim Burton, Kevin Bacon, Kevin Sorbo, Nicki Minaj, Jessica Biel, Anne Hathaway, Kirsten Dunst, Kelly Clarkson, LeAnn Rimes.

Personality and Romance: 6 Guas born in the year of the Dog are a harmonious mix of Metal and Earth energy; these men and women are affectionate, loyal, attractive, antisocial/loners, and they have a keen sense of justice. By and large, they are quite cynical of the world, but they shine when they engage in noble, charitable works or "feel-good" causes. While 6 Gua Dogs are not overly ambitious or materialistic, they are diligent and dedicated workers, often rising to great heights due to this. 6 Gua Dogs can be blissfully naïve and innocent which can make them vulnerable or even fragile in romantic relationships. Although these men and women make the most loyal and best of friends, they tend to be self-righteous, taking a great deal of pride in being honest, faithful, correct, and proper. Often, they come across as holier-than-thou. While the 6 Gua Dogs are warm and personable, they generally have a very pessimistic view of life and are always expecting the worst to happen. They make devoted and loving partners, but they do require lots of reassurance and attention in the relationship.

The Best Stuff: When 6 Gua Dogs are fully exhibiting their best qualities, they are honest, intelligent, straightforward, loyal, attractive, amiable, unpretentious, sociable, open-minded, idealistic, moralistic, practical, affectionate, and *doggedly* determined, with a sense of justice and fair play.

The Worst Stuff: When 6 Gua Dogs move to the darker side of their nature, they can be cynical, lazy, cold, judgmental, over-thinkers, loners, pessimistic, worriers, stubborn, and quarrelsome.

Career: Some of the best professions for 6 Gua Dogs where they may attain wealth, fame, or fulfillment are as scientists, interior designers, professors, politicians, nurses, judges, doctors, teachers, IT professionals, goldsmiths, excavators, lawyers, government employees, and lecturers, or in technology.

Best Matches: Those part of the West Life Group (2, 6, 7, or 8 Life Guas); excellent matches are 7 Guas born in the year of the Tiger or Horse. The 9 Guas may try to control or pressure you except those born in the year of the Dog. Avoid any Life Gua born in the year of the Dragon, as this is considered a direct clash with your energy.

6 Gua as a Pig
There are no 6 Guas ever born in the year of the Pig.

The 7 Guas
7 Gua as a Rat
Men Only!
Talkative, Sexual, Charming
Elements: Yin Metal and Yang Water
Years Occurring: 1912, 1948, 1984, 2020
There are no 7 Gua females ever born in the year of the Rat.

Famous 7 Gua Rat Men: Gene Kelly, Perry Como, Karl Malden, Art Linkletter, Steven Tyler, James Taylor, Ozzy Osbourne, Cat Stevens, Terry Bradshaw, Alice Cooper, Prince Charles, Ted Nugent, Mikhail Baryshnikov, Gérard Depardieu, Jeremy Irons, Al Gore, Andrew Lloyd Webber, Wolf Blitzer, Richard Simmons, Jean Reno, Trey Songz, Fernando Torres, Prince Harry, LeBron James, Mark Zuckerberg.

Personality and Romance: The 7 Guas born in the year of the Rat are a harmonious mix of Metal and Water energy; these men are charming, confident, witty, talkative, and have engaging personalities. They are usually very interesting men and make great partners and lovers. Sometimes insecure, 7 Gua Rats tend to be restless, impulsive, and need a great deal of praise and flattery; be cognizant of not injuring their sensitive egos with direct or even implied criticism. While these men are not great risk-takers, they make inventive entrepreneurs, good negotiators, and clever tacticians.

7 Gua Rats love the pleasures of life—good food, good sex, good conversation, and the like. They can be fully charged at the beginning of a relationship, romantic and sentimental; they love to take care of their partners. These men take marriage very seriously and are faithful in romantic relationships. They can be charismatic, smooth-talking, or have a razor-sharp tongue—especially if backed into a corner, where they may also become aggressive.

The Best Stuff: When 7 Gua Rats are fully exhibiting their best qualities, they are forthright, disciplined, systematic, meticulous, charismatic, hardworking, industrious, charming, eloquent, sociable, and shrewd.

The Worst Stuff: When 7 Gua Rats move to the darker side of their nature, they can be manipulative, cruel, dictatorial, rigid, selfish, obstinate, critical, over-ambitious, ruthless, intolerant, scheming, and childish.

Career: Some of the best professions for 7 Gua Rats where they may attain wealth, fame, or fulfillment, are as/in writers, actors, advisors, politicians, engineers, directors, administrators, researchers, race car drivers, police officers, lawyers, and lecturers, and in metal mining, excavation, the Internet, and metal jewelry.

Best Matches: Those part of the West Life Group (2, 6, 7, or 8 Life Guas); *excellent* matches are 6 Guas born in the year of the Monkey or Rat. The 9 Guas may try to control or pressure you except those born in the year of the Dragon. Avoid any Life Gua born in the year of the Horse as this is considered a direct clash with your energy.

7 Gua as an Ox

No 7 Guas are ever born in the year of the Ox.

7 Gua as a Tiger

Women Only!

Impulsive, Sexy, Passionate

Elements: Yin Metal and Yang Wood

Years Occurring: 1902, 1938, 1974, 2010, 2046

There are no 7 Gua males ever born in the year of the Tiger.

Famous 7 Gua Tiger Women: Natalie Wood, Claudia Cardinale, Diana Rigg, Connie Stevens, Eva Mendes, Victoria Beckham, Penélope Cruz, Kate Moss, Jenna Jameson, Jillian Michaels, Hilary Swank, Kimberly "Lil' Kim" Jones, Amy Fisher, Alanis Morissette, Elizabeth Banks, Victoria Silvstedt.

Personality and Romance: 7 Gua women born in the year of the Tiger are an inauspicious mix of Metal and Wood energy, causing inner turbulence and unrest. These women are passionate, impulsive, protective, enthusiastic, and bold with exciting, powerful, sexual allure. The 7 Gua Tigers tackle things with enthusiasm, optimism, and determination that ensure their success in work or projects. They make talented and efficient leaders and are the most loyal and generous of friends. They are huge risk-takers, spontaneous, independent, and they like to be on top! In the areas of love and romance, these women often get carried away with their passions, making them victims of love gone bad; at times they can fall into the charms of manipulative and immoral men. The 7 Gua Tigers may tend toward the excessive and extremes—too much sex, too much food, too many radical ideas or opinions, and so forth. They may have many lovers as they get bored very easily, especially if the heartthrob of the moment turns out to be predictable. In the end, they long for a mate that is constant, steady, and allows the natural instincts of a tigress to blossom—protective mothers and loyal, passionate wives.

The Best Stuff: When 7 Gua Tigers are fully exhibiting their best qualities, they are unpredictable, rebellious, colorful, powerful, passionate, daring, impulsive, vigorous, stimulating, sincere, affectionate, humanitarian, and generous.

The Worst Stuff: When 7 Gua Tigers move to the darker side of their nature, they can be restless, reckless, impatient, quick-tempered, obstinate, and selfish.

Career: Some of the best professions for the 7 Gua Tigers where they may attain wealth, fame, or fulfillment are in advertising, travel, art, comedy, medicine, culinary arts, engineering, IT, goldsmithing, excavation, web development, justice, metal jewelry, and working with sports equipment, or as a chauffeur.

Best Matches: Those part of the West Life Group (2, 6, 7, or 8 Life Guas); excellent matches are 6 Guas born in the year of the Tiger or Horse. 9 Guas may try to control or pressure you except those born in the year of the Dog. Avoid any Life Gua born in the year of the Monkey as this is considered a direct clash with your energy.

7 Gua as a Rabbit

Men Only!

Refined, Charming, Nervous

Elements: Yin Metal and Yin Wood

Years Occurring: 1903, 1939, 1975, 2011, 2047

There are no 7 Gua females ever born in the year of the Rabbit.

Famous 7 Gua Rabbit Men: Bob Hope, Bing Crosby, Marvin Gaye, Neil Sedaka, George Hamilton, Francis Ford Coppola, Enrique Iglesias, David Beckham, Tiger Woods, Tobey Maguire, 50 Cent, Ray Lewis, Russell Brand, Michael Bublé, and Johnny Galecki.

Personality and Romance: The 7 Gua men born in the year of the Rabbit are an inauspicious mix of Metal and Wood energy, causing some internal chaos and instability. These men are diplomatic, well-mannered, shrewd, sensuous, and stylish. They are always conscious of their image, making sure they come off impeccable. 7 Gua Rabbit males tend to be very materialistic and could even be described as genuine snobs—having the right address, right clothes, the best associates, and so forth are essential. Not known for being spontaneous, these men are careful planners in almost all areas of their life, including romantic relationships as well. Generally they will only choose a spouse that in their estimation is worthy and suitable—meeting all the criteria to secure the right image. The 7 Gua Rabbits must be alert not to overindulge in the pleasures of life such as food, drink, money, and sex; they must keep a balanced lifestyle. While extremely charming, they can be fast- or smooth-talking, or have a razor-sharp tongue. These men are also naturally sensuous and highly sexual but they will powerfully commit to the right partner.

The Best Stuff: When 7 Gua Rabbits are fully exhibiting their best qualities, they are gracious, kind, sensitive, soft-spoken, amiable, elegant, reserved, cautious, artistic, thorough, tender, self-assured, astute, compassionate, and flexible.

The Worst stuff: When 7 Gua Rabbits move to the darker side of their nature, they can be moody, detached, superficial, self-indulgent, opportunistic, and lazy.

Career: Some of the best professions for 7 Gua Rabbits where they may attain wealth, fame, or fulfillment are in cultivation, health care, justice, politics, estate management, engineering, IT, gold-smithing, machinery, metal, mining, hi-tech goods, law, metal jewelry, and lecturing.

Best Matches: Those part of the West Life Group (2, 6, 7, or 8 Life Guas); excellent matches are 6 Guas born in the year of the Pig or Rabbit. 9 Guas may try to control or pressure you except those born in the year of the Goat. Avoid any Life Gua born in the year of the Rooster as this is considered a direct clash with your energy.

7 Gua as a Dragon
There are no 7 Guas ever born in the year of the Dragon.

7 Gua as a Snake
Women Only!
Seductive, Talkative, Regal
Elements: Yin Metal and Yin Fire
Years Occurring: 1929, 1965, 2001, 2037
There are no 7 Gua males ever born in the year of the Snake.

Famous 7 Gua Snake Women: Audrey Hepburn, Grace Kelly, Jacqueline Kennedy, Barbara Walters, Shania Twain, Katarina Witt, Brooke Shields, Elizabeth Hurley, Sarah Jessica Parker, Linda Evangelista, Paulina Porizkova, Princess Stéphanie of Monaco, Connie Nielsen, Kyra Sedgwick, Heidi Fleiss, Constance Marie, J. K. Rowling.

Personality and Romance: 7 Gua women born in the year of the Snake are an inauspicious mix of Metal and Fire energy, causing some emotional inner turmoil. These women are highly intelligent, deep thinkers, alluring, and very dignified. Often unaware of their potent attraction, they move through life innocently casting a spell with their charm and feminine sexuality. If they pursue an academic or scholastic profession, they will achieve great success and fame. The 7 Gua Snake women love exquisite things—homes, jewelry, clothes, jets—all the trappings of a life filled with luxury and beauty. They are masters of the waiting game, and it often pays off with a brilliant marriage that brings them wealth and status. These women are often irresistible and men can fall passionately in love with them; they tend to be youthful in behavior or appearance. They are comfortable in the spotlight and are good at acting and speaking in front of the camera or on the radio. In romantic relationships, 7 Gua Snakes enjoy being wooed and lavished with attention. In marriage they make good partners with no particular need for deep independence; rather, security is what they crave.

The Best Stuff: When 7 Gua Snakes are fully exhibiting their best qualities, they are deep thinkers, wise, mystic, graceful, soft-spoken, sensual, creative, prudent, shrewd, ambitious, elegant, cautious, responsible, calm, strong, constant, and purposeful.

The Worst Stuff: When 7 Gua Snakes move to the darker side of their nature, they can be loners, poor communicators, possessive, hedonistic, self-doubting, distrustful, and mendacious.

Career: Some of the best professions for 7 Gua Snakes where they may attain wealth, fame, or fulfillment are in science, investigation, astrology, stage magic, sociology, agriculture, medicine, engineering, computers, excavation, hi-tech goods, law, metal jewelry, government service, sports equipment, and as lecturers.

Best Matches: Those part of the West Life Group (2, 6, 7 or 8 Life Guas); *excellent* matches are 6 Guas born in the year of the Snake or Rooster. The 9 Guas may try to control or pressure you except those born in the year of the Ox. Avoid any Life Gua born in the year of the Pig as this is considered a direct clash with your energy.

7 Gua as a Horse
Men Only!
Independent, Magnetic, Talkative
Elements: Yin Metal and Yang Fire
Years Occurring: 1894, 1930, 1966, 2002, 2038
There are no 7 Gua females ever born in the year of the Horse.

Famous 7 Gua Horse Men: Jack Benny, Clint Eastwood, Ray Charles, Sean Connery, Shel Silverstein, Richard Harris, Warren Buffett,

John Cusack, Adam Sandler, Mike Tyson, Luke Perry, Troy Aikman, Kiefer Sutherland, David Schwimmer, Billy Zane, Jon Favreau, Michael Imperioli, Billy Burke, Donal Logue, Jeffrey Dean Morgan, Matthew Fox.

Personality and Romance: 7 Gua men born in the year of the Horse have an inauspicious mix of Metal and Fire energy, causing some internal chaos and instability. These men are fiercely independent, proud, outspoken, and may have a fiery or touchy temperment. They tend to be restless and need an outlet for their incredible energy and spirit. 7 Gua Horse men tend to act on inspired ideas without hesitation, often getting carried away by the excitement of something new. Because these men are often brimming with ideas, energy and time may get scattered. In romantic relationships, they love the thrill and exhilaration of romance, sometimes setting aside their usual responsible and hard-working habits to pursue a whirlwind of new emotions. However, when settled down, they make excellent husbands and great providers. With a tendency to overindulge in the pleasures of life such as food, drink, money, and sex, they must strive to keep a balanced existence. They can be fast- or smooth-talking, or have razor-sharp tongues.

The Best Stuff: When 7 Gua Horses are fully exhibiting their best qualities, they are cheerful, popular, quick-witted, changeable, earthy, perceptive, talkative, agile both mentally and physically, magnetic, intelligent, astute, flexible, and open-minded.

The Worst Stuff: When 7 Gua Horses move to the darker side of their nature, they can be fickle, anxious, rude, gullible, stubborn, crabby, unstable, and wishy-washy.

Career: Some of the best professions for 7 Gua Horses where they may attain wealth, fame, or fulfillment are in publicity, sales, journalism, translation, performing arts, library sciences, philosophy, teaching, culinary arts, law enforcement, engineering, goldsmithing, judging, metal jewelry, government service, sports equipment, and lecturing.

Best Matches: Those part of the West Life Group (2, 6, 7, or 8 Life Guas); excellent matches are 6 Guas born in the year of the Tiger or Horse. 9 Guas may try to control or pressure you except those born in the year of the Dog. Avoid any Life Gua born in the year of the Rat as this is considered a direct clash with your energy.

7 Gua as a Goat

There are no 7 Guas ever born in the year of the Goat.

7 Gua as a Monkey

Women Only!
Lightning Quick, Unconventional, Playful
Elements: Yin Metal and Yang Metal
Years Occurring: 1920, 1956, 2010, 2028
There are no 7 Gua males ever born in the year of the Monkey.

Famous 7 Gua Monkey Women: Maureen O'Hara, Shelley Winters, Bo Derek, Dana Delany, Kim Cattrall, Patti Hansen, Carrie Fisher, Geena Davis, Sela Ward, Lisa Hartman, Linda Hamilton, Jerry Hall, Paula Zahn, LaToya Jackson, Dorothy Hamill, Lisa Niemi Swayze, Koo Stark, Rita Wilson.

Personality and Romance: The 7 Gua women born in the year of the Monkey have an auspicious mix of yin and yang Metal, bringing a radiant inner confidence! These ladies are gracious, generous, unconventional, and they make loyal and entertaining friends. They also can be talkative, lively, and nervous. 7 Gua Monkeys are often blessed with very good looks and sensuous beauty. Comfortable in the spotlight, the 7 Guas are good at acting and speaking in front of the camera or on the radio. These women love their freedom and may be hard to pin down; they're quick witted and will slip through your fingers at any attempt of constraint. The 7 Gua Monkeys also have a strong tendency to overindulge in the pleasures of life: food, drink, money, and sex—they must strive to keep balanced. If you bore these charming ladies, they'll move onto a new lover, but an excellent partner can make them commit in every way.

The Best Stuff: When 7 Gua Monkeys are fully exhibiting their best qualities, they are inventive, motivating, improvising, quick-witted, inquisitive, flexible, innovative, problem-solving, self-assured, sociable, polite, dignified, competitive, objective, factual, and intellectual.

The Worst Stuff: When 7 Gua Monkeys move to the darker side of their nature, they can be egotistical, vain, selfish, cunning, jealous, excessive, and suspicious.

Career: Some of the best professions for the 7 Gua Monkeys where they may attain wealth, fame, or fulfillment are in banking, science, engineering, stock market trading, film directing, medicine, engineering, IT, goldsmithing, hardware, law, justice, metal jewelry, sports equipment, and seminars.

Best Matches: Those part of the West Life Group (2, 6, 7, or 8 Life Guas); excellent matches are 6 Guas born in the year of the Monkey or Rat. 9 Guas may try to control or pressure you except those born in the year of the Dragon. Avoid any Life Gua born in the year of the Tiger, as this is considered a direct clash with your energy.

7 Gua as a Rooster

Men Only!
Lightning Quick, Sexual, Charming
Elements: Yin Metal and Yin Metal
Years Occurring: 1921, 1957, 1993, 2029
There are no 7 Gua females ever born in the year of the Rooster.

Famous 7 Gua Rooster Men: Charles Bronson, Louis Jourdan, Mario Lanza, Prince Philip, Peter Ustinov, Sugar Ray Robinson, Vince Gill, Dolph Lundgren, Daniel Day-Lewis, Donny Osmond, Christopher Lambert, Matt Lauer, Falco, Ray Romano, Spike Lee.

Personality and Romance: The 7 Gua men born in the year of the Rooster are an auspicious mix of yin and yang Metal energy, giving them steely confidence! These men are resilient, clever, and very macho; they enjoy strutting around and crowing, but under their gruffness lie hearts of gold. However, they are not "dandies"; they have substance and depth. 7 Gua Roosters can be amazingly creative, rebellious, productive, and use speech to their advantage; they can be fast- or smooth-talkers, or have razor-sharp tongues. They may be talented at imitating voices as well. These men are very comfortable with power making great leaders and CEOs, anywhere their considerable management and organizational skills may be put to use. In romantic relationships, they tend toward infidelity; they are quite guilt-free and comfortable courting several women at a time—they're real heart-breakers! However, if they do marry, they seldom desert their families, and they make great providers. With a strong tendency to overindulge in the pleasures of life such as food, drink, money, and sex, they must make an effort to keep a balanced life. 7 Gua Roosters are very social, charming, and charismatic; they create stimulating, informative conversation wherever they go.

The Best Stuff: When 7 Gua Roosters are fully exhibiting their best qualities, they are neat, meticulous, organized, self-assured, decisive, conservative, critical, perfectionist, alert, zealous, practical, scientific, and responsible.

The Worst Stuff: When 7 Gua Roosters move to the darker side of their nature, they can be overzealous and critical, puritanical, excessive, egotistical, abrasive, and opinionated.

Career: Some of the best professions for 7 Gua Roosters where they may attain wealth, fame, or fulfillment are in hospitality, public relations, professional sports, journalism, travel writing, fire fighting, medicine, philosophy, computers, metal mining, law, metal jewelry, government service, sports equipment, and public speaking.

Best Matches: Those part of the West Life Group (2, 6, 7, or 8 Life Guas); excellent matches are 6 Guas born in the year of the Snake or Rooster. 9 Guas may try to control or pressure you except those born in the year of the Ox. Avoid any Life Gua born in the year of the Rabbit as this is considered a direct clash with your energy.

7 Gua as a Dog
There are no 7 Guas ever born in the year of the Dog.

7 Gua as a Pig
Women Only!
Accumulators, Intelligent, Affectionate
Elements: Yin Metal and Yin Water
Years Occurring: 1911, 1947, 1983, 2019, 2055
There are no 7 Gua males ever born in the year of the Pig.

Famous 7 Gua Pig Women: Lucille Ball, Ginger Rogers, Jaclyn Smith, Cheryl Tiegs, Teri Garr, Barbara Bach, Hillary Rodham Clinton, Sally Struthers, Glenn Close, Camilla Parker-Bowles, Marisa Berenson, Danielle Steel, Elisabeth Broderick, Deidre Hall, Emmylou Harris, Mila Kunis, Emily Blunt, Amy Winehouse.

Personality and Romance: 7 Gua women born in the year of the Pig are a very auspicious mix of Metal and Water energy, bringing them unexpected blessings and unique gifts and talents. These women are affectionate, peace-loving, hardworking, intelligent, and passionate. 7 Gua Pigs are often blessed with very good looks and sensuous beauty; however they tend to be naïve and can be used by unscrupulous, immoral men. These women are very social, charming, and charismatic; they create stimulating, informative conversation wherever they go. They can be fast-talkers, smooth-talkers, or have razor-sharp tongues, and they may also use their voice as a way to fame. 7 Gua Pigs can be vulnerable in the mouth, throat, or lungs and must be careful not to smoke or engage in drug use. With a strong tendency to overindulge in the pleasures of life such as food, drink, money, and sex, they must strive to keep things and their bodies balanced.

The Best Stuff: When 7 Gua Pigs are fully exhibiting their best qualities, they are honest, uncomplicated, gallant, sturdy, sociable, peace-loving, patient, loyal, hardworking, trusting, sincere, calm, understanding, thoughtful, scrupulous, passionate, and intelligent.

The Worst Stuff: When 7 Gua Pigs move to the darker side of their nature, they can be naïve, over-reliant, self-indulgent, gullible, fatalistic, excessive, and materialistic.

Career: Some of the best professions for 7 Gua Pigs where they may attain wealth, fame, or fulfillment are in medicine, philosophy, teaching, culinary arts, law enforcement, engineering, computers, goldsmithing, hi-tech goods, web development, law, metal jewelry, government service, sports equipment, and lecturing.

Best Matches: Those part of the West Life Group (2, 6, 7, or 8 Life Guas); excellent matches are 6 Guas born in the year of the Pig or Rabbit. 9 Guas may try to control or pressure you except those born in the year of the Goat. Avoid any Life Gua born in the year of the Snake as this is considered a direct clash with your energy.

The 8 Guas
8 Gua as a Rat
Women Only!
Witty, Sexual, Magnetic
Elements: Yang Earth and Yang Water
Years Occurring: 1912, 1936, 1948, 1984, 2008, 2020, 2044
There are no 8 Gua males ever born in the year of the Rat.

Famous 8 Gua Rat Women: Eva Braun, Sonja Henie, Julia Child, Doris Duke, Ursula Andress, Mary Tyler Moore, Ruth Buzzi, Princess Elizabeth of Yugoslavia, Stevie Nicks, Grace Jones, Barbara Hershey, Margot Kidder, Kathy Bates, Barbara Mandrell, JoBeth Williams, Tina Sinatra, Scarlett Johansson, Katy Perry, Khloé Kardashian, Cheryl Burke, Ashlee Simpson, Kelly Osbourne.

Personality and Romance: The 8 Gua women born in the year of the Rat are a combination of Earth and Water energy, which causes some emotional tension. These women are steadfast, witty, magnetic, hardworking, vivacious, and dynamic. While the 8 Gua Rats may resist change, they can deftly handle trouble without falling apart. They tend to be a bit old-fashioned in relationships, wanting marriage and babies above a career. They fear being alone and must always have a man in their life. Even when life is bringing them success and independence, these women will give it up to have a spouse and security. These women are full of energy, talkative, expressive, and charming; however they can become aggressive when provoked. They are talented with things of the earth—construction, real estate, and landscaping. They move homes and jobs a great deal and love to travel. They are loyal in relationships, finding it hard to break away and go forward. A good partner needs to be able to keep up with this high-energy personality.

The Best Stuff: When 8 Gua Rats are fully exhibiting their best qualities, they are forthright, disciplined, systematic, meticulous, charismatic, hardworking, industrious, charming, eloquent, sociable, noble, and shrewd.

The Worst Stuff: When 8 Gua Rats move to the darker side of their nature, they can be manipulative, cruel, dictatorial, rigid, selfish, obstinate, critical, stubborn, over-ambitious, ruthless, intolerant, and scheming.

Career: Some of the best professions for 8 Gua Rats where they may attain wealth, fame, or fulfillment are as writers, counselors, lawyers, politicians, designers, directors, entrepreneurs, stand-up comedians, historians, or race car drivers, or in publishing, real estate, construction, architecture, human resources, and OB-GYN.

Best Matches: Those part of the West Life Group (2, 6, 7, or 8 Life Guas); *excellent* matches are 2 Guas born in the year of the Monkey or Rat; 9 Guas born in the year of the Dragon. 3 and 4 Guas may try to control or pressure you. Avoid any Life Gua born in the year of the Horse as this is considered a direct clash with your energy.

8 Gua as an Ox
There are no 8 Guas, male or female, ever born in the year of the Ox.

8 Gua as a Tiger
Men Only!
Risk-takers, Dazzling, Independent
Elements: Yang Earth and Yang Wood
Years Occurring: 1902, 1938, 1974, 2010, 2046
There are no 8 Gua females ever born in the year of the Tiger.

Famous 8 Gua Tiger Men: John Steinbeck, Bobby Jones, Oliver Reed, Ted Turner, Karl Lagerfeld, Bill Withers, Peter Jennings, Elliott

Gould, Leonardo DiCaprio, Joaquin Phoenix, Ryan Seacrest, Ryan Phillippe, Jimmy Fallon, CeeLo Green.

Personality and Romance: The 8 Gua men born in the year of the Tiger are an inauspicious mix of Earth and Wood energy, creating inner turmoil and restlessness. These men are action-oriented, big risk-takers, tempestuous, independent, and unpredictable. 8 Gua Tigers can be quite irresistible; you'll always feel an air of excitement around them and may get carried away by their confidence and ambition. They are adventurous, highly social, and they have unforgettable charm! These men have energy so intense and primal that it can overpower people. However, they are deeply sensitive and protective. While there's never a dull moment with these men, be prepared if you fall in love with one. They are high-maintenance and will require lots of energy and attention. 8 Gua Tigers crave excitement, love the outdoors and nature, and enjoy building things where their dynamic energy can find an outlet.

The Best Stuff: When 8 Gua Tigers are fully exhibiting their best qualities, they are unpredictable, rebellious, colorful, powerful, passionate, daring, impulsive, vigorous, stimulating, sincere, affectionate, humanitarian, and generous.

The Worst Stuff: When 8 Gua Tigers move to the darker side of their nature, they can be restless, reckless, impatient, quick-tempered, obstinate, and selfish.

Career: Some of the best professions for 8 Gua Tigers where they may attain wealth, fame, or fulfillment are in design, politics, law enforcement, travel writing, exploration, business executive positions, acting, property, real estate, construction, consultancy, hospitality, architecture, pottery, stoneworking, and OB-GYN.

Best Matches: Those part of the West Life Group (2, 6, 7, or 8 Life Guas); excellent matches are 2 Guas born in the year of the Tiger or Horse, or 9 Guas born in the year of the Dog. 3 and 4 Guas may try to control or pressure you. Avoid any Life Gua born in the year of the Monkey, as this is considered a direct clash with your energy.

8 Gua as a Rabbit
Women Only!
Virtuous, Materialistic, Social
Elements: Yang Earth and Yin Wood
Years Occurring: 1903, 1939, 1963, 1975, 1999, 2011, 2035, 2047
There are no 8 Gua males ever born in the year of the Rabbit.

Famous 8 Gua Rabbit Women: Claudette Colbert, Tina Turner, Ali MacGraw, Dusty Springfield, Dixie Carter, Elizabeth Ashley, Whitney Houston, Brigitte Nielsen, Vanessa Williams, Nicollette Sheridan, Lisa Kudrow, Keely Shaye Smith, Tatum O'Neal, Jeanne Tripplehorn, Natasha Richardson, Angelina Jolie, Charlize Theron, Eva Longoria, Drew Barrymore, Kate Winslet.

Personality and Romance: 8 Gua women born in the year of the Rabbit are an inauspicious mix of Earth and Wood energy, triggering inner conflict and insecurities. These women are virtuous, diplomatic, modest, tactful, soft-spoken, and elegant. Social acceptance is very important to them, and they desire material things in the world—grand homes, good marriages, successful husbands who brings status, good careers—the objective is to look picture perfect. Later in life, they may even become hoarders. However, the 8 Gua Rabbits are down to earth, enjoying a life of order and peace. Their energy is quick as lightning, but they also make excellent listeners and can make others feel calmed in their presence. These women may have unrealistic expectations and need partners who will not take advantage of them. They are attracted to and talented with matters related to the earth—real estate (especially raw land and mountainous regions), construction, landscaping, and planting.

These ladies will need time alone to recharge their energy, otherwise they may tend towards depression.

The Best Stuff: When 8 Gua Rabbits are fully exhibiting their best qualities, they are diplomatic, intuitive, social, refined, classy, soft-spoken, elegant, reserved, well-mannered, stylish, clever, and naturally sensuous.

The Worst Stuff: When 8 Gua Rabbits move to the darker side of their nature, they can be stubborn, moody, detached, superficial, self-indulgent, opportunistic, and lazy.

Career: Some of the best professions for 8 Gua Rabbits where they may attain wealth, fame, or fulfillment are in literature, public relations, justice and law, cultivation, education, culture, politics, real estate, construction, consultancy, hospitality, architecture, human resources, farming, and OB-GYN.

Best Matches: Those part of the West Life Group (2, 6, 7, or 8 Life Guas); excellent matches are 2 Guas born in the year of the Pig or Rabbit, or 9 Guas born in the year of the Goat. The 3 and 4 Guas may try to control or pressure you. Avoid any Life Gua born in the year of the Rooster, as this is considered a direct clash with your energy.

8 Gua as a Dragon
There are no 8 Guas ever born in the year of the Dragon.

8 Gua as a Snake
Men Only!
Seductive, Intelligent, Sensitive
Elements: Yang Earth and Yin Fire
Years Occurring: 1929, 1965, 2001, 2037
There are no 8 Gua females ever born in the year of the Snake.

Famous 8 Gua Snake Men: Ike Jones, Christopher Plummer, Bob Newhart, Max von Sydow, André Previn, Salman Khan, Charlie

Sheen, Slash, Robert Downey Jr., Ben Stiller, Sean Patrick Flanery, Chris Rock, Martin Lawrence, Dougray Scott, Scottie Pippin, Kevin James, Shahrukh Khan.

Personality and Romance: 8 Gua men born in the year of the Snake are a mix of Earth and Fire energy, an auspicious mix that gives them lots of personal power. These men are sensitive, stubborn, intelligent, and they're masters at the waiting game. They can become spiritual seekers and "trek the mountains in search of answers" or to find themselves. They are consummate seducers and tend to be possessive and jealous in relationships with lovers and partners. One of their best qualities is how they reserve and use their internal energy for powerful results. 8 Gua Snakes tend to resist change; they can deftly handle trouble without falling apart. These men work very hard but have a tendency to get bored with routine and will regularly job hop. They are great thinkers, and solving complex problems is stimulating to them; where most would crack under pressure and deadlines, they do well. They are geared for success and often become very rich, gathering worldly honors, recognition, and status.

The Best Stuff: When 8 Gua Snakes are fully exhibiting their best qualities, they are deep thinkers, wise, mystic, sensual, creative, shrewd, ambitious, elegant, cautious, responsible, calm, strong, dependable, and purposeful.

The Worst Stuff: When 8 Gua Snakes move to the darker side of their nature, they can be hoarders, stubborn, self-righteous, short-tempered, poor communicators, possessive, hedonistic, self-doubting, distrustful, and mendacious.

Career: Some of the best professions for 8 Gua Snakes where they may attain wealth, fame, or fulfillment are as a scientist, analyst, astrologer, dietician, entrepeneur, farmer, or in real estate, construction, consultancy, hotels, architecture, recruitment, quarrying, politics, law, and OB-GYN.

Best Matches: Those part of the West Life Group (2, 6, 7, or 8 Life
Guas); excellent matches are 2 Guas born in the year of the Snake
or Rooster, or 9 Guas born in the year of the Ox. The 3 and 4 Guas
may try to control or pressure you. Avoid any Life Gua born in the
year of the Pig, as this is considered a direct clash with your energy.

8 Gua as a Horse

Women Only!
Confident, Proud, Stubborn
Elements: Yang Earth and Yang Fire
Years Occurring: 1918, 1930, 1954, 1966, 1990, 2002, 2026, 2038
There are no 8 Gua males ever born in the year of the Horse.

Famous 8 Gua Horse Women: Rita Hayworth, Pearl Bailey, Ingmar
Bergman, Betty Ford, Tippi Hedren, Joanne Woodward, Princess
Margaret, Lesley-Anne Down, Ellen Barkin, Kathleen Turner, Chris
Evert, Annie Lennox, Condoleezza Rice, Margaux Hemingway,
Halle Berry, Samantha Fox, Salma Hayek, Janet Jackson, Sophie
Marceau, Cindy Crawford, Sinéad O'Connor, Robin Wright, Cyn-
thia Nixon, Kristen Stewart, Emma Watson, Jennifer Lawrence.

Personality and Romance: 8 Gua women born in the year of the Horse
are an auspicious mix of Earth and Fire energy, giving them a
great deal of self-assurance and self-worth. These ladies are warm-
hearted and generous but fiercely independent; trying to control or
break her spirit will not end well. The 8 Gua Horses are champions
of causes, require lots of activity, and have a desire for adventure.
They have a mind of their own and are usually highly principled
and moral—lying and being dishonest is not part of her character.
These women are rather bossy and earthy; usually very successful, they have no need to parade around their material wealth.
They tend to be hypersensitive, complex, stubborn and dependable—making good wives and spouses only when they respect

their strong, patient mate. These women also have a little "save the world" energy. They do tend to fall hard and fast in relationships, but get a great deal mellower later in life.

The Best Stuff: When 8 Gua Horses are fully exhibiting their best qualities, they are cheerful, popular, quick-witted, changeable, earthy, stubborn, perceptive, talkative, agile both mentally and physically, magnetic, intelligent, astute, flexible, and open-minded.

The Worst Stuff: When 8 Gua Horses move to the darker side of their nature, they can be fickle, anxious, rude, gullible, stubborn, overly sensitive, lack stability, intolerant, and bossy.

Career: Some of the best professions for 8 Gua Horses where they may attain wealth, fame, or fulfillment are as a sales representative, journalist, language instructor, librarian, or pilot, or in real estate, construction, consultancy, hospitality, insurance, architecture, pottery, recruitment, quarry, farming, and OB-GYN.

Best Matches: Those part of the West Life Group (2, 6, 7, or 8 Life Guas); excellent matches are 2 Guas born in the year of the Tiger or Horse, and 9 Guas born in the year of the Dog. The 3 and 4 Guas may try to control or pressure you. Avoid any Life Gua born in the year of the Rat, as this is considered a direct clash with your energy.

8 Gua as a Goat
There are no 8 Guas ever born in the year of the Goat.

8 Gua as a Monkey
Men Only!
Lightning Quick, Playful, Generous
Elements: Yang Earth and Yang Metal
Years Occurring: 1920, 1956, 1992, 2028
There are no 8 Gua females ever born in the year of the Monkey.

Famous 8 Gua Monkey Men: Yul Brynner, Montgomery Clift, Mickey Rooney, Walter Matthau, Tony Randall, Dwight Yoakam, Chris Isaak, Tom Hanks, Andy Garcia, Kenny G, David Copperfield, Eric Roberts, Björn Borg, David E. Kelley, Randy Jackson, Joe Montana, Bryan Cranston, Sugar Ray Leonard, Taylor Lautner, Josh Hutcherson, Nick Jonas.

Personality and Romance: 8 Gua men who are born in the year of the Monkey are an auspicious mix of Earth and Metal energy, giving them a great deal of inner power and confidence. These men are witty, intelligent, and have magnetic personalities. Although they can be playful, mischievous, and love a practical joke, they are also stubborn and competitive. While these men can often be extravagant suitors—think champagne, diamonds, and furs—they love their freedom and will not settle down in marriage easily. The 8 Gua Monkeys are hardworking, great risk-takers, and are survivors of difficult situations usually due to their charm and considerable social skills. They have integrity and may become spiritual seekers, and "trek the mountains in search of answers" or to find themselves. These men are fast learners and crafty opportunists; they have many interests and need partners who are capable of stimulating them. Later in life they may become eccentric or hoarders. While 8 Gua Monkeys tend to resist change, they can deftly handle trouble without falling apart. They are geared for success and often become very rich with worldly honors, recognition, and status.

The Best Stuff: When 8 Gua Monkeys are fully exhibiting their best qualities, they are inventors, motivators, improvisers, quick-witted, inquisitive, flexible, innovative, problem solvers, self-assured, sociable, polite, dignified, competitive, successful, earthy, objective, factual, and intellectual.

The Worst Stuff: When 8 Gua Monkeys move to the darker side of their nature, they can be hoarders, self-righteous, stubborn, short-tempered, egotistical, vain, selfish, cunning, jealous, impudent, impulsive, and suspicious.

Career: Some of the best professions for 8 Gua Monkeys where they may attain wealth, fame or fulfillment, are in accounting science, engineering, stock market trading, film directing, jewelry, sales, real estate, construction, earthenware, consultancy, hotel, insurance, architecture, quarry, human resources, and OB-GYN.

Best Matches: Those part of the West Life Group (2, 6, 7, or 8 Life Guas); excellent matches are 2 Guas born in the year of the Monkey or Rat, or 9 Guas born in the year of the Dragon. The 3 and 4 Guas may try to control or pressure you. Avoid any Life Gua born in the year of the Tiger as this is considered a direct clash with your energy.

8 Gua as a Rooster

Women Only!
Confident, Purposeful, Social
Elements: Yang Earth and Yin Metal
Years Occurring: 1909, 1921, 1945, 1957, 1981, 1993, 2017, 2029, 2053
There are no 8 Gua males ever born in the year of the Rooster.

Famous 8 Gua Rooster Women: Queen Juliana, Jessica Tandy, Jane Russell, Lana Turner, Priscilla Presley, Jaclyn Smith, Carly Simon, Goldie Hawn, Bette Midler, Diane Sawyer, Rita Coolidge, Linda Hunt, Vanna White, Faye Resnick, Rachel Ward, Melanie Griffith, Denise Austin, Caroline Kennedy, Gloria Estefan, Jessica Alba, Beyoncé Knowles, Britney Spears, Duchess Kate Middleton, Paris Hilton, Serena Williams, Natalie Portman, Anna Kournikova, Jennifer Hudson, Ivanka Trump, Victoria Justice.

Personality and Romance: 8 Gua women born in the year of the Rooster are an auspicious mix of Earth and Metal energy, giving them purpose and great inner confidence. These ladies are hardworking, talented, charming, resourceful, loyal, honest, and open; they're very comfortable with power and prestige. 8 Gua Roosters love deeply and when wounded or disappointed, create a wall of protection against the offenders. However, they do not wear their hearts on their sleeves; you'll not see drama queen displays of emotion. They generally take life seriously and are filled with laser-sharp purpose and efficiency. These women dislike snobby, condescending people and are equally unimpressed with blatant social climbers. 8 Gua Roosters love challenges and will tackle them with vigor (intimidation if necessary) and considerable power. They are famously stubborn but not vindictive, nor do they hold grudges. So talented are these ladies, there is almost no profession they can't excel in or master, and they will manage it with efficiency and resolute independence. They are geared for success and often become very rich with worldly honors, recognition, and status. Prone to "telling it like it is," they will need a partner who is not overly sensitive.

The Best Stuff: When 8 Gua Roosters are fully exhibiting their best qualities, they are purposeful, neat, meticulous, organized, self-assured, decisive, conservative, perfectionist, observant, zealous, practical, scientific, talented, social, honest, loyal, responsible, and have hearts of gold.

The Worst Stuff: When 8 Gua Roosters move to the darker side of their nature, they can be stubborn, overzealous, critical, puritanical, intimidating, egotistical, abrasive, and opinionated.

Career: Some of the best professions for 8 Gua Roosters where they may attain wealth, fame, or fulfillment are in restaurants, hairdressing, public relations, professional athletics, journalism, dentistry, surgery, the military, fire fighting, real estate, construction, consultancy, hospitality, architecture, quarry, and OB-GYN.

Best Matches: Those part of the West Life Group (2, 6, 7, or 8 Life Guas); excellent matches are 2 Guas born in the year of the Snake or Rooster, or 9 Guas born in the year of the Ox. The 3 and 4 Guas may try to control or pressure you. Avoid any Life Gua born in the year of the Rabbit, as this is considered a direct clash with your energy.

8 Gua as a Dog
There are no 8 Guas ever born in the year of the Dog.

8 Gua as a Pig
Men Only!
Accumulators, Intelligent, Affectionate
Elements: Yang Earth and Yin Water
Years Occurring: 1911, 1947, 1983, 2019, 2055
There are no 8 Gua females ever born in the year of the Pig.

Famous 8 Gua Pig Men: Ronald Reagan, L. Ron Hubbard, Jack Ruby, Arnold Schwarzenegger, Carlos Santana, Don Henley, Elton John, Meatloaf, O. J. Simpson, David Letterman, Kevin Kline, Larry David, Salman Rushdie, Stephen King, Sam Neill, Henry Cavill, Andrew Garfield, Aaron Rodgers, Chris Hemsworth, Jesse Eisenberg.

Personality and Romance: 8 Gua men who are born in the year of the Pig are an inauspicious mix of Earth and Water energy, causing them inner turmoil and insecurity. These men are intelligent, perceptive, affectionate, highly sexual, and they make great partners. The pig's "pot belly" makes them great accumulators of wealth, energy, or wisdom. Although these men can be stubborn, they have a dependable, steadfast nature. They tend to have a great deal of integrity and are vey attracted to all things spiritual. They can become spiritual seekers, and "trek the mountain in search of answers" or to find themselves. Professionally, these men are industrious and productive; they're not afraid to try to do what interests them, as they have a great sense of responsibility, creativity, and rich imagination. They are geared for success and often become very rich with worldly honors, recognition, and status.

The Best Stuff: When 8 Gua Pigs are fully exhibiting their best qualities, they are honest, gallant, sturdy, noble, sociable, peace-loving, patient, loyal, hard-working, trusting, sincere, calm, understanding, thoughtful, scrupulous, passionate, and intelligent.

The Worst Stuff: When 8 Gua Pigs move to the darker side of their nature, they can be naïve, over-reliant, materialistic, procrastinators, gullible, passive, lazy, overly meek/apologetic, fatalistic, depressed, and self-indulgent.

Career: Some of the best professions for 8 Gua Pigs where they may attain wealth, fame, or fulfillment, are in or as entertainers, caterers, doctors, farmers, or veterinarians, or in transportation, entertainment, retail, hospitality, real estate, construction, consultancy, architecture, pottery, human resources, and OB-GYN.

Best Matches: Those part of the West Life Group (2, 6, 7, or 8 Life Guas); excellent matches are 2 Guas born in the year of the Pig or Rabbit, or 9 Guas born in the year of the Goat. The 3 and 4 Guas may try to control or pressure you. Avoid any Life Gua born in the year of the Snake as this is considered a direct clash with your energy.

The 9 Guas
9 Gua as a Rat
There are no 9 Guas ever born in the year of the Rat.

9 Gua as an Ox

Men and Women!

Confident, Brilliant, Loyal

Elements: Yin Fire and Yin Earth

Years Occurring for Males: 1901, 1937, 1973, 2009, 2045

Years Occurring for Females: 1913, 1949, 1985, 2021

Famous 9 Gua Oxen Men and Women: Walt Disney, Louis Armstrong, Rosa Parks, Vivien Leigh, Jack Nicholson, Warren Beatty, Morgan Freeman, Bill Cosby, Anthony Hopkins, Dustin Hoffman, George Carlin, Ridley Scott, Joyce DeWitt, Shelley Long, Whoopi Goldberg, Twiggy, Sigourney Weaver, Meryl Streep, Ivana Trump, Vera Wang, Yasmin Khan, Annie Leibovitz, Paul Walker, Akon, Adrien Brody, Nick Lachey, Peter Facinelli, Neil Patrick Harris, Peter Andre, Ashley Tisdale, Bar Refaeli, Ciara, Amanda Seyfried, Keira Knightley, Carey Mulligan.

Personality and Romance: 9 Gua men and women who were born in the year of the Ox are an auspicious mix of Fire and Earth energy, creating inner confidence and stability. These men and women are honest, patriotic, ambitious, family-oriented, free-spirited, and highly intelligent. They are famously diligent, determined, and hard-working. 9 Gua Oxen are not influenced by others and do things according to their own ideas and abilities. Before taking action to do anything, they will have a specific plan and detailed steps. Add to this their physical strength, and these people have the ability to enjoy great success. 9 Gua Oxen have a sharp, brilliant intellect. They can also be wise, loyal, and sentimental. Blessed with a fiery spirit and energy, these people have a decidedly adventurous streak. They are not particularly romantic, preferring to take a more practical approach to selecting a spouse. They prefer their own counsel over that of others, and would rather develop life-long relationships than casual ones.

With concentrated and focused effort, they can reach great heights of achievements and standing in the world.

The Best Stuff: When 9 Gua Oxen are fully exhibiting their best qualities, they are radiant, steadfast, loyal, social, methodical, patient, hardworking, ambitious, conventional, steady, modest, logical, resolute, and tenacious.

The Worst Stuff: When 9 Gua Oxen move to the darker side of their nature, they can be paranoid, unforgiving, ruthless, domineering, psychotic, unstable, stubborn, narrow-minded, materialistic, rigid, and demanding.

Career: Some of the best professions for 9 Gua Oxen where they may attain wealth, fame, or fulfillment are in medicine, religion, manufacturing, pharmacy, engineering, politics, real estate, interior design, public speaking, chemicals, optical, cosmetics, television, beauty, war correspondence, and the military.

Best Matches: Those part of the East Life Group (1, 3, 4, or 9 Life Guas); excellent matches are 3 Guas born in the year of the Ox. Regarding the West Life Group, 9 Guas support the 2 and 8 Guas and may control the 6 and 7 Guas. Avoid any Life Gua born in the year of the Goat as this is considered a direct clash with your energy.

9 Gua as a Tiger

There are no 9 Guas ever born in the year of the Tiger.

9 Gua as a Rabbit

There are no 9 Guas ever born in the Year of the Rabbit.

9 Gua as a Dragon

Men and Women!

Powerful, Brilliant, Loyal

Elements: Yin Fire and Yang Earth

Years Occurring for Males: 1928, 1964, 2000, 2036

Years Occurring for Females: 1904, 1940, 1976, 2012, 2048

Famous 9 Gua Dragon Men and Women: Joan Crawford, Greer Garson, Eddie Fisher, Burt Bacharach, Jimmy Dean, Andy Warhol, Raquel Welch, Jill St. John, Elke Sommer, Nancy Sinatra, Dionne Warwick, Keanu Reeves, Lenny Kravitz, Russell Crowe, Matt Dillon, Rob Lowe, Ty Pennington, Michael McDonald, Clive Owen, Djimon Hounsou, Bobby Flay, Melissa Rauch, Reese Witherspoon, Piper Perabo, Diane Kruger, Alicia Silverstone, Rashida Jones, Kelly Clarkson, Keri Russell, Isla Fisher, Naomie Harris.

Personality and Romance: The 9 Gua men and women born in the year of the Dragon are an auspicious mix of Fire and Earth energy, bringing them great personal power. Chinese culture reveres the mythical dragon as the mightiest and most sacred creature. These men and women enjoy things on a grand scale and play by their own rules. They are vibrant, courageous, tenacious, intelligent, enthusiastic, confident, impetuous, and charismatic. 9 Guas have a sharp, brilliant intellect; they can also be wise, loyal, and sentimental. The 9 Gua Dragon women are captivating and are not modest or unassuming—you *will* notice her as she enters a room. The male 9 Gua Dragons have supreme egos; they are dashing, hugely ambitious, and born winners. Blessed with a fiery spirit and energy, these Guas have a permanent adventurous streak. The female 9 Guas are usually beautiful like divas or goddesses. 9 Gua Dragons may have their head in the clouds at times, but they are usually very grounded. In the search for the ideal partner, they might find themselves often hesitant to move forward in a relationship and/or unwilling to make a permanent commitment. When they do, however, it is their intention that it be lasting. 9 Gua Dragons are likely to have a warm, giving personality. They can be very generous to their loved ones and make loyal life partners. Because dragons can have hot tempers, they need a tough-skinned spouse.

The Best Stuff: When 9 Gua Dragons are fully exhibiting their best qualities, they are intellectual, magnanimous, stately, vigorous, strong, self-assured, brilliant, proud, noble, direct, dignified, zealous, fiery, passionate, decisive, pioneering, ambitious, generous, and loyal.

The Worst Stuff: When 9 Gua Dragons move to the darker side of their nature, they can be paranoid, unstable, rash, psychotic, arrogant, imperious, tyrannical, demanding, eccentric, grandiloquent, extremely bombastic, prejudiced, dogmatic, overbearing, violent, impetuous, and brash.

Career: Some of the best professions for 9 Gua Dragons where they may attain wealth, fame, or fulfillment, are in law, the arts, entrepreneurship, medicine, invention, computer analysis, law, engineering, architecture, broking, public speaking, fuel/oil, chemicals, advertising, television, restaurants, beauty, and war correspondence.

Best Matches: Those part of the East Life Group (1, 3, 4, or 9 Life Guas); excellent matches are 3 Guas born in the year of the Dragon. Regarding the West Life Group, the 9 Guas support the 2 and 8 Guas and may control the 6 and 7 Guas. Avoid any Life Gua born in the year of the Dog as this is considered a direct clash with your energy.

9 Gua as a Snake

There are no 9 Guas ever born in the year of the Snake.

9 Gua as a Horse

There are no 9 Guas ever born in the year of the Horse.

9 Gua as a Goat

Men and Women!
Gentle, Cunning, Classy
Elements: Yin Fire and Yin Earth
Years Occurring for Males: 1919, 1955, 1991, 2027
Years Occurring for Females: 1931, 1967, 2003, 2039

Famous 9 Gua Goat Men and Women: Nat "King" Cole, Liberace, Jack Palance, Anita Ekberg, Angie Dickinson, Mitzi Gaynor, Leslie Caron, Rita Moreno, Della Reese, Steve Jobs, Bill Gates, Billy Idol, Bruce Willis, David Lee Roth, Billy Bob Thornton, Dodi Fayed, Tom Bergeron, Gary Sinise, Kelsey Grammer, Yun-Fat Chow, Willem Dafoe, Jeff Daniels, Dana Carvey, Pamela Anderson, Nicole Kidman, Courtney Thorne-Smith, Faith Hill, Anna Nicole Smith, Toni Braxton, Julia Roberts, Carrie-Anne Moss, Mira Sorvino, Laura Dern, Kristen Johnston, Joely Fisher, Rebecca Ramos, Mitchel Musso, Jason Dolley, Hunter Hayes.

Personality and Romance: 9 Gua men and women born in the year of the Goat are a mix of Fire and Earth energy, giving them inner confidence and stability. They are shy, gentle, calm, intelligent, cunning, charming, crafty, sympathetic, and tend to be dreamers. While they love being social, they do not crave attention, preferring to be observant and autonomous. They are just as happy to be left alone or to stay at home. 9 Gua Goats like to be fashionable and will spend money on presenting a first-class appearance; however they are rarely snobbish, even when they have tons of material wealth and the finer things in life. 9 Guas have a sharp, brilliant intellect; they can also be wise, loyal, and sentimental. The 9 Gua Goat women are usually very beautiful, like divas or goddesses, and may even have an ethereal air about them. These men and women are extremely reliable and steadfast; even under undue pressure they remain calm. They have nurturing personalities and are very giving people; intensely private, it takes some time and effort to know them. They have a small inner circle, but will work hard for friends and loved ones.

The Best Stuff: When 9 Gua Goats are fully exhibiting their best qualities, they are righteous, sincere, sympathetic, mild-mannered, shy, artistic, creative, gentle, compassionate, understanding, mothering, determined, peaceful, and generous.

The Worst Stuff: When 9 Gua Goats move to the darker side of their nature, they can be crafty, cunning, moody, indecisive, over-passive, worriers, pessimistic, overly sensitive, and whiny.

Career: Some of the best professions for 9 Gua Goats where they may attain wealth, fame, or fulfillment are in law, religion, chemicals, optics, cosmetics, advertising, and television, or as an entrepeneur, doctor, journalist, inventor, computer analyst, engineer, architect, or soldier.

Best Matches: Those part of the East Life Group (1, 3, 4, or 9 Life Guas); an excellent match are 3 Guas born in a Goat year. Regarding the West Life Group, 9 Guas support the 2 and 8 Guas but may control the 6 and 7 Guas. Avoid any Life Gua born in the year of the Ox, as this is considered a direct clash with your energy.

9 Gua as a Monkey
There are no 9 Guas ever born in the year of the Monkey.

9 Gua as a Rooster
There are no 9 Guas ever born in the year of the Rooster.

9 Gua as a Dog
Men and Women!
Social, Loyal, Passionate
Elements: Yin Fire and Yang Earth
Years Occurring for Males: 1910, 1946, 1982, 2018, 2054
Years Occurring for Females: 1922, 1958, 1994, 2030

Famous 9 Gua Dog Men and Women: Jacques Cousteau, David Niven, Artie Shaw, Ava Gardner, Doris Day, Judy Garland, Betty White, Cyd Charisse, Sylvester Stallone, David Gilmour, Barry Gibb, Bill Clinton, Al Green, Tim Curry, Alan Rickman, Keith Moon, Timothy Dalton, Jimmy Buffett, Donald Trump, Daryl Hall, Tommy Lee Jones, Steven Spielberg, George W. Bush, Danny Glover, André the Giant, Ben Vereen, Madonna, Sharon Stone, Jamie Lee Curtis, Michelle Pfeiffer, Ellen DeGeneres, Marg Helgenberger, Andie MacDowell, Anita Baker, Annette Bening, Angela Bassett, Nancy Grace, Lil' Wayne, Ne-Yo, Prince William, Justin Bieber.

Personality and Romance: 9 Gua men and women born in the year of the Dog are a mix of Earth and Fire energy, creating an inner fiery passion and stability. They are generous, faithful, loyal, pessimistic, introspective, sincere, amiable, loving, kind, and devoted. Due to bearing a strong sense of loyalty and sincerity, they will do everything for the person they think is most important. 9 Gua Dogs are born with a good nature, not inclined toward criminal behavior or seeking gain through dishonest means. They simply require a quiet life and a good family to help them forget the ugliness and evil in the world. They are always ready to help others, even to the detriment of their own interests, and when they find themselves betrayed by cunning people, they will feel shocked and hurt. 9 Gua Dogs are consummate worriers and are generally pessimistic about the world around them, always fully expecting something bad around the corner. However, they have a sharp, brilliant intellect and can also be wise, loyal, and sentimental. Whatever they focus and turn their attention to, they will develop competence; they'll always find a way to complete an assignment. In romantic relationships, 9 Gua Dogs require lots of emotional support and attention. They find it difficult to trust others, and many are often scared off by the dog's insecure, worrisome, and anxious nature.

The Best Stuff: When 9 Gua Dogs are fully exhibiting their best qualities, they are honest, intelligent, straightforward, loyal, attractive, amiable, unpretentious, sociable, open-minded, idealistic, moralistic, practical, affectionate, and have a strong sense of justice.

The Worst Stuff: When 9 Gua Dogs move to the darker side of their nature, they can be cynical, lazy, cold, paranoid, judgmental, *dogging*, pessimistic, worriers, stubborn, and quarrelsome.

Career: Some of the best professions for 9 Gua Dogs where they may attain wealth, fame, or fulfillment are in education, social work, research, campaigns, counseling, interior design, academics, politics, nurse, fuel/oil, advertising, television, restaurants, lighting, beauty, and war correspondence.

Best Matches: Those part of the East Life Group (1, 3, 4, or 9 Life Guas); an excellent match is a 3 Gua born in the year of the Dog. Regarding the West Life Group, 9 Guas support the 2 and 8 Guas but may control the 6 and 7 Guas. Avoid any Life Gua born in the year of the Dragon, as this is considered a direct clash with your energy.

9 Gua as a Pig

There are no 9 Guas ever born in the year of the Pig.

The Life-Gua Zodiac Personalities system is a unique way to peer into our energy and that which attracts and repels us. The information is useful, not only in romantic relationships, but with family members, coworkers, children, bosses, business partners, and past spouses or lovers. Having insights into our proclivities is useful…and sometimes disconcerting, as few people readily admit that at times our behavior can veer toward the negative.

Remember that the Life Gua Zodiac Personalities aspect of Eight Mansions is not about using your good and bad directions; rather it is all about the relationships with ourselves and others in our sphere. In order to understand relationships even further, let's explore the Flying Star system, which is excellent at revealing how the energy of our home or office can influence people's behavior, good and bad. Flying Stars has very specific ways in which to activate energy—both exterior and interior—to beckon harmony, prosperity, romance, and luck in love!

Part III
Flying Stars

Six

....

Using Flying Stars to Understand Relationships

....

It is the stars, the stars above us govern our conditions.
William Shakespeare

Flying Stars is one of the most exciting and powerful Feng Shui systems in modern-day practice. It's part of a major branch of Classical Feng Shui and has been around without much modification for more than 400 years.[10] The actual name for this method is *Xuan Kong Fei Xing* (pronounced "shoon kong fay sing"), which means "subtle mysteries of time and space" or "mysterious void." It is also referred to as "time dimension Feng Shui" as it so accurately depicts the energy/events of a structure in the past, present, and future. This excellent system is superior for understanding relationships and people's behavior in a living

---

10. The two main branches of Classical Feng Shui are San He and San Yuan; Feng Shui Masters use both of these major schools/branches with their numerous formulas, methods and techniques and one big body of knowledge and practice.

space, day after day, year after year. While there have been several books on Flying Stars in recent years, most Americans have barely heard of it, being more familiar with the Westernized styles of Feng Shui such as the Eight Life Aspirations. Flying Stars is an advanced system designed to address the issue of time. The ancient masters who were responsible for creating it wanted to know what happens to a structure as it moves through time, and more importantly, how would it affect the occupants. Flying Stars is a system fully developed to do just that and explain why no structure can forever enjoy good or bad Feng Shui as it cycles through time. Depending on the specific compass direction that your home faces, it will have a Natal Star chart, much like an astrological chart for a person. While Eight Mansions revolve around people, Flying Stars focuses on buildings; both use direction.

Flying Stars is considered an advanced system but by following the recommendations in either chapter 8 or 9 you will be able to successfully activate the energy of your living space as soon as you locate your unique Natal Star chart.

Flying Stars was developed in the Ming and Ching Dynasties. There are six big schools of the Flying Star system, but all are very similar in their approach and interpretation based on classic Chinese texts.[11] They all share the same goal, to analyze the energy of the building/home and adjust the energy to support the occupants.

So what are the "stars"? The stars are simply the numbers 1 through 9. They also have an earthly correlation to the seven real stars of the Big Dipper (aka Ursa Major) with two imaginary ones. Each star has unique qualities and energy that can influence behavior and events. For example, some stars indicate wealth, sickness, romance, scholarly pursuits, writing, fame, divorce, and so forth. It is obvious that some stars are auspicious, while others are very negative.

---

11. The Six Big Schools of Flying Stars are 1) Wu Chang Pai, 2) Chen Nan Pai,
    3) Su Chou Pai, 4) Shang Yu Pai, 5) Siang Chuo Pai, and 6) Kuang Tong Pai.

Cycle	Period	Years	Trigram/Gua
Upper	1	1864-1884	Kan
	2	1884-1904	Kun
	3	1904-1924	Chen
Middle	4	1924-1944	Xun/Sun
	5	1944-1964	No Trigram
	6	1964-1984	Chien/Qian
Lower	7	1984-2004	Dui/Tui
	8	2004-2024	Gen/Ken
	9	2024-2044	Li

Figure 12: The San Yuan 180-year Cycle of Time.

Flying Stars is based on huge time cycles and planetary alignments. According to the ancient Chinese scholars, the planets in our solar system align in a straight line once every 179 or 180 years. It is believed that the first observation of this phenomenon was around 2500 BCE.

In Feng Shui this called a megacycle of time. The Chinese next divided this 180-year cycle into three 60-year cycles (called Upper, Middle, and Lower). The 60-year cycles were once more divided into 20-year increments called periods or ages. Each period is assigned a number (1 through 9) and a trigram (except 5, which has no trigram) that has a unique energy it exhibits for 20 years. Why 20-year periods? Interestingly, they also observed that the Milky Way shifted every 20 years thus affecting the luck of a building or home and human beings. See the chart below giving an example of the nine 20-year periods comprising the 180-year megacycle of time covering the years from 1864 to 2043.

As you can see, we are currently in Period 8 and will be until February 3, 2023; using the solar calendar, the Chinese New Year is February 4 of any given year. Period 9 will start February 4, 2024. The ruling energy or influence is always the number and associated trigram of the period. For example, eight is king for Period 8! The number eight is always venerated by the Chinese because it has noble energy in general, and secondly it makes a homophone with "wealth" (*bā* in Chinese). In chapters 8 and 9 you will find all the Flying Stars charts from 1984 to 2024. This covers two 20-year periods, and we will be only discussing Periods 8 and 7, as most homes fall into these two time periods.

Finding Your Home's Flying Star Chart

How do you know which Flying Star chart is correct for your house? There are two important factors that must be determined in order to locate the correct chart for your house: the facing direction and your move-in date. Once you have found the right chart for your house, think of it as a permanent energy map of your space and how energy is distributed; once determined you will refer to either chapter 8 or 9.

Determine the Facing

You will need a fairly accurate compass to get the correct degree your home faces. Most smartphones have compass apps, but remember these phones do not have magnets in them as a traditional compass would. The "compasses" on your phone will only be as good as the app, usually using a combination of GPS and the phone's accelerometer. Defer to a traditional magnetic compass if you doubt the reading. What I do like about smartphone compasses is that they give you a digital readout and direction.

Take your compass measurement/degree from the front door if it faces the road. More than 80 percent of homes will have the door facing the road, and be located pretty much in the center of the house. In these homes, taking your compass direction will be straightforward. If the door does not face the road, stand in the middle of your front yard or garden to determine how your house faces. Any side doors or angled doors— even if they seem to face the road—cannot be used to measure from to determine the facing in this system (see Figure 13). The general rule for determining the facing is where the most yang energy is; the truth is almost nothing competes with the energy of a street. For those who live in apartment buildings, use the main door/entrance as the facing direction; superimpose the correct chart/direction over your floor plan.

In Flying Stars there are only 24 possible facing directions. How is this derived? Each of the eight directions (north, south, northwest, and so forth; each direction has 45 degrees) are sub-divided into three sectors (8 x 3=24). Each of the sub-sectors is 15 degrees of that direction. As a result you'll have South 1, South 2, and South 3, for example. Each is comprised of 15 degrees, and this is how these directions are referred to in Feng Shui.

Even though there are 24 facings, there are only 16 Flying Star charts for each period, since the last two sub-divided sectors share the same Natal chart. In other words, South 2 or South 3 will have the same exact chart in any given period. It will be simple to locate your chart once you have the facing degree; all the charts are clearly indicated by the degrees and will tell you which charts are South 1, East 2, Southwest 1, and so forth. Make sure you have taken an accurate compass direction of your house so you have the correct Flying Star chart—you will be setting into motion new energy!

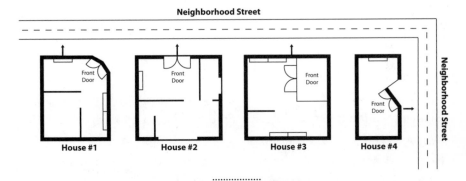

Figure 13: Determining the facing. The arrows point to the correct facing direction which is toward the road; measure this direction with a compass to find your Flying Star chart. In houses 1, 3, and 4, the front door cannot be used to determine the facing.

Move-In Date

There is much controversy regarding whether to use the actual construction date or the move-in date when determining a building's period. To this day, Feng Shui Masters still actively debate this in Hong Kong and other areas of the world. Grandmaster Yap has seen these discussions get very heated indeed, everyone shouting that they are right! Primarily, masters in Hong Kong prefer the construction date, while those in Malaysia, Singapore, and Taiwan use the move-in date. Since I'm in the lineage of Grandmaster Yap, I use move-in date and find it extremely reliable and accurate.

Use the following information to determine what period your home belongs to:

- Your home is a Period 7, if you moved in between February 4, 1984 to February 3, 2004.

- Your home is a Period 8 if you moved in between February 4, 2004 to February 3, 2024.

Exceptions for Period 7 homes are if major renovations took place *after* February 4, 2004. What constitutes a major renovation? Removing the entire roof (some small percentage must be exposed to the open sky at least for a few hours), major interior remodeling, renovating the front entrance and door, painting the entire inside and outside at the same time, remodeling the kitchen or bathrooms, installing one or more skylights, changing all the floors at the same time, adding on a room, or adding an attached garage. All of these things cause a major shift in energy, and therefore your Flying Star chart will change. So if you did any of these things or a combination of them (after February 4, 2004) and you moved in Period 7, your home will now be a Period 8 chart. If you moved into your house after 2004, and have done or are currently doing some renovations, your home is still a Period 8. So what does a Flying Star chart look like?

Components of a Flying Star Chart

Remember, the Flying Star chart of a property is simply an energy map of the building. Feng Shui Masters use this chart to make accurate predictions on relationships, romance potential, success in a career, when a promotion or marriage may take place, lawsuits—anything that may happen in the human experience. A Flying Star chart is a nine-square grid with three numbers in each square. These three numbers are either a facing, mountain, or time star.

Facing Star. Also known as "water stars," these numbers are located in the upper right-hand corner in all nine palaces (squares) of the chart. These stars affect money, finance, and career. Good stars indicate wealth-luck, while bad stars denote money loss.

Mountain Star. Also known as "sitting stars," these numbers are located in the upper left-hand corner in all nine palaces of the chart. Mountain stars influence luck where people, health, career, fertility, and employees are concerned.

Time Star. Also known as the "base star," this number indicates the period to which the chart belongs. It is the single star below the facing and mountain stars.

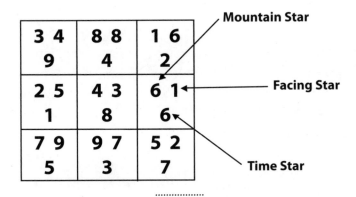

Figure 14: Components of a Flying Star chart.

To keep things simple and consistent throughout the book, I will use the terms *facing star* and *mountain star*. In order to fully understand the soul of Flying Stars, you must know the meaning that each star portends. In this system, the good stars—which are also wealth stars—are 1, 6, 8, and 9 whether they are facing or mountain stars. The 4 Star is good for romance, writing, study, publishing, fame, and sexual energy. Please note that the 2, 3, 5, and 7 are very bad stars that can deliver sickness, lawsuits, bankruptcy, and robbery respectively. The stars that relate to romance, sex, love affairs, and enticements regarding the opposite sex are 1, 4, 6, and 7; these are called "Peach Blossom" stars.

Star 5 is considered the worst star, considered evil because it has no direction, thus making it a wild card and unpredictable. It does, however, possess immense power. Bad stars are only good in their period; otherwise, they are considered inauspicious. In other words, the 5 star is only advantageous in Period 5, and the same goes for the 2, 3, and 7 stars. When a Flying Star chart is analyzed, several important factors are taken into consideration: the nature of the star (good or bad), the landforms in your immediate environment, and the interior layout of your living space.

If the external formations support the energy of the chart, you will get a positive result. An auspicious formation can bring good fortune, while landforms that do not support the chart can attract misfortune. The chart can only "come alive" and bestow benevolent energy when the interior environment and external landforms support it. The following are the positive and negative aspects of the nine stars, the star symbol indicate the current, good stars. The bolded text gives the outcomes for Period 8.

Star	Element	Nature of the Nine Stars (for Period 8)
1	WATER	**Indicates money and knowledge.** Research, thinking, knowledge, intelligence, examination, scholarly, good government positions, promotion, studies, distinction, and abundance.
2	EARTH	**Indicates sickness.** Difficulty in childbirth, dying young, bad illness. Sickness in the stomach, abdominal problems, abortion, and miscarriages.
3	WOOD	**Indicates lawsuits and fighting.** Insanity, asthma, hurting the wife, gossip, slander, prosecution, trials by law, legal problems, arguments, breathing problems, and theft.
4	WOOD	**Indicates romance and writing.** Knowledge, passion, romance, wisdom, harmony, success in exams, honesty, good authority, beautiful children, and fame.
5	EARTH	**Indicates disasters, cancer, and bankruptcy.** Lawsuits by the government, calamity, catastrophe, lawsuits, setbacks, disease, death, and grave misfortune.
6	METAL	**Indicates power and authority.** Government, nobility, distinction, respect, fame, honors, activity, success, good money decisions, and a world-famous son.
7	METAL	**Indicates robbery and theft.** Government lawsuits, jailed, indictment, and fires.
8	EARTH	**Indicates wealth and investments.** Riches, finance, good reserves, investments are excellent, gentle people, loyalty, and cultivation.
9	FIRE	**Indicates achievements and promotions.** Advancement, graduation, reputation, emotion, great smarts, good scores on government exams, a middle son acquiring wealth, great achievements, accomplishments, and status.

Figure 15: The Nature of the Stars.

Flying Star Charts

Flying Stars Feng Shui makes a crucial connection between the orientation of a building, the move-in date, the present time, and the luck of the occupants. Ensuring that the energy from the stars is extracted prudently exterior and interior to your homesite is the heart of evaluating and activating the Flying Star chart. In addition to the permanent Natal chart of the house, there are "visiting" stars that only visit for a year or a month in certain areas of your home; furthermore there are daily and hourly stars. However considering their very short blips in time, giving them serious consideration would be a bit much, therefore I've not included them in the book. Master Yap's personal feeling regarding daily and hourly stars was to "get a life"; by the time they're analyzed, the news is old.

It's important to note that the visiting annual and monthly stars can trigger the energy of certain stars or star combinations; in chapters 8 and 9 you'll notice that I have alerted you when additional romance energy is visiting for the year. More importantly, I have made recommendations to significantly change the energy of your home for Period 8 and Period 7 homes, including all 16 charts for both periods. The recommendations take into consideration Eight Mansions, Advanced Eight Mansions, Flying Stars—basically *all* systems which are part of the San He and San Yuan branches. The suggestions will tell you how to activate the exterior and interior of your home, thus automatically extracting romance, harmony, prosperity, and excellent relationships. Getting the exterior environment correct is one of the most important things you can do in Feng Shui. You can have a perfectly wonderful, relationship potential chart, and it can be made null and void by bad landforms or not activating it properly according to the Flying Star chart.

All 16 Flying Star charts in any given period will fall into four basic structures:

- **Double Stars Meet at Facing** *(Shuang Xing Dao Xiang)*

- **Double Stars Meet at Sitting** *(Shuang Xing Dao Zuo)*

- **Prosperous Sitting and Facing** *(Wang Shan Wang Shui)*

- **Reverse Formation** *(a.k.a Up the Mountain, Down the River)*

The basic structure of the chart is what ultimately determines how it should be activated; otherwise your chart will not "come alive."

Enhancing Relationships, Prosperity, and Harmony

How to Use Chapters 8 and 9

Implementing the recommendations in either chapter 8 or 9 is the next best thing to having a Feng Shui Master visit your residence. You will need to collect vital information concerning your home before you refer to chapter 8 or 9; first you will need to know the exact degree your home faces. Next you will need to decide which period your home belongs to as described earlier in this chapter. Let's start with the compass reading. Once you have that degree, refer to the chart below. For example, if your reading is 205°, your house faces Southwest 1; if it's 43°, your house faces Northeast 2.

Now that you have the correct facing direction and period, you can go right to the information concerning your house. For Period 8 homes, use chapter 8; Period 7 homes, go to chapter 9.

Have your floor plan in front of you divided up in nine sectors as shown in Figure 17; the example is for a Period 8, West 3 chart and a 4 Life Gua. Overlay all the eight directions, your Eight Mansions, and the Flying Stars. Each of the Flying Star charts has where all the directions should be placed in the black area. By having this information on your floor plan, you will be able to make notes of the possible placements of water, beds, desks and so on as you read the recommendations. There may be limitations or restrictions due to doors, closets, sliding glass doors, and so forth; however there are several placements to choose from.

The Bad Stuff

When I was first learning Classical Feng Shui, it seemed like there was a lot of "bad stuff"; I wondered why the Chinese focused so much on the negative. We in the West tend to focus on the positive, so I was perplexed. However, I quickly understood the reasoning and significance of this aspect in a site assessment. Classical Feng Shui has an extremely long history in which the masters could observe and then document results with razor-sharp accuracy. In the end, the purpose was to determine if you had negative formations, then to avoid or quash them.

General Direction	Exact Direction	Facing Name	Energy or Animal	Compass Degrees
South	S1	Bing	Yang Fire	157.6–172.5
	S2	Wu	HORSE	172.6–187.5
	S3	Ting	Yin Fire	187.6–202.5
Southwest	SW1	Wei	GOAT	202.6–217.5
	SW2	Kun	Earth	217.6–232.5
	SW3	Shen	MONKEY	232.6–247.5
West	W1	Geng	Yang Metal	247.6–262.5
	W2	You	ROOSTER	262.6–277.5
	W3	Xin	Yin Metal	277.6–292.5
Northwest	NW1	Xu	DOG	292.6–307.5
	NW2	Chien	Metal	307.6–322.5
	NW3	Hai	PIG	322.6–337.5
North	N1	Ren	Yang Water	337.6–352.5
	N2	Tzi	RAT	352.6–7.5
	N3	Kwei	Yin Water	7.6–22.5
Northeast	NE1	Chou	OX	22.6–37.5
	NE2	Gen	Earth	37.6–52.5
	NE3	Yin	TIGER	52.6–67.5
East	E1	Jia	Yang Wood	67.6–82.5
	E2	Mao	RABBIT	82.6–97.5
	E3	Yi	Yin Wood	97.6–112.5
Southeast	SE1	Chen	DRAGON	112.6–127.5
	SE2	Xun	Wood	127.6–142.5
	SE3	Su	SNAKE	142.6–157.5

Figure 16: The 24 Possible Facing Directions.

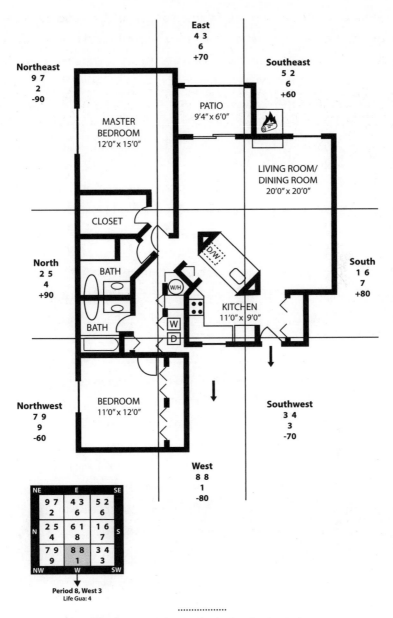

Figure 17: Example Floor Plan for Period 8.

Being aware of and avoiding or correcting landforms/energy that indicate money loss, divorce, lawsuits, disease, ill health, affairs, and so forth ensures good Feng Shui and good events in the occupants' lives. Please pay attention to—but not dwell on—the possible negative features of your chart. Having this knowledge is power in your pocket, equally as important now as it was in ancient times.

Therefore, in addition to very detailed information on the Natal Star charts, you will be alerted to several possible negative scenarios that will affect the harmony of the house, and in fact all relationships (romantic, family, and business), which include **Eight Roads of Destruction** (divorce/bankruptcy), **Goat Blade Water** (affairs, drug use, alcoholism, and gambling), **Eight Killing Forces** (bloody crimes of passion/accidents), and **Peach Blossom Sha Roads** (extramarital/scandalous affairs, bankruptcy, illicit sexting, and divorce)—all which are known as bad landforms because they involve a mountain, water, roads, or water exits.

Renovation and Ground-Digging Taboos

Each year, it is taboo to renovate or dig in the ground in certain directions/sectors of your home site. This would include installing a pool, adding on a room, remodeling bathrooms/kitchens, removing huge trees/stumps, adding a detached garage, digging a decorative water feature, or installing a sprinkler system; all involve shaking/digging into the earth or the house (hammering or demolition). Replacing annual flowers, normal tree trimming, house painting, or locating a fountain will *not* disturb the energy. There are four shas (afflictions) that visit each year; the Three Killings, the Grand Duke Jupiter, and the Five Yellow are the most serious.[12] Please

---

12. The four annual shas or afflictions are the Three Killings (Sam Sart), the Five Yellow (Wu Wang), the Grand Duke Jupiter (Tia Sui), and the Year Breaker (Sui Po). For more detailed information, refer to *Classical Feng Shui for Wealth and Abundance*. If you must renovate or have already paid for the construction of a pool, Feng Shui Masters will use the Great Sun formula to find dates to begin construction to protect you from harmful results.

refer to the chart below if you plan to renovate in these areas or to excavate for a large water feature or move the ground; all proper placement of water can be found in chapters 8 or 9 depending on your home's facing.

When there are two or more afflictions visiting in one sector, it is best to wait to renovate or dig until the next year; for example, notice that in 2015 the Three Killings and the Five Yellow visit the west. Disturbing the west in that year may bring money loss, divorce, blood-related accidents, bankruptcy, violence, or severe injuries. 2008 saw a very rare occurrence—the south direction had three out of four of the afflictions: the Three Killings, the Five Yellow, and the Year Breaker.

Do Not Renovate or Dig in these Sectors/Directions			
Year	Grand Duke Jupiter Involves 15°	Three Killings Involves 75°	The 5 Yellow Involves 45°
2014	South 2	North 1, 2, 3 plus NE 1 and NW 3	Northwest
2015	Southwest 1	West 1, 2, 3 plus NW 1 and SW 3	West
2016	Southwest 3	South 1, 2, 3 plus SE 3 and SW 1	Northeast
2017	West 2	East 1, 2, 3 plus NE 3 and SE 1	South
2018	Northwest 1	North 1, 2, 3 plus NE 1 and NW 3	North
2019	Northwest 3	West 1, 2, 3 plus NW 1 and SW 3	Southwest
2020	North 2	South 1, 2, 3 plus SE 3 and SW 1	East
2021	Northeast 1	East 1, 2, 3 plus NE 3 and SE 1	Southeast
2022	Northeast 3	North 1, 2, 3 plus NE 1 and NW 3	Center
2023	East 2	West 1, 2, 3 plus NW 1 and SW 3	Northwest
2024	Southeast 1	South 1, 2, 3 plus SE 3 and SW 1	West

Figure 18: Renovation or Digging Taboos.

The Master Bedroom

There are two ways to enhance relationships, harmony, and prosperity in the bedroom: location and direction; the *direction* of the bed will give you the most powerful results. Additionally, both stars (mountain and facing) get "activated" while sleeping. Most other areas of the home such as doors, desk facing, fireplaces, water features, ovens, and stove knobs will *only* activate the facing star! Keeping that in mind, if you are able to choose a good location *and* direction your luck will double.

Large wall mirrors, ceiling mirrors, mirrored closet doors, or a water feature in the master bedroom can incite affairs; either spouse may feel unsatisfied and be tempted to cheat. The rule is, while lying in bed, if you can see yourself in a mirror, it must be addressed. The best solution to mirrored closet doors is to replace them with wooden ones if possible. At the very least, cover them with paint intended for metal surfaces, paste over with high-end wallpaper or fabric, or install drapes to cover them while sleeping. Other mirrors can be moved within the room; water features should be completely removed.

———

Flying Stars has generated enormous world-wide interest in the last 20 years, and having some knowledge of this exciting system is worth the effort. Just as with the Eight Mansions, Flying Stars also has many facets—the Natal Star chart, annual visiting stars, monthly stars, the renovation taboos, and unique time periods. The next chapter features special Flying Star charts and other techniques such as Three Harmony Doorways and the Peach Blossom to enhance romance and relationships.

Seven

·······················

Feng Shui Secrets to Enhance Romantic Love and Relationships

·······················

To love someone deeply gives you strength.
Being loved by someone deeply gives you courage.

Lao Tzu

In this chapter I'll give you some techniques Feng Shui Masters use to enhance relationships; you will be pleasantly surprised that they go beyond paintings of love birds, use of red or purple paint, candles, wedding photos, and love charms. In fact, these are not methods used in Classical Feng Shui at all, but are the commercialized methods of Western Feng Shui. Maybe you've tried them and placed all the right things in the "marriage corner"…and got zero results.

According to this more symbolic type of Feng Shui, some of the more popular objects to place in the "marriage corner" are a picture of mandarin ducks, geese, the double happiness sign, a mountain peony, a lute, magpie, or crystals in the window. There are two reasons why results are lackluster: Western Feng Shui is not authentic and neither are the "love cures," and they take a cookie-cutter, one-size-fits-all approach, with everyone having the same marriage corner. To get results with Feng Shui, it must be specific to you and your home—this means the exact direction your home faces, your birthday, and when you moved in.

This chapter is devoted to romantic relationships because of the huge interest in how this works in Feng Shui. Feng Shui Masters were not matchmakers, nor is that their function in our times. Basically, you will have to make some effort to help yourself in this area (using your "man or woman luck"). This means you will have to do some personal work if you keep attracting the wrong kind of lover or partner.

Repeating the same negative patterns and behaviors (and not liking the results) is a clear indication for change. If you are in this type of cycle, even the homes you unconsciously choose can indicate trouble with relationships such as bad romance, fatal attractions, abuse, losing your job, or fighting with relatives and neighbors. The house and the events you have experienced can be a blatant wake-up call if we pay attention. Everything changes with understanding; all of our relationship experiences give us information, wisdom, and hope. You will, no doubt, notice that a lot of the techniques involve real water, roads, driveways, or sidewalks—this is because these things either hold energy or are purveyors of energy.

Relationship Luck Techniques

"Peach Blossom" (Tao Hua) or the "Flower of Romance" Direction

The Peach Blossom or the Flower of Romance is a Feng Shui technique that uses direction (a specific 15-degree increment) and is based on the animal year in which you were born. Mind you, this is not the Peach Blossom Sha Road we discussed earlier in chapter 3! This technique is used to attract an exciting new lover/partner or to get a marriage proposal from a serious relationship. It can be used by both men and women. It is never used for married people to stimulate romance; there are other techniques for that; this book discusses them all. If married couples use the Peach Blossom technique, a third party or "outsider" may show up. This is known as a Peach Blossom Sha romance; just remember that in Feng Shui, the word *sha* is never good.

In Chinese culture, peach blossoms are descriptors for mainly two things: a beautiful woman and romance. In ancient China, a home was often surrounded by a wall for protection. Servants ran everyday errands, and the family's matriarch rarely went outside the home without her husband. Sometimes when a woman left her husband, she had to literally jump over the wall. When this happened it was said that the "beautiful peach blossom jumped over the wall." In Feng Shui, the term "peach blossom" primarily indicates romance. But it can also have connotations of love, wine, music, dancing, parties, poetry, and the good life in general.

Remember this is a method that is used to attract a new romantic partner to your life, and it not designed to bring harmony to those relationships in trouble. There are other techniques better suited for that such as activating your +70 and good stars. It is best used for:

- Single people looking for new love interests;

- A woman waiting for a marriage proposal; and

- Singles looking to increase "attractiveness" or the power to attract.

Now, how do you find your Peach Blossom direction, and how do you activate it? It is important to understand that this technique is not as powerful as the Eight Mansions system, which is your personal relationship direction (+70). However, results can definitely be had.

To locate your personal Peach Blossom direction, find the animal year in which you were born. Use the Eight Mansions chart in chapter 4 if you don't already know it. Your Peach Blossom sector depends on your animal sign. If you are a Monkey, Rat, or Dragon, your Peach Blossom sector is West 2. If you are a Pig, Rabbit, or Goat, your Peach Blossom sector is North 2. For the Tiger, Horse, and Dog it is the East 2 sector. Finally for the Snake, Rooster, and Ox it is the South 2 sector. What does the "2" mean? It is the exact 15 degrees in the middle of that direction. For example, if your Peach Blossom is the East it will be between 82 and 97 degrees. See Figure 19 for exact Peach Blossom degrees.

Now let's talk about how to activate the 15 degrees that is your actual Peach Blossom. This is done by simply placing fresh flowers in your Peach Blossom area. While people think it's the flowers—usually roses, the universal flower for love—that activate the Peach Blossom, it's actually the *water* in the vase that will stimulate the energy! That said, don't place a small fountain in lieu of a vase of flowers. This is not an appropriate method to activate your Peach Blossom direction.

Before you activate your Peach Blossom direction, make sure there are no married people in the house who share the same direction as you do, as this may cause affairs. I was just learning Classical Feng Shui in 1996 when I was introduced to the Peach Blossom method. I was anxious to try it on a dear friend who was single. He had lost his wife to cancer a couple of years earlier and was finally ready to meet someone who could be a potential partner. I did a Feng Shui evaluation of his whole house, but asked him to activate his Peach Blossom direction as well. Shortly afterward, several of us (including my friend) were attending a spiritual workshop in the Carolinas where he met a beautiful woman from Colorado. My friend lived in the Seattle area. They married a year later. Sometimes it's just about the timing, so perfect, so "peachy."

You will need a simple compass to find the 15 degrees that is your Peach Blossom location. Keep in mind, every room of the house has an east, west, south and so forth. If you can, place fresh flowers in your bedroom or in a well-loved room in your Peach Blossom direction/location, ideally where you can see them often. Never use artificial flowers to activate your Peach Blossom. Replace dead/dying flowers and keep the water clear and clean. Try it for at least 60 to 90 days to gauge the results.

The Animal Years (Animal Trine)	Peach Blossom to Attract Romance (Direction or Location)
Tiger, Horse, or Dog	Rabbit (East 2) between 82° to 97°
Snake, Rooster, or Ox	Horse (South 2) between 172° to 187°
Monkey, Rat, or Dragon	Rooster (West 2) 262° to 277°
Pig, Rabbit, or Goat	Rat (North 2) 352° to 7°

Figure 19: Peach Blossom Directions.

As a note of interest, Rabbit, Horse, Rooster, and Rat are considered Peach Blossom years. The next Peach Blossom year is the Rooster in 2017. Peach Blossom years carry strong romance potential—they can be particularly important for those born in those years! You may also experience more romance if you are part of the triad or trine of energy. For example, you may not be born in a Rooster year, but you are connected to the Snake-Rooster-Ox triad, so if you are born in either Snake or Ox years, you will also feel the strong effect of the 2017 Peach Blossom Year.

MASTER'S TIP

There are a lot of techniques for enhancing relationships; this one is really simple to implement and can be used by both men and women. Place fresh flowers in your Peach Blossom area. Never keep dead flowers or artificial flowers in your Peach Blossom location/direction.

The Pearl String Formations
(Lin Shu San Poon Gua)

Pearl Strings are one of several very special Flying Star charts; when activated properly they enhance prosperity, relationships, and household harmony. Some Masters call these wonderful formations the *Continuous Bead Formations*. The Pearl Strings will only be in homes and buildings that face northwest, southwest, southeast, and northeast. There are two types of Pearl String formations—one that enhances prosperity and one that supports relationships.

No matter which type of Pearl String formation you have, they both must be supported by a mountain in front and water at the back. A mountain in front could be a real hill, mound, or small mountain. If do not live near mountains or hills, one may be simulated with courtyard walls, landscaping mounds, boulders, or a combination of these. These special charts must also have water at the back. If you have it reversed—water in the front and a mountain behind you—then it is not considered auspicious. These charts are only fortunate in their Period and will last 20 years, at most. For example, all the Pearl Strings for Period 7 are past luck now that we are fully in Period 8 as of February 4, 2004. In order to extract harmony, prosperity, and relationship-luck from these homes, the powerful 8 energy must be activated. These special charts occur four times in Period 7 (Southeast 2, Southeast 3, Northwest 2, and Northwest 3), and only twice in Period 8 (Southeast 1 and Northwest 1).

MASTER'S TIP

In order to fully capture the luck that the Pearl String Charts offer, you must place a mountain in the front and water at the back.

Combination of Ten Formations
(He Shih Chu)

All special Flying Star charts need to be activated in specific ways. When done so properly they can bring prosperity, harmonious relationships, prestige, standing in the community, and powerful connections. As with many cultures around the world, the number ten is consider auspicious. There are two types—one to support prosperity and the other that enhances relationships. In all nine palaces of the Star chart, either the mountain star and time star will add to ten, or the facing star and time star add to ten.

Either one is very auspicious; they are lucky in their period and will last, at most, 20 years. Those Combinations of Ten for Period 7 have fallen out of luck and these charts must be extracted in special ways to be viable in Period 8.

Some say that these special charts override any negative aspects of a house. However, this simply is not true. The potential of these charts can be totally negated by bad landforms scenarios described in chapter 3; I've seen this happen many times. So before you activate your special chart, correct any bad landforms. These special charts occur four times in Period 7 (South 2, South 3, and North 2, and North 3) and only twice in Period 8 (Southwest 1 and Northeast 1).

MASTER'S TIP

These lucky buildings and homes must have the proper external features to bring you prosperity, harmony, great relationships, and prestige! Refer to chapter 8 to see how to activate the Combination of Ten charts correctly.

Parent String Gua Formations
(Fu Mu San Poon Gua)

This special Flying Star chart is also called the Three Combinations, and is said to represent the Cosmic Trinity—heaven, earth, and man (or father, mother, and son). Some Masters believe these charts to be so auspicious that they will transcend all nine periods. However, this is simply not true and a bit exaggerated. They too, will only last twenty years and are activated exactly like the Pearl Strings—mountain in front and water at the back.

These charts may be identified by having, in all nine palaces, one of these combinations of numbers—1 4 7, or 2 5 8, or 3 6 9. They will appear in no particular order; in other words it doesn't matter if the number is the mountain, facing, or time star. The three combinations must be grouped as described above, and must occur in every palace to be a Parent String chart.

If activated properly, these charts are famous for bringing great relationships, prosperity, high standing in the community, harmony, and lots of opportunities to rise in the world. These charts are very rare and do not occur at all in Period 7. However, in Period 8 there are four occurrences (Southwest 2, Southwest 3, Northeast 2, and Northeast 3).

MASTER'S TIP

In order to fully capture the luck that the Parent String charts offer, you must place a mountain in the front and water at the back; they are activated exactly like the Pearl String charts. If you have a Parent String formation, refer to chapter 8 to see how to correctly activate these wonderful charts.

Three Harmony Doorways

Despite the name, it does not require three doors to enhance relationship-luck with this technique. It will involve only one door and some type of pathway, road or driveway. How does it work? Depending on the direction the door faces, a "pathway of chi" can be designed to come from a specific direction so that these two features (door direction and path direction) bring a harmonious energy to the home.

The Three Harmony Doorway	
Door Direction *(Select a well-used or important door)*	**Sidewalk, Driveway, or Road** *(Sidewalk must be six to eight feet from the selected direction before curving back toward the door)*
Northeast 3, South 2, Northwest 1	Southwest 3, North 2, or Southeast 1
Northwest 3, East 2, Southwest 1	Southeast 3, West 2, or Northeast 1
Southwest 3, North 2, or Southeast 1	Northeast 3, South 2, Northwest 1
Southeast 3, West 2, or Northeast 1	Northwest 3, East 2, Southwest 1

Figure 20: The Three Harmony Doorway.

The Three Harmony Doorways bring harmonious relationship-luck to the household as the name implies. I like to use this technique for any house that it is practical to do so. Most homes already have the driveway poured, so you can only use the driveway in new-home construction. For homes that already exist, pathways and sidewalks are much more practical and easy to implement. A Feng Shui Master or practitioner may recommend this method for married couples, business partners, single people, shopping centers, or anywhere he/she feels needs the "harmony" boost. It is also known to bring nobility to the household or business. When implementing this formula, choose a well-used or important door—usually the front door or back door. The sidewalk should come from one of the coordinating directions; make it at least six to eight feet before curving back towards the selected door.

More on Peach Blossoms

In Feng Shui, this term is used to describe romantic or sexy energy, also known as the Flower of Romance. There are several different types of Peach Blossoms described in the book; first are the Peach Blossom Sha (road/water) formations which indicate affairs, adultery, and scandals when roads or water is placed in certain areas of a home (discussed in detail in chapter 3). Next is the Peach Blossom technique which is used to activate certain directions with flowers as discussed in this chapter for good romance or a proposal of marriage. And finally there are Peach Blossom combinations; these are certain combination of stars (numbers) that indicate romance, both good and bad such as (1, 4); (1, 6); (1, 7); (4, 1); the results depend on how they are activated and the overall energy of your living space.

As you can see, relationships, sex, and romance are given a great deal of consideration in Feng Shui as this often determined whether a household would be stable and harmonious or a scandalous, drama-filled train wreck! The term "peach blossom" is one of the most used terms concerning relationships, sex, and romance in Classical Feng Shui.

———

Before proceeding, please review "How to Use Chapters 8 and 9" in chapter 6 to begin changing the energy of your home! Remember, only one chart will apply to your home, the rest can be used to alter the energy of friends and family's homes.

Eight

·····················

Period 8 Charts:
How to Extract Love,
Prosperity, and Harmony

·····················

Kissing is like drinking salty water:
you drink and your thirst increases.
Ancient Chinese Proverb

We are currently in Period 8 which is extremely auspicious; however your Flying Star chart must be properly set into motion to receive benefit. The following information will guide you how to activate the *exterior* and *interior* to do just that. Please be diligent in correcting any bad formations discussed in chapter 3 or otherwise your great chart and its energy cannot be completely realized!

PERIOD 8

South 1 (157.6° to 172. 5°)

Facing Name: **Bing**

Chart: **Double Stars Meet at Sitting**
(Shuang Xing Dao Zuo)

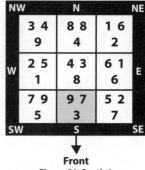

NW	N	NE
3 4 9	8 8 4	1 6 2
2 5 1	4 3 8	6 1 6
7 9 5	9 7 3	5 2 7

W · E (left/right labels), SW · S · SE (bottom labels)

↓ **Front**

Figure 21: South 1

Romancing the Chart

This chart has three areas to enhance romance, relationships, and love-luck. They are the northwest (4 facing star), northeast (1, 6 Peach Blossom combo), and east (6, 1 Peach Blossom combo). Very strong romance energy combines together in the northwest and east in 2015; in 2017, in the northeast; and in 2018, in the south and northwest. Wealth, prosperity, and relationship harmony are energies automatically invoked by placing water and a mountain in the north.

Activating the External Environment
Needs Water and Mountain in the North

This house has two prosperous 8's at the back of the property known as Double Stars Meet at Sitting. Install two important features to extract the relationship and prosperous energy—solid backing *and* big water at the back of the property (north). The water could be a pool, pond, waterfall, huge fountain, or lake. Be aware that if you have a large water feature in the northwest sector of your garden, it could bring affairs. However, if the house has excellent Feng Shui, then water in this area can bring luck and opportunities in publishing and writing, and enhance a public persona. For those living in an apartment, high-rise building, townhome, condominium, or a rented space where you not able to install a water feature outdoors, place one indoors in the recommended area. Also, a tall, heavy statue or two can serve equally as well and activate the excellent mountain energy.

The south-facing homes support relationships/connections, writing, entrepreneurs, and success in scholarly pursuits. This is especially true if there is important and significant backing such as a natural mountain/hill, or solid fencing. There is a potential Eight Roads of Destruction if there is a road or real water coming from/exiting the southeast direction; they are notorious for bringing extramarital/scandalous affairs, bankruptcy, and divorce. This house also has a potential Goat Blade Water formation if there is a road/driveway or real water coming from or exiting certain areas of the south direction. For this house, it would resemble a T-Juncture (south direction). You will know if you have this formation as it will indicate affairs, drug use, alcoholism, and gambling.

Activating the Interior Environment
Master Bedroom

There are two ways to enhance relationships, harmony, and prosperity in the bedroom—location and direction; the *direction* of the bed will give you the most powerful results. The north, south (second floor), northeast, and east have good mountain stars with auspicious chi and are excellent areas to locate the master bedroom. **Bed Directions:** For the most potent relationship-luck, place your headboard/bed to the north (1, 3, 4, or 9 Guas only), northeast (2, 6, 7, or 8 Guas only), or east direction (all Guas). The above bed directions have good mountain and facing star combinations that will enhance relationships. The northwest direction may also be used by all Guas, however be warned that that it is a strong Peach Blossom combination, especially for men who may find themselves literally hounded by women, and that it could produce undesirable results if your Feng Shui is not good.

If you choose your relationship direction (+70) coupled with one of the above recommendations, it will yield powerful results. For example, east has strong, good Peach Blossom energy; this is also the 4 Gua's +70. For 1 Guas, choose the north; this arrangement indicates recognition at work, a promotion, or meeting a partner through work or at the workplace as this is their relationship direction (+70) and the north has prosperity energy as well.

Take special caution regarding the west and southeast; do not use if at all possible. If the master bedroom is already located there, make sure that the bed direction is not also west or southeast. If so, reposition immediately; activating this direction indicates cancer, bankruptcy, divorce, and all types of mishaps and disasters. Additionally, use a soft neutral color palette— whites, creams, taupes, and metal colors such as silver and bronze. Avoid fire colors (reds, pinks, purples, or oranges) in the artwork, rugs, bedding, or wall color. These precautions will ensure harmony in the household.

Home Office

For the best relationship harmony, business opportunities, and romance- luck, face your desk/body to the north (1, 3, 4, or 9 Guas only), northeast (2, 6, 7, or 8 Guas only), or east, northwest, and southwest directions (all Guas). Remember the north is not a good direction for beds, desks, or doors for those in the West Life group. Choose one of these facing directions coupled with your +70 (relationship) direction if at all possible. Here are some examples: the 7 Guas can face northeast, as it has strong romance energy and it's their +70; the 4 Guas can face east, it has the "flower of romance" energy and it's their +70; the 2 Guas can face north- west, it has romance energy (4 facing star) and it's their +70 direction.

Kitchen/Stove/Firemouth + Toilets

The best directions for the stove knobs are north, east, or southwest. To activate romance, the stove knobs can also face northwest. You will strug- gle with relationships if there is a stove or toilet located in your +70 sector of the house. This also makes it difficult to conceive children. Review the chart to find your unique relationship direction. Select and use a toilet located in one of your negative sectors of the house (-90, -80, -70, or -60).

Best Doors in the House

For great relationships, opportunities, and prosperity, always use and activate good doors; the best ones for this chart are facing to the north, northeast, east, northwest, and southwest. If one of these directions is also your +70, you will be very lucky with relationships! A west-facing door in this chart is the worst of the worst; avoid it if at all possible. It has the evil 5 facing star and can attract all types of disasters. If this is your only door, you will need to cure it with lots of metal near or directly on the door itself. Brass, bronze, copper, pewter, and stainless steel are some high-vibrating metals to use.

PERIOD 8

South 2 (172.6° to 187.5°)

   Facing Names: **Wu** and the **Horse**

South 3 (187.6° to 202.5°)

   Facing Name: **Ting**

Chart: **Double Stars Meet at Facing**
   (Shuang Xing Dao Xiang)

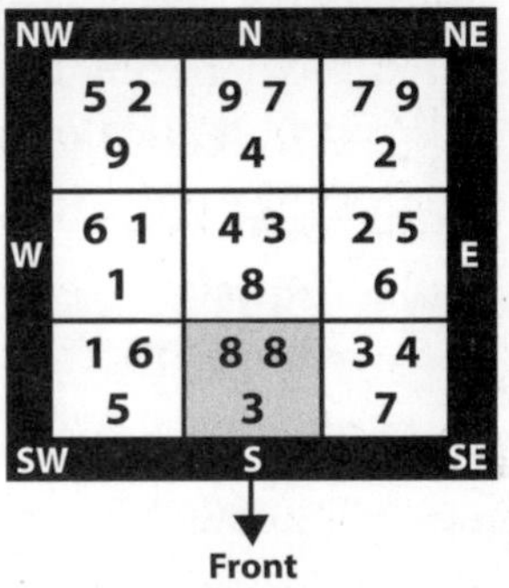

NW	N	NE
5 2 9	9 7 4	7 9 2
6 1 1	4 3 8	2 5 6
1 6 5	8 8 3	3 4 7
SW	S	SE

W (left) · E (right)

↓ **Front**

Figure 22: South 2 & 3

Romancing the Chart

This chart has three areas to enhance romance, relationships, and love-luck. They are southeast (4 facing star), southwest (1, 6 Peach Blossom combo), and west (6, 1 Peach Blossom combo). Very strong romance energy combines together in the southwest in 2014; in 2016, in the west; 2017, northeast; and in 2018, it will be in the south. These areas will be fully extracted by following the recommendations below. Wealth, prosperity, and relationship harmony are energies automatically invoked by placing water and a mountain in the south.

Activating the Exterior Environment
Needs Mountain and Water in Front

This house has the current prosperity energy of two 8s in the front and is known as **Double Stars Meet at Facing** and can bring great relationships and money. It is important to activate this chart by installing a mountain and water. The "mountain" can be higher ground, courtyard walls, landscape mounds, boulders (with no sharp or jagged edges), or any combination (the mountain should be three feet or higher). A water fountain, pond, or stream may be placed in the front. If you live in a home where you are not able to place an outdoor water feature, place one inside in the recommended area (consider a wall fountain).

For homes that face South 2, there is a possible Eight Killing Forces if there is a mountain located in the northwest direction; this formation will unsettle relationships in the house. These homes also may have a Peach Blossom Sha Road formation if there is real water or a road coming from the east. The Peach Blossom Sha Roads are famous for bringing sexual scandals, bad romance, illicit affairs, unrequited love, and extramarital liaisons.

For homes that face South 3, there is a possible Goat Blade Water formation if there is a road or water coming from or exiting the southeast. You will know if you have this formation as it will indicate affairs, drug use, alcoholism, and gambling. There is also a possible Eight Roads of Destruction if there is a road or water coming from/exiting the southwest direction. Eight Roads of Destruction are notorious for bringing extramarital/scandalous affairs, bankruptcy, and divorce.

Activating the Interior Environment
Master Bedrooms

There are two ways to enhance relationships, harmony, and prosperity in the bedroom—location and direction; the direction of the bed will give you the most powerful results. Locate your bedroom in the south (second floor), north, west, or southwest as these sectors have good mountain stars with auspicious energy. **Bed Directions:** For the most potent relationship-luck, and for homes that face South 2, place your head-board/bed to the south or southeast (1, 3, 4, or 9 Guas only) or the west or southwest (2, 6, 7, or 8 Guas only). If the home faces South 3, place your headboard/bed to the west, south, or southwest (all Guas)! Southeast is especially good for 3 Guas, as this is their unique relationship direction (+70) and the 4 facing star known for its romance energy. However, if you choose southeast, be warned that it is a strong Peach Blossom combination, especially for men who may find themselves hounded by women. It is still possible that this direction could produce undesirable results if your Feng Shui is not good. For a 1 Life Gua, south is their +70 and extremely prosperous energy. Activating this direction indicates a partner with wealth or meeting a partner through work or at the workplace.

Take special caution regarding the east and northwest; do not use if at all possible. If the master bedroom is already located there, make sure that the bed direction is not also east or northwest. If so, reposition immediately. Activating this direction indicates cancer, bankruptcy, divorce, death, and all types of mishaps and disasters. Place some decorative metal art objects in the room made of bronze, copper, or brass—nothing with sharp, jagged edges; round shapes are the best. Additionally, use a soft neutral color palette—whites, creams, taupes, and metal colors such as silver and bronze are good as well. Avoid fire colors (reds, pinks purples, or oranges) in the artwork, rugs, bedding, or wall color. These precautions will ensure harmony in the household.

Home Office

For the best relationship-luck and if the home faces South 2, face your desk/body to the south or southeast (1, 3, 4 or 9 Guas only) or the west, northeast, or southwest (2, 6, 7, or 8 Guas only). If the home faces South 3, place your desk/face to the northeast, west, south, southeast, or southwest (all Guas). Choose one of these facing directions coupled with your +70 (relationship) direction if possible. For example, if you are a 6 Gua, choose southwest, your +70 (relationship direction) and a strong Peach

Blossom combination. Likewise, if you are a 3 Gua, choose southeast, as this has the 4 romance star and is your +70 (relationship direction).

Kitchen/Stove/Firemouth + Toilets

The best directions for the stove knobs are south, west, or northeast. If the stove knobs face southeast, it will activate a romance star. You will struggle with relationships if there is a stove or toilet located in your +70 sector of the house, and divorce is a high risk. This also makes it difficult to conceive children. Select a toilet located in one of your negative sectors of the house (-90, -80, -70, or -60).

Best Doors in the House

For great relationships, opportunities and prosperity—always use and activate good doors; the best ones for this chart are facing to the south, southeast, west, northeast, and southwest. If one of these directions is also your +70, you will be very lucky with relationships. An east-facing door in this chart is the worst of the worst; avoid if at all possible. It has the evil 5 facing star and its energy can attract all types of disasters. If this is your only door—coming and going—you will need to cure it with lots of metal near or directly on the door itself. Brass, bronze, copper, pewter, and stainless steel are good metals to use.

PERIOD 8

Southwest 1 (202.6° to 217.5°)
  Facing Names: **Wei** and the **Goat**

Very Special Chart: **Combination of Ten** *(He Shih Chu)* and **Prosperous Sitting and Facing** *(Wang Shan Wang Shui)*

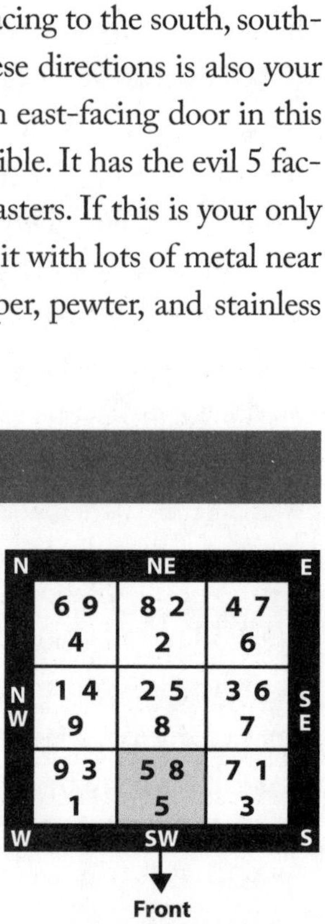

N		NE		E
	6 9	8 2	4 7	
	4	2	6	
N W	1 4	2 5	3 6	S E
	9	8	7	
	9 3	5 8	7 1	
	1	5	3	
W		SW		S

Front
Figure 23: Southwest 1

Romancing the Chart

This chart has two areas to enhance romance, sexual energy, relationships, and love-luck. They are the northwest (1, 4 Peach Blossom combo) and the south (7, 1 Peach Blossom combo). Very strong romance energy combines together in the northwest and east in 2015; in 2016, in the southeast; and in 2018, it in the south and northwest. These areas will be fully extracted by following the recommendations below. Wealth, prosperity, and relationship-harmony are energies automatically invoked by placing water in the southwest and a mountain in the northeast.

Activating the Exterior Environment
Needs Water in Front, Mountain in Back

This chart is one of the most auspicious charts of Period 8, with two special aspects known as a **Combination of Ten** and **Prosperous Sitting and Facing**. The property is extremely lucky for all types of relationships—love, romance, employees, and networking. The southwest-facing properties are also known for turning bad fortunes into lucrative opportunities via powerful connections.

A Combination of Ten chart is where either the mountain star or facing star adds to ten with the time star. The time star is the single number below the mountain star and facing star. When they add to ten with the mountain star, it is very auspicious for relationships, often called "lucky for people." This southwest-facing chart is one that will support and enhance relationships—personal, family, and business. Having a significant backing is the key to fully realizing the chart's potential.

Obviously, if you have a hill or mountain at the back of your house, this is extremely auspicious! If not, you can create a "mountain" at the back with a very high and solid fence, dense landscaping, high ground, and so forth. If you have water here, there will likely be serious illness in the house, and you'll have lost your opportunity to correctly extract the people/relationship-luck available with this chart. If you wish to install a pool in the backyard for privacy, locate it instead in the north corner; however be aware this will activate a Peach Blossom Sha situation if the water touches between 352° and 357°. This house is best served by *not* placing water anywhere at the back of the property. However, if you must have a pool at the back or there is a lake or some natural water feature, consult a professional so you can avoid the Peach Blossom Sha position which is only 15 degrees of north.

It is important that this home have a beautiful water feature such as a stream, koi pond, waterfall, or fountain at the front of the property, place it as center of your garden as possible however do not directly align or block the front door. If your home faces a natural lake, ocean, river, or pond—and you have substantial support at the back—then this chart is fully activated. These essential exterior forms will bring incredible opportunities and luck to the occupants. Remember, the emphasis should be kept to the back of the property, not the front. Make the back of your home as important, solid, and substantial as possible.

Also note that if you have a large water feature in the northwest sector of your garden, it could bring illicit affairs, love triangles, and scandals. However, if the house has excellent energy and sound Feng Shui, the water can bring luck in publishing, writing, and enhance a public persona. If you are unable to install an exterior water feature, then place one inside near the front door; wall fountains are very popular and are diverse in design, cost, and availability.

There is a possible Peach Blossom Sha Road if there is real water or a road in certain areas of the north direction/location. The Peach Blossom Sha Road formations are famous for bringing sexual scandals, bad romance, illicit affairs, unrequited love, and extramarital liaisons.

Activating the Interior Environment
Master Bedroom
There are two ways to enhance relationships, harmony, and prosperity in the bedroom—location and direction; the direction of the bed will give you

the most powerful results. To enhance relationship/romance-luck, locate your bedroom in the north, northwest, east, west, or northeast; these sectors have good mountain stars with auspicious energy. **Bed Directions:** For even more potent relationship-luck, place your headboard/bed to the north (1, 3, 4, or 9 Guas only), south, or northwest direction (all Guas). All the above bed directions have good mountain and facing star combinations, or star combos that have Peach Blossom energy that will enhance relationships. If you choose south (7, 1 combo) for your bed, your overall Feng Shui must be good; this combination is a Peach Blossom that can turn bad if not. Choose one of these facing directions coupled with your +70 (relationship) direction if possible. For example, if you are a 2 Gua, the northwest is your +70 and has a Peach Blossom combination that is very strong for sex and romance. If you are a 9 Gua, angle your bed to the north—it is your +70 and has a good star combination.

Home Office

For the best relationship harmony and luck, face north or southeast (1, 3, 4, or 9 Guas only), or south, northwest, or southwest direction (all Guas). Choose one of these facing directions coupled with your +70 (relationship) direction if possible. For example if you are a 1 Gua, face south—this has romance energy and it's your +70 (relationship) direction. If you are a 2 Gua, face northwest. This is your relationship direction (+70) and it has a strong Peach Blossom combo. If you are a 6 Gua, you could face southwest, as this is your +70 and the stars relate to wealth. This arrangement indicates recognition at work, a promotion, or meeting a partner through work or at the workplace.

Kitchen/Stove/Firemouth+ Toilets

To enhance nobility, wealth and relationships, the stove knobs (firemouth) should face south or southwest; northwest will enhance romance for all Guas. If the stove knobs face north, it may hurt the father/man of the house. You will struggle with relationships if there is a stove or toilet located in your +70 sector of the house. Select a toilet located in one of your negative sectors of the house (-90, -80, -70, or -60).

Best Doors in the House

For great relationships, opportunities, and prosperity—always use and activate good doors; the best ones for this chart are facing north, southeast, south, northwest, and southwest. If one of these directions is also your +70, you will be very lucky with relationships and romance!

PERIOD 8

Southwest 2 (217.6° to 232.5°)
  Facing Name: **Kun**

Southwest 3 (232.6° to 247.5°)
  Facing Names: **Shen** and the **Monkey**

Very Special Chart: **Parent String**
  (Fu Mo San Poon Gua)

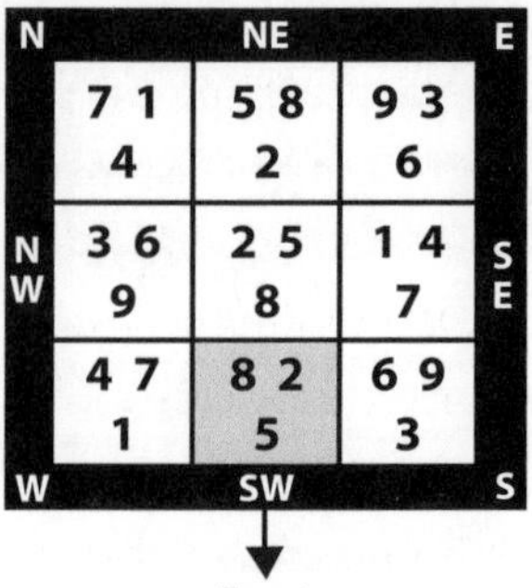

N		NE		E
	7 1 4	5 8 2	9 3 6	
NW	3 6 9	2 5 8	1 4 7	SE
	4 7 1	8 2 5	6 9 3	
W		SW		S

↓
Front
Figure 24: Southwest 2 & 3

Romancing the Chart

This chart has two areas to enhance romance, relationships, and love-luck. They are the the southeast (1, 4 Peach Blossom combo) and the north (7, 1 Peach Blossom combo). These areas become intensified when strong romance energy combines together in the north in 2015, the southeast and west in 2016, the northeast in 2017, and the south and northwest in 2018. Wealth, prosperity, and relationship harmony are energies automatically invoked by placing water in the northeast and a mountain in the southwest.

Activating the Exterior Environment
Needs Mountain in Front, Water in Back

Homes that face these directions (Southwest 2 and 3) have a special chart known as a **Parent String** formation said to bring triple good luck! When properly activated—a mountain in front, and water at the back—it brings a "string" of auspicious opportunities for money, relationships and health. The "mountain" can be higher ground, courtyard walls, landscape mounds, boulders (no sharp or jagged edges), or any combination (the mountain should be three feet or higher). Install a gorgeous water feature at the back of your house with a waterfall, large fountain, pond, or swimming pool. Keep it in the center of the garden. If you do not have a garden/yard, place two heavy stone statues on either side of the front door (interior or exterior), or a fountain at the back of your apartment, condo, or high-rise home (outdoors or interior). Metal on or near the front door is also recommended. Parent String homes are purported to turn bad fortunes into dazzling opportunities and attracting vast fortunes very quickly, creating powerful families!

Southwest 2 homes have a possible Eight Roads of Destruction if there is a road/water coming from/exiting certain areas of the south and west. Eight Roads of Destruction are notorious for bringing extramarital or scandalous affairs, bankruptcy, and divorce.

Southwest 3 facing properties may have an Eight Killings formation if there is a mountain coming from the east that will unsettle household relationships. This facing may also have a possible Peach Blossom Sha Road if there is real water or a road in the west location/direction. The Peach Blossom Sha Road formations are famous for bringing sexual scandals, bad romance, illicit affairs, unrequited love, and extramarital liaisons.

Activating the Interior Environment
Master Bedroom

There are two ways to enhance relationships, harmony, and prosperity in the bedroom—location and direction; the direction of the bed will give you the most powerful results. To enhance relationship/romance-luck, locate your bedroom in the south, southeast, southwest, west, or east sectors of the house, as these sectors have good mountain stars with auspicious energy. **Bed Directions**: For the most potent relationship-luck, and homes that face Southwest 2, place your headboard/bed to the northwest (2, 6, 7, or 8 Guas only and who are also lawyers or judges), or north, southeast, or south (1, 3, 4, or 9 Guas only) directions. If you choose north (7, 1 combo) for your bed, your overall Feng Shui must be good, as this combination is a Peach Blossom that can turn bad if not.

For homes that face Southwest 3, place the headboard/bed to the southeast or south (all Guas); these directions have good facing and mountain star combinations that will enhance relationships, prosperity, and harmony in the house. The northwest and north in this chart are acceptable but not excellent. Choose one of these directions coupled with your +70 (relationship) direction if possible. For example, if you are a 3 Gua, choose the southeast direction and place your bed on that wall; not only it is a very strong romance combination, this is your personal relationship direction (+70) as well! Likewise, if you are a 9 Gua, choose and angle your bed to the north, as this is your +70. It has potent sexual and romance energy.

Home Office

For the best relationship harmony in homes that face Southwest 2, face your desk/body to the northeast or northwest (2, 6, 7, or 8 Guas only), or north, southeast, or south (1, 3, 4, or 9 Guas only). For homes that face Southwest 3 face your desk/body to the northeast, northwest, southeast, or south (all Guas), and north (1, 3, 4, or 9 Guas only) as these directions have good facing stars with wealth and harmonious relationship energy. Choose one of these facing directions coupled with your +70 (relationship) direction if possible. For example if you are a 3 Gua, face to the southeast, as it's your +70 and has very strong romance energy which is also good for the writing and publishing business.

Kitchen/Stove/Firemouth + Toilets

The best directions for the stove knobs are northeast, south, or north as these sectors have good facing stars for wealth and harmony. To enhance romance or to attract a good partner, have the knobs face the southeast direction. You will struggle with relationships if there is a stove or toilet located in your +70 sector of the house. Select a toilet located in one of your negative sectors of the house (-90, -80, -70, or -60).

The Best Doors in the House

For great relationships, opportunities, and prosperity, always use and activate good doors; the best ones for this chart are facing the northeast, northwest, north, southeast, and south. Select one of these doors based on your Life Gua. If one of these directions is also your +70, you will be very lucky in relationships and romance!

PERIOD 8

West 1 (247.6° to 262.5°)
    Facing Name: **Geng**

Chart: **Double Stars Meet at Sitting**
    (Shuang Xing Dao Zuo)

Romancing the Chart

This chart has two areas to enhance romance, relationships, and love-luck. They are the north (1, 6 Peach Blossom combo) and the northeast (4 facing star). These areas become intensified when strong romance energy combines

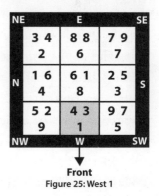

Figure 25: West 1

together in the west and southeast in 2016; in 2017 it is the northeast. These areas will be fully extracted by following the recommendations below. Wealth, prosperity, and relationship harmony are energies automatically invoked by placing water and a mountain in the east.

Activating the Exterior Environment
Needs Mountain and Water in Back

This facing has the prosperous 8s at the back of the property known as **Double Stars Meet at Sitting**. You will need to have substantial support at the back of your site. This may be accomplished with a solid wall or fence comprised of stucco, brick, or stone; even smartly designed, tiered landscaping or a series of stacked terraces would work brilliantly. While designing this important feature, incorporate a large water feature in proportion to the size of your home and garden in the back. If you live in an apartment, high-rise, townhome, condo, or rented space and are not able to install an outdoor water feature, place one inside at the back of your space. Large, heavy bookcases or armoires can also represent your mountain; they should be placed on the back wall as well. West-facing properties produce well-educated, intelligent, polite, and charming people who can become very wealthy in good business management or by getting involved in politics.

The house does have a possible Eight Roads of Destruction formation if there is a road/driveway coming from or exiting the southwest. This formation can destroy good business relationships, devastate people's lives, and kill wealth and harmony! This house also has a potential Goat Blade Water formation if there is a road/driveway or real water coming from or exiting certain areas of the west. You will know if you have this formation as it will indicate affairs, drug use, alcoholism, and gambling.

Activating the Interior Environment
Master Bedroom

There are two ways to enhance relationships, harmony, and prosperity in the bedroom—location and direction; the direction of the bed will give you the most powerful results. To enhance relationship/romance-luck, locate your bedroom in the north, east, west, or southwest as these sectors have good mountain stars with auspicious energy. **Bed Directions:** For the most potent relationship-luck, place your headboard/bed to the north (1, 3, 4, or 9 Guas only), northeast (2, 6, 7, or 8 Guas) or northeast (between 52° to 67°) for those part of the East Life Group (1, 3, 4, or 9 Guas); the northeast direction has strong Peach Blossom energy particularly for males, and indicates being swarmed by female attention. However, take care to use the above 15-degree increment if you are East Life group to ensure a good result. Those part of the West Life group are automatically support by this direction. East is also excellent for all Guas to use. Choose one of the above recommended facing directions coupled with your +70 (relationship) direction if possible. For example, if you are 4 Gua, the East is exceptional—it's your +70 and has wealth energy. This arrangement indicates recognition at work, a promotion, or meeting a partner through work or at the workplace.

Take special caution regarding the south and northwest—do not use either if at all possible. If the master bedroom is already located there, make sure that the bed direction is not also south or northwest. If so, reposition immediately; activating this direction indicates cancer, bankruptcy, divorce, death, and all types of mishaps and disasters. Additionally, use a soft neutral color palette—whites, creams, taupes, and metal colors such as silver or bronze are good as well. Avoid fire colors (reds, purples, pinks, or oranges) in the artwork, rugs, bedding, or wall color. These precautions will ensure harmony in the household.

Home Office
To enhance relationship-luck, face your desk/body to the north or southeast (1, 3, 4, or 9 Guas only), northeast (2, 6, 7, and 8 Guas only) or east (all Guas); these directions have good facing stars with very auspicious energy that will enhance prosperity, relationship harmony, or romance. Choose one of these facing directions coupled with your +70 (relationship) direction if possible. For example, if you are a 9 Gua, choose north,

as it has good Peach Blossom energy and it's your +70. Or if you are a 7 Gua, choose to face northeast—it has romance energy and it's your +70.

Kitchen/Stove/Firemouth + Toilets

To activate romance, harmony, and prosperity the stove knobs can face to the east or southeast directions as these sectors have good facing stars. You will struggle with relationships if there is a stove or toilet located in your +70 sector of the house. Select a toilet located in one of your negative sectors of the house (-90, -80, -70, or -60).

Best Doors in the House

For great relationships, opportunities, and prosperity—always use and activate good doors; the best ones for this chart are facing to the north, northeast, east, and southeast. Select one of these doors based on your Life Gua. If one of these directions is also your +70, you will be very lucky with relationships and romance. A south-facing door in this chart is the worst of the worst; avoid if at all possible. It has the evil 5 facing star and its energy can attract all types of disasters. If this is your only door—coming and going—you will need to cure it with lots of metal near or directly on the door itself. Brass, bronze, copper, pewter, and stainless steel are some high-vibrating metals to use.

PERIOD 8

West 2 (262.6° to 277.5°)
   Facing Names: **You** and the **Rooster**

West 3 (277.6° to 292.5°)
   Facing Name: **Xin**

Chart: **Double Stars Meet at Facing**
   (Shuang Xing Dao Xiang)

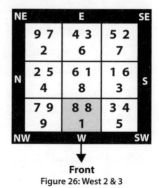

Front
Figure 26: West 2 & 3

Romancing the Chart

This chart has two areas to enhance romance, sexual energy, relationships, and love-luck. They are the south (1, 6 Peach Blossom combo) and southwest (4 facing star). These areas become intensified when strong romance energy combines together in the southwest in 2014, northwest in 2015, west in 2016, and the south in 2017. Wealth, prosperity, and relationship harmony are energies automatically invoked by placing water and a mountain in the west.

Activating the Exterior Environment
Needs Mountain and Water in Front

This chart has the prosperous 8s at the front of the site known as the **Double Stars Meet at Facing.** In order to fully extract the relationship and prosperity potential, you will need to have both a mountain and water in the front garden. The "mountain" can be higher ground, courtyard walls, landscape mounds, boulders (no sharp or jagged edges), or any combination (the mountain should be three feet or higher.) Install a beautiful water feature such as a fountain, stream, or koi pond in the front as well. If you are unable to install these features exterior of your home, place a fountain inside near the door. A tall, heavy piece of furniture in the west could serve as a good mountain. If there is a large body of water—natural or manmade—in the north, this could indicate divorce, money-loss, widowhood, abortions, and grave misfortune. With correct activation, west-facing homes produce dynamic individuals who will be successful and able to accumulate great wealth rather quickly. It also supports outstanding academic achievements and super athletes.

The West 2 homes also have a possible Eight Killing Forces if there is mountain chi coming from the southeast. If there is real water or a road in the south location/direction there could be the ill-fated Peach Blossom Sha Road formation to the West 2 facing properties. The Peach Blossom Sha Road formations are famous for bringing sexual scandals, bad romance, illicit affairs, unrequited love, and extramarital liaisons.

The West 3 facing homes have a possible Eight Roads of Destruction formation if there is a road/driveway coming from or exiting the northwest direction. This formation can destroy good business relationships, devastate people's lives, and harm your finances. This house also has a potential Goat Blade Water formation if there is a road/driveway or real water coming from or exiting certain areas of the southwest direction. You will know if you have this formation as it will indicate affairs, drug use, alcoholism, and gambling.

Activating the Interior Environment
Master Bedroom

There are two ways to enhance relationships, harmony, and prosperity in the bedroom—location and direction. The direction of the bed will give you the most powerful results. To enhance relationship/romance- luck, locate your bedroom in the west (second floor), south, east, or northeast, these sectors have good mountain stars. **Bed Directions:** For the most potent relationship-luck, and for homes that face West 2, place your headboard/bed to the west or southwest (2, 6, 7, or 8 Guas only), or south (1, 3, 4, or 9 Guas only) directions. For homes that face West 3, place your headboard/bed to the south, southwest, or west (all Guas); these directions have good facing and mountain star combinations that will enhance relationships, prosperity, and harmony in the house. If you choose the east direction, be warned that it is a strong Peach Blossom combination, especially for men who may find themselves literally hounded by women, and that it could produce undesirable results if your Feng Shui is not good.

Choose one of these facing directions coupled with your +70 (relationship) direction if possible. For example, if you are an 8 Gua, place your bed/headboard on the west wall; this is your +70 and prosperity energy. This arrangement indicates recognition at work, a promotion, or meeting a partner through work or at the workplace. If you are a 1 Gua, place your bed/headboard on the south wall; this is your +70 and it has good Peach Blossom energy.

Take special caution regarding the north and southwest; do not use these directions if at all possible. If the master bedroom is already located there, make sure that the bed direction is not also north or southeast. If so, reposition immediately; activating this direction indicates cancer, bankruptcy, divorce, death, and all types of mishaps and disasters. Additionally, use a soft neutral color palette—whites, creams, taupes, and metal colors such as silver and bronze are good as well. No fire colors (reds, pinks, purples, or oranges) in the artwork, rugs, bedding, or wall color. These precautions will ensure harmony in the household.

Home Office
For the best relationship harmony in homes that are West 2, face your desk/body to the west, southwest, northwest, (2, 6, 7, or 8 Guas only), or south (1, 3, 4, or 9 Guas only) directions. For homes that face West 3, place your desk/face to the south, southwest, west, or northwest (all Guas) as these directions have good facing stars with auspicious energy. Choose one of these facing directions coupled with your +70 (relationship) direction if possible. For example, if you are a 6 Gua, face southwest; this is your +70 and has romance, writing, and publishing energy.

Kitchen/Stove/Firemouth + Toilets
To enhance relationships, prosperity, and harmony, the best directions for the stove knobs are west, southwest, or northwest. You will struggle with relationships if there is a stove or toilet located in your +70 sector of the house. Select a toilet located in one of your negative sectors of the house (-90, -80, -70, or -60).

Best Doors in the House
For great relationships, opportunities, and prosperity—always use and activate good doors; the best ones for this chart are facing to the west, southwest, northwest, and south. If one of these directions is also your +70, you will be very lucky with relationships and romance! A north-facing

door in this chart is the worst of the worst; avoid if at all possible. It has the evil 5 facing star and its energy can attract all types of disasters. If this is your only door—coming and going—you will need to cure it with lots of metal near or directly on the door itself. Brass, bronze, copper, pewter, and stainless steel are some high-vibrating metals to use.

PERIOD 8

Northwest 1 (292.6° to 307.5°)

Facing Name: **Xu** and the **Dog**

Very Special Chart: **Pearl String**
(Lin Cu San Poon Gua)

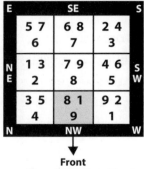

Figure 27: Northwest 1

Romancing the Chart

This chart has two areas to enhance romance, sexual energy, relationships, and love-luck. They are the south (4 facing star) and the southwest (4 mountain star). These areas become intensified when strong romance energy combines together in the northwest in 2015, northeast in 2017, and south in 2018. Wealth, prosperity, and relationship harmony are energies automatically invoked by placing water in the southeast and a mountain in the northwest.

Activating the Exterior Environment
Needs Mountain in Front, Water in Back

Northwest 1 is a very auspicious formation called a **Pearl String**; many Masters refer to it as the Continuous Bead Formation. Either way, it is activated by a mountain in front, and water at the back. The "mountain" can be higher ground, courtyard walls, landscape mounds, boulders (no sharp or jagged edges) or any combination (the mountain should be three feet or higher). Keep these features as center of the garden as possible, but do not block the front door. Place water at the back by installing a pool, waterfall/pond, koi pond, fountain, or jacuzzi. If you are unable to activate this chart on the exterior, place water on the back wall (wall fountain or large fish tank) and add two heavy objects on either side of the front door (interior or exterior). It is said that when activated properly, this chart can bring the occupants triple good luck/opportunities.

There is a Peach Blossom Sha Road if there is real water or a road in the east location/direction. The Peach Blossom Sha Road formations are famous for bringing sexual scandals, bad romance, illicit affairs, unrequited love, and extramarital liaisons.

Activating the Interior Environment
Master Bedroom
There are two ways to enhance relationships, harmony, and prosperity in the bedroom—location and direction; the direction of the bed will give you the most powerful results. To enhance relationship/romance-luck, locate your bedroom in the southeast, west, northeast, southwest, or northwest (second floor) as these rooms have good mountain stars with auspicious energy. **Bed Directions**: For even more potent relationship-luck, place your headboard/bed to the northwest or southwest (all Guas), or southeast (1, 3, 4, or 9 Guas only). Choose one of these facing directions coupled with your +70 (relationship) direction if possible. For example if you are a 3 Gua, choose the southeast direction, as it has great energy and it's your relationship direction (+70). For 2 Guas, choose northwest, it has superior energy and it's your +70.

Home Office
For relationship-luck, prosperity, and harmony place your desk/face to the northwest, south, and southwest (all Guas), or southeast (1, 3, 4, or 9 Guas only). Choose one of these facing directions coupled with your +70 (relationship) direction if possible. For example, if you are a 2 Gua, choose the northwest—it is your relationship direction (+70). This arrangement indicates recognition at work, a promotion, or meeting a partner through work or at the workplace.

Kitchen/Stove/Firemouth + Toilets

The best directions for the stove knobs are northwest, south, or southeast. If the knobs face south, this will stimulate the romance star and help attract a partner. You will struggle with relationships if there is a stove or toilet located in your +70 sector of the house. Select a toilet located in one of your negative sectors of the house (-90, -80, -70, or -60).

Best Doors in the House

For great relationships, opportunities, and prosperity—always use and activate good doors; the best ones for this chart are facing to the northwest, south, southwest, and southeast. If one of these directions is also your +70, you will be very lucky with money and relationships! A north-facing door, in this chart, is the worst of the worst; avoid if at all possible. It has the evil 5 facing star, whose energy attracts all types of disasters. If this is your only door—coming and going—you will need to cure it with lots of metal to or directly on the door itself. Brass, bronze, copper, pewter, and stainless steel are some high-vibrating metals to use.

PERIOD 8

Northwest 2 (307.6° to 322.5°)
   Facing Name: **Chien**

Northwest 3 (322.6° to 337.5°)
   Facing Names: **Hai** and the **Pig**

Special Chart: **Prosperous Sitting and Facing** *(Wang Shan Wang Shui)*

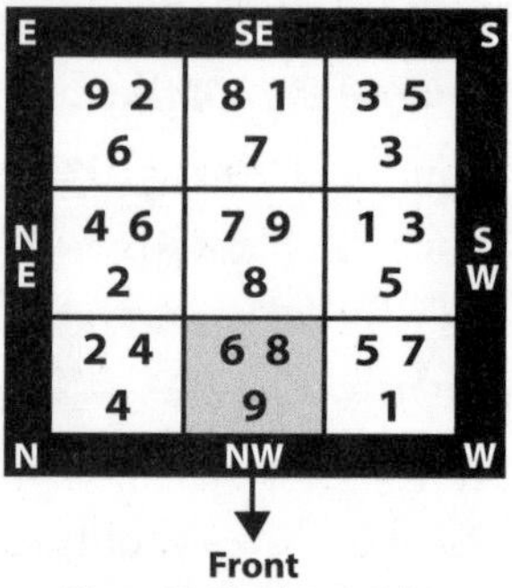

E	SE	S
9 2 **6**	8 1 **7**	3 5 **3**
4 6 **2**	7 9 **8**	1 3 **5**
2 4 **4**	6 8 **9**	5 7 **1**

(N / NE on left, S / SW / W on right, N / NW / W on bottom)

↓
Front
Figure 28: Northwest 2 & 3

Romancing the Chart

This chart has two areas to enhance romance, sexual energy, relationships, and love-luck. They are the north (4 facing star) and the northeast (4 mountain star). Other areas become intensified when strong romance energy combines together in the northwest in 2015, west in 2016, and northeast in 2017. Wealth, prosperity, and relationship harmony are energies automatically invoked by placing water in the northwest and a mountain in the southeast.

Activating the Exterior Environment
Needs Water in Front, Mountain in Back

This chart is extremely advantageous and is known as **Prosperous Sitting and Facing**; it is also affectionately called "lucky for people, lucky for money." To fully extract the wonderful energy potential of this chart, place a water feature in the front and make sure there is significant, solid backing emulating the energy of a mountain at the back of the property. A tall, solid fence comprised of brick, wood, stucco, stone, or any combination thereof is excellent. Beautiful retaining walls or tiered landscaping also activate the back perfectly. If there is a natural mountain, hill, or mound, you are indeed blessed. In the event that you live in an apartment, high-rise, townhome, condo or a rented space and are not able to place an outdoor water feature, install one inside near the front door. Place tall, heavy bookcases or an armoire on the back wall (southeast). If you have a back patio, then place heavy stone planters or statues there to represent your "mountain."

For homes that face Northwest 2, there is a possible Eight Roads of Destruction if you have a road coming from/exiting from either the west or north; they are notorious for bringing extramarital/scandalous affairs, bankruptcy, and divorce. Northwest 3 facing homes could have an Eight Killing Forces if mountain energy comes from the south; this formation will unsettle relationships in the house and attract blood-related accidents. The Northwest 3 homes can also have a Peach Blossom Sha Road formation if there is real water or a road in the north location/direction; these formations can bring sexual scandals, bad romance, illicit affairs, unrequited love, and extramarital liaisons.

Activating the Interior Environment
Master Bedroom

There are two ways to enhance relationships, harmony, and prosperity in the bedroom—location and direction; the direction of the bed will give you the most powerful results. To enhance relationship/romance-luck, locate your bedroom in the east, southeast, southwest, northeast, or northwest (second floor) as these rooms all have good mountain stars with auspicious energy. **Bed Directions**: For even more potent relationship-luck, and for homes that face Northwest 2, place your headboard/bed to the northwest and northeast (2, 6, 7, or 8 Guas only), or southeast (1, 3, 4, or 9 Guas only). For homes that face Northwest 3, place your headboard/bed to the northwest, southeast, or northeast (all Guas); these directions have good facing and mountain star combinations that will enhance relationships, prosperity, and harmony in the house.

Home Office

For the best relationship luck, harmony, and prosperity, and for homes that face Northwest 2, place your desk/face northwest and northeast (2, 6, 7, or 8 Guas only), or southeast and north (1, 3, 4, or 9 Guas only). For homes that face Northwest 3, place your desk/face northwest, southeast, or northeast (all Guas only) or north (1, 3, 4 or 9 Guas only). Choose one of these facing directions coupled with your +70 (relationship) direction if possible. For example if you are a 3 Gua, face the southeast as this is your relationship direction. Also, this arrangement indicates recognition at work, a promotion, or meeting a partner through work or at the workplace.

Kitchen/Stove/Firemouth + Toilets

For household harmony and prosperity, the best directions for the stove knobs are the northwest, north, or southeast as these are good facing stars that are activated by fire. Relationships will be difficult if your stove or toilet is located in your +70 (relationship) sector of the house. If you have either of these scenarios, relocate the stove and use another toilet. Choose a toilet in your negative sectors of the house (-90, -80, -70, or -60).

Best Doors in the House

For great relationships, opportunities, and prosperity—always use and activate good doors; the best ones for this chart are facing northwest, northeast, southeast, and north. If one of these directions is also your +70, you will be very lucky in relationships and romance! In this chart, a south-facing door is the worst of the worst; avoid if at all possible. It has the evil 5 facing star and it's quite powerful in the south. If this is your only door—coming and going—you will need to cure it with lots of metal near or directly on the door itself. Brass, bronze, copper, pewter, and stainless steel are some high-vibrating metals to use.

PERIOD 8

North 1 (337.6° to 352.5°)
  Facing Name: **Ren**

Chart: **Double Stars Meet at Facing**
  (Shuang Xing Dao Xiang)

Romancing the Chart

This chart has two areas to enhance romance, sexual energy, relationships, and love-luck. They are the east (1, 6 Peach Blossom combo) and the northeast (6, 1 Peach Blossom combo).

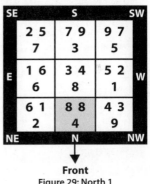

SE	S	SW
2 5 7	7 9 3	9 7 5
1 6 6	3 4 8	5 2 1
6 1 2	8 8 4	4 3 9
NE	N	NW

E (left side) · W (right side)

↓
Front
Figure 29: North 1

These areas become intensified when strong romance energy combines together in the northwest and east in 2015, northeast in 2017, and south in 2018. Wealth, prosperity, and relationship harmony are energies automatically invoked by placing water and a mountain in the north.

Activating the Exterior Environment
Needs Water and Mountain in Front

With the two prosperous 8s in the front of the property, known as **Double Stars Meet at Facing,** place a mountain and water in the front garden to fully extract the auspicious energy. You can kill two birds with one stone if you install a tall, heavy stone fountain near (but not blocking) the front door.

The "mountain" can be higher ground, courtyard walls, landscape mounds, boulders (no sharp or jagged edges), or any combination (the mountain should be three feet or higher). The water feature may be a stream, koi pond, waterfall (flowing toward the house, not away from it), or fountain. If you are unable to place these features exterior to your site, install a water fountain near the front door inside. Place two heavy statues or stone planters on either side of the front door (inside or out). North-facing properties indicate success, charismatic people, and excellent relationship and wealth luck. North is one of the best facings for all those in the East Life group (1, 3, 4, or 9 Guas), and you will benefit greatly by living in one.

There is a possible Eight Roads of Destruction with this facing if there is a road coming from/exiting the northwest; they are notorious for bringing extramarital/scandalous affairs, bankruptcy, and divorce. This house also has a potential Goat Blade Water formation if there is a road/driveway or real water coming from or exiting certain areas of the northwest direction. You will know if you have this formation as it will indicate affairs, drug use, alcoholism, and gambling.

Activating the Interior Environment
Master Bedroom

There are two ways to enhance relationships, harmony, and prosperity in the bedroom—location and direction; the direction of the bed will give you the most powerful results. To enhance relationship/romance-luck, locate the master bedroom in the east, southwest, north (second floor), or northeast sectors of the house as they are good mountain stars with auspicious energy. **Bed Directions:** For even more potent relationship-luck, place your headboard/bed to the north (1, 3, 4, or 9 Guas only), east (all Guas), or northeast (2, 6, 7, or 8 Guas only). Choose one of these facing directions coupled with your +70 (relationship) direction if possible. For example, if you are a 4 Gua, choose east; it's your +70 and it has good Peach Blossom energy. For 7 Guas, choose the northeast, as it has excellent romance energy and it's your relationship direction (+70).

Take special caution regarding the west and southeast; do not use if at all possible. If the master bedroom is already located there, make sure that the bed direction is not also west or southeast. If so, reposition immediately; activating this direction indicates cancer, bankruptcy, divorce, death, and all types of mishaps and disasters. Additionally, use a soft neutral color palette—whites, creams, taupes, and metal colors such as silver or bronze are good as well. No fire colors (reds, purples, pinks, or oranges) in the artwork, rugs, bedding, or wall color. These precautions will ensure harmony in the household.

Home Office

To enhance prosperity, relationships, and romance, place your desk/face to the north (1, 3, 4, or 9 Guas only), east (all Guas), northeast (2, 6, 7, or 8 Guas only), or south (all Guas except 6 and 7). Choose one of these facing directions coupled with your +70 (relationship) direction if possible. For example, if you are a 7 Gua, face to the northeast—it has good romance energy and it's your +70. If you are a 9 Gua, face to the north; this arrangement indicates recognition at work, a promotion, or meeting a partner through work or at the workplace.

Kitchen/Stove/Firemouth + Toilets

The best directions for the stove knobs are north, northeast, and south as these directions have facing stars that support prosperity and harmony and are activated by the fire. You will struggle with relationships if there is a stove or toilet located in your +70 sector of the house. Select a toilet located in one of your negative sectors of the house (-90, -80, -70, or -60).

Best Doors in the House

For great relationships, opportunities, and prosperity—always use and activate good doors; the best ones for this chart are facing the north, east, northeast, and south. If one of these directions is also your +70, you will be very lucky in relationships and romance! A southeast-facing door is the worst of the worst in this chart; avoid if at all possible. It has the evil 5 facing star and its energy attracts all types of disasters. If this is your only door—coming and going—you will need to cure it with lots of metal near or directly on the door itself. Brass, bronze, copper, pewter, and stainless steel are some high-vibrating metals to use.

PERIOD 8

North 2 (352.6° to 7.5°)

Facing Names: **Tzi** and the **Rat**

North 3 (7.6° to 22.5)

Facing Name: **Kwei**

Chart: **Double Stars Meet at Sitting** *(Shuang Xing Dao Zuo)*

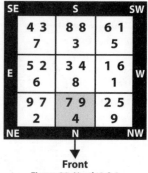

Front

Figure 30: North 2 & 3

Romancing the Chart

This chart has two areas to enhance romance, sexual energy, relationships, and love-luck.

They are the west (1, 6 Peach Blossom combo) and the southwest (6, 1 Peach Blossom combo). These areas become intensified when strong romance energy combines together in the west in 2016, northeast in 2017, and south in 2018. Wealth, prosperity, and relationship harmony are energies automatically invoked by placing water and a mountain in the south.

Activating the Exterior Environment
Needs Mountain and Water in Back

This chart has the two 8s at the back known as **Double Stars Meet at Sitting;** two important features are needed to fully realize the powerful, positive energy of this chart—a mountain and water. Install a pool with a rock waterfall and both elements will be fully represented at the rear of the site. Make sure the house has substantial backing with high ground, or terraced landscaping against a solid fence or wall. Keep the water as central as possible. If there is a natural hill or mountain already at the back, this is extremely auspicious.

If you are unable to activate this chart on the exterior level, install a water fountain near the back door. Place two stone planters or statues outside if you have a balcony or patio. If not, place them near the back door inside your living space. The north-facing charts can bring the occupants success in business and business relationships that will take them all over the world.

North 2 properties also could have a Peach Blossom Sha Road if there is real water or a road in the west location or direction. The Peach Blossom Sha Road formations are famous for bringing sexual scandals, bad romance, illicit affairs, unrequited love, and extramarital liaisons.

For homes that face North 3, there is a possible Eight Roads of Destruction if you have a road/driveway coming from or exiting the northeast direction. This formation is notorious for bringing extramarital/scandalous affairs, bankruptcy, and divorce. This house also has a potential Goat Blade Water formation if there is a road/driveway or real water coming from or exiting certain areas of the north direction. You will know if you have this formation as it will indicate affairs, drug use, alcoholism, and gambling.

Activating the Interior Environment
Master Bedroom

There are two ways to enhance relationships, harmony, and prosperity in the bedroom—location and direction. The direction of the bed will give you the most powerful results. To enhance relationship/romance-luck, locate your bedroom in the south, southwest, southeast, west, or northeast as all of these areas have good mountain stars with auspicious energy. **Bed Directions**: For even more potent relationship-luck, and for homes that face North 2, place your headboard/bed to the south (1, 3, 4, or 9 Guas only), or southwest or west (2, 6, 7, or 8 Guas only). If the home faces to North 3, place your headboard/bed to the south, west, or southwest (all Guas). Choose one of the above directions that is also your +70 direction to get the best results in enhancing relationships. For example, the 8 Guas should choose the west—it has great romance energy and it's their +70.

Take special caution regarding the northwest and east; do not use if at all possible. If the master bedroom is already located there, make sure that the bed direction is not also northwest or east. If so, reposition immediately; activating this direction indicates cancer, bankruptcy, divorce, death, and all types of mishaps and disasters. Additionally, use a soft neutral color palette—whites, creams, taupes, and metal colors such as silver or bronze are good as well. Avoid fire colors (reds, purples, pinks, or oranges) in the artwork, rugs, bedding, or wall color. These precautions will ensure harmony in the household.

Home Office

To enhance harmony, prosperity, and romance for North 2 properties, place your desk/face to the south, southeast, or north (1, 3, 4, or 9 Guas only), or southwest or west (2, 6, 7, or 8 Guas only). If the home faces North 3, place your desk/face to the south, west, or southwest (all Guas), and north (1, 3, 4, or 9 Guas only). Choose one of the above directions that is your +70 direction. For example, if you are a 6 Gua, face southwest, as it has good romance energy and it's your +70. If you are a 1 Gua, face south while sitting at your desk; this arrangement indicates recognition at work, a promotion, or meeting a partner through work or at the workplace.

Kitchen/Stove/Firemouth + Toilets

To increase household harmony, the best directions to activate with the stove knob direction are the south, north, or southwest. You will "burn up" and harm your relationships if there is a stove or toilet located in your +70 sector of the house. Select a toilet located in one of your negative sectors of the house (-90, -80, -70, or -60).

Best Doors in the House

For great relationships, opportunities and prosperity—always use and activate good doors; the best ones for this chart are facing to the south, north, southwest, and west. If one of these directions is also your +70, you will be very lucky in relationships and romance! In this chart, a northwest-facing door is the worst of the worst; avoid if at all possible. It has the evil 5 facing star and its energy attracts all types of disasters. If this is your only door coming and going, you will need to cure it with lots of metal next to or directly on the door itself. Brass, bronze, copper, pewter, and stainless steel are some high-vibrating metals to use.

PERIOD 8

Northeast 1 (22.6° to 37.5°)

Facing Names: **Chou** and the **Ox**

Very Special Chart: **Combination of Ten** *(He Shih Chu)* and **Prosperous Sitting and Facing** *(Wang Shan Wang Shui)*

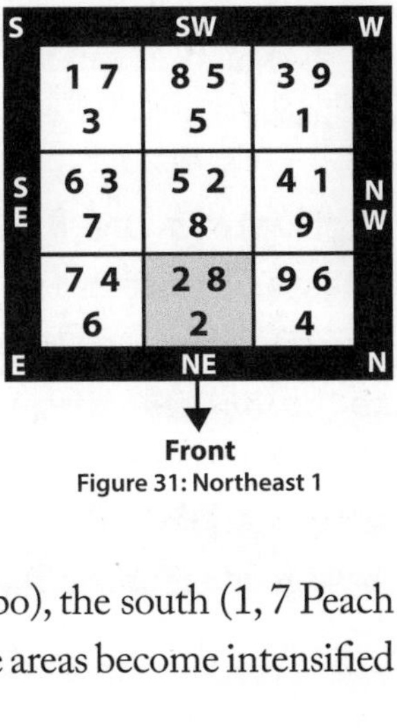

S	SW		W
1 7 **3**	8 5 **5**	3 9 **1**	
6 3 **7**	5 2 **8**	4 1 **9**	
7 4 **6**	2 8 **2**	9 6 **4**	
E	NE		N

Front

Figure 31: Northeast 1

Romancing the Chart

This chart has three areas to enhance romance, sexual energy, relationships, and love-luck.

They are the northwest (4, 1 Peach Blossom combo), the south (1, 7 Peach Blossom combo), and the east (4 facing star). These areas become intensified when strong romance energy combines together in the northwest and east in 2015, the west in 2016, the northeast in 2017, and the south in 2018. Wealth, prosperity, and relationship harmony are energies automatically invoked by placing water in the northeast and a mountain in the southwest.

Activating the Exterior Environment
Needs Water in Front, Mountain in Back

This is one of the most auspicious charts of Period 8 boasting two very special aspects; it's a **Combination of Ten** *and* **Prosperous Sitting and Facing**. The Northeast 1 chart is therefore extremely lucky for both people and money! To fully activate the enormous potential of this chart, you will need substantial backing such as a solid fence comprised of stucco, brick, rock, or wood—or any combination of these elements. Installing tiered or terraced garden beds in front of the solid fence will magnify the effect. Place a beautiful water feature such as a stream, koi pond, water fountain, or waterfall in the front that flows toward the home.

If you are unable to place these features exterior of your home, then install a water fountain near the front door inside. Place two heavy stone planters or statues near the back door or on the balcony or patio if you have one. If there is real water or a road in the south location or direction, there is a possible Peach Blossom Sha Road, which is famous for bringing sexual scandals, bad romance, illicit affairs, unrequited love, and extramarital liaisons.

Activating the Interior Environment
Master Bedroom

There are two ways to enhance relationships, harmony, and prosperity in the bedroom—location and direction; the direction of the bed will give you the most powerful results. To enhance relationship/romance-luck, locate your bedroom in the south, southwest, north, or southeast, as these areas all have good mountain stars with auspicious energy. **Bed Directions:** For even more potent relationship-luck, place your headboard/bed to the northwest (all Guas), or north (1, 3, 4, or 9 Guas only) directions. Choose one of the above directions that is also your +70 and you will get the best result in enhancing relationships. The northwest has good Peach Blossom energy—especially for women—and all Guas may use it, however it is particularly potent for 2 Guas as it is their +70 direction. The south also has strong Peach Blossom energy and can be used; however the overall Feng Shui of your home must be good, otherwise it can turn bad and bring affairs and sweet-talking con men your way.

Home Office

To enhance romance, harmony, and prosperity, while sitting at your desk, face northeast (2, 6, 7, or 8 Guas only), northwest, east, and west (all Guas), or north (1, 3, 4, or 9 Guas only) directions. Choose one of these facing directions coupled with your +70; for example if you are a 2 Gua, face the northwest as it has strong romance/writing energy and it's your relationship direction (+70). If you are a 7 Gua, face northeast—this arrangement indicates recognition at work, a promotion, or meeting a partner through work or at the workplace.

Kitchen/Stove/Firemouth + Toilets

To enhance household harmony, prosperity, and romance the stove knobs should face northeast, east, northwest, or west. You will have difficulty with relationships if there is a stove or toilet located in your +70 sector of the house. Select a toilet located in one of your negative sectors of the house (-90, -80, -70, or -60).

Best Doors in the House

For great relationships, opportunities, and prosperity, always use and activate good doors; the best ones for this chart are facing northeast, northwest, west, north, and east. If one of these directions is also your +70, you will be very lucky in relationships! A southwest-facing door, in this chart, is the worst of the worst; avoid if at all possible. It has the evil 5 facing star and it's quite powerful in the southwest. If this is your only door coming and going, you will need to cure it with lots of metal next to or directly on the door itself. Brass, bronze, copper, pewter, and stainless steel are some high-vibrating metals to use.

PERIOD 8

Northeast 2 (37.6° to 52.5°)
    Facing Name: **Gen**

Northeast 3 (52.6° to 67.5°)
    Facing Names: **Yin** and the **Tiger**

Very Special Chart: **Parent String**
    (Fu Mu San Poon Gua)

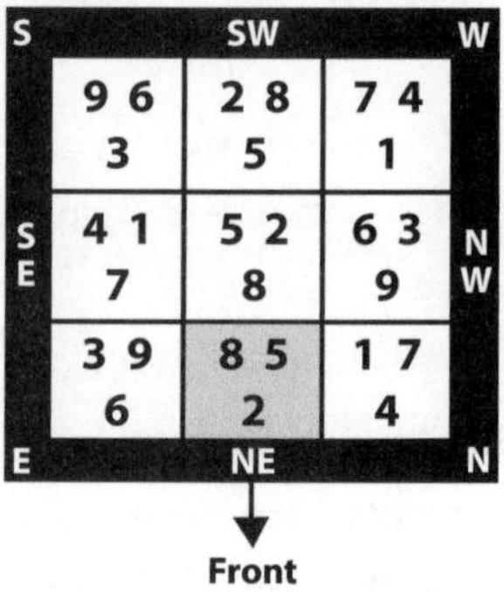

S	SW	W
9 6	2 8	7 4
3	5	1
4 1	5 2	6 3
7	8	9
3 9	8 5	1 7
6	2	4
E	NE	N

SE (left side), NW (right side)

↓
Front
Figure 32: Northeast 2 & 3

Romancing the Chart

This chart has three areas to enhance romance, sexual energy, relationships, and love-luck.

They are the southeast (4, 1 Peach Blossom combo), the north (1, 7 Peach Blossom combo), and the west (4 facing star). These areas become intensified when strong romance energy visits the west and southeast in 2016, and the south in 2018. Wealth, prosperity, and relationship harmony are energies automatically invoked by placing water in the southwest and a mountain in the northeast.

Activating the Exterior Environment
Needs Mountain in Front, Water in Back

This chart is one of the special charts called a **Parent String**; they are purported to transcend all time periods and can bring triple good luck! However, they must activated in a very specific way—a mountain in the front and water at the back. The "mountain" can be higher ground, courtyard walls, landscape mounds, boulders (no sharp or jagged edges) or any combination (the mountain should be three feet or higher). Keep the mountain as centered in the garden as possible without blocking the front door or place the mountain on the right-hand side (as you are looking out the front door). Install a beautiful water feature such as a pool, waterfall, koi pond, or small fountain in the center of the back garden.

If you are unable to install mountain and water features to your home's exterior, place a water fountain inside near the back door or on the balcony or patio if you have one. Near the front door, install two heavy stone planters or statues (inside or out). A tall armoire or bookcases may also represent your internal mountain. Properties that face northeast can produce open-minded and kind-hearted people, intelligent children, and the householders can amass fortunes.

For homes facing Northeast 2 there is a possible Eight Roads of Destruction if you have a road/driveway coming from and exiting the north and east directions. This formation can destroy good business relationships, devastate people's lives, and kill wealth and harmony! For the Northeast 3 facing properties there is a possible Eight Killing Forces if there is a mountain in front of the property on the left-hand side; this formation will unsettle relationships in the house. There is a possible Peach Blossom Sha formation if there is a road or real water coming from the east; this formation is notorious for bringing sex scandals, bad romance, illicit affairs, unrequited love, and extramarital liaisons.

Activating the Interior Environment
Master Bedroom

There are two ways to enhance relationships, harmony, and prosperity in the bedroom—location and direction; the direction of the bed will give you the most powerful results. To enhance relationship/romance-luck, locate your bedroom in the south, north, northwest, or northeast (second floor) as these areas have good mountain stars with great energy. **Bed Directions:** For even more potent relationship-luck for homes that face Northeast 2, place your headboard/bed to the southeast or south (1, 3, 4, or 9 Guas only) as these directions have good facing and mountain star combinations. For homes that face Northeast 3, place your headboard to the southeast or south directions (all Guas). The north may also be used for the East Life group (1, 3, 4 or 9 Guas), as this is a strong Peach Blossom combination, and if your overall Feng Shui is not sound, it could turn bad, bringing lots of affairs and sweet-talking cons to you. For 3 Guas, choose southeast direction as it has good Peach Blossom energy and it's your +70.

Home Office

For homes that face Northeast 2, place your desk/face to the southwest or west (2, 6, 7, or 8 Guas only), southeast, south, or east (1, 3, 4, or 9 Guas only) as these directions have good facing stars with romance, relationship harmony, and prosperity energy. For homes that face Northeast 3, place your desk/face to the southwest, west, southeast, south, or east, as these directions support all Guas. Choose one of these directions that is also your +70; for example, if you are a 3 Gua, face southeast, as it has strong, good romance energy and is your relationship direction (+70).

Kitchen/Stove/Firemouth + Toilets

The best directions for the stove knobs are southeast, southwest, west, or east as these directions will activate household harmony, romance, and prosperity. You will have difficulties with relationships if there is a stove or toilet located in your +70 sector of the house. Select a toilet located in one of your negative sectors of the house (-90, -80, -70, or -60).

Best Doors in the House

For great relationships, opportunities, and prosperity—always use and activate good doors; the best ones for this chart are facing west, southwest, southeast, south, and east. If one of these directions is also your +70, you will be very lucky with relationships! Unfortunately, the northeast-facing front door in this chart is the worst of the worst; avoid if at all possible. It has the evil 5 facing star and it's quite powerful in this direction. If this is your only door coming and going, you will need to cure it with lots of metal near or directly on the door itself. Brass, bronze, copper, pewter, and stainless steel are some high-vibrating metals to use.

PERIOD 8

East 1 (67.6° to 82.5°)

Facing Name: **Jia**

Chart: **Double Stars Meet at Facing**
(Shuang Xing Dao Xiang)

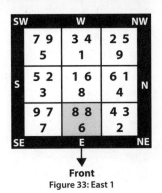

Figure 33: East 1

Romancing the Chart

This chart has two areas to enhance romance, sexual energy, relationships, and love-luck. They are the north (6, 1 Peach Blossom combo) and the west (4 facing star). The west area becomes intensified with romance energy in 2016. In 2017, the north is visited by more romance/Peach Blossom energy. Wealth, prosperity, and relationship harmony are energies automatically invoked by placing water and a mountain in the east.

Activating the Exterior Environment
Need Water and Mountain in Front

This chart has the two 8s at the front of the property known as **Double Stars Meet at Facing**. In order to fully capture the great energy located at the front of the property, you will need both a mountain and water. The "mountain" can be higher ground, courtyard walls, landscape mounds, boulders (no sharp or jagged edges) or any combination (the mountain should be three feet or higher). Install a water feature such as a koi pond, waterfall, or pond in the front garden. You could place a large, tall, stone fountain in the front yard and this would fulfill the criteria of the mountain *and* water.

If you are unable to implement these features exterior to your site, then install a water fountain near the front door, such as a wall fountain. Place two stone statues or planters near the front door either inside or out. Tall armoires or bookcases near the front door could also represent your internal mountain.

There is a possible Eight Roads of Destruction formation if you have a road/driveway coming from or exiting the northeast direction; they are notorious for bringing extramarital/scandalous affairs, bankruptcy, and divorce. This house also has a potential Goat Blade Water formation if there is a road/driveway or real water coming from or exiting certain areas of the east direction. You will know if you have this formation as it will indicate affairs, drug use, alcoholism and gambling.

Activating the Interior Environment
Master Bedroom

There are two ways to enhance relationships, harmony and prosperity in the bedroom—location and direction; the *direction* of the bed will give you the most powerful results. To enhance relationship/romance-luck, locate your bedroom in the north, east, or southeast as these areas have good mountain stars with great energy. **Bed Directions:** For even more potent relationship-luck, place your headboard/bed to the north (1, 3, 4, or 9 Guas only), or the east direction (all Guas). All Guas may also choose the west direction, however be warned that it is a strong Peach Blossom combination, especially for men, who may find themselves literally hounded by women, and that it could produce undesirable results if your Feng Shui is not good. If you choose your relationship direction (+70), it will speed things up a bit; for example if you are a 9 Gua, choose north as this is your relationship direction and has good Peach Blossom energy.

Take special caution regarding the northwest and south; do not use if at all possible. If the master bedroom is already located there, make sure that the bed direction is not also northwest or south. If so, reposition immediately; activating these directions indicates cancer, bankruptcy, divorce, death, and all types of mishaps and disasters. Additionally, use a soft neutral color palette—whites, creams, taupes, and metal colors such as silver and bronze are good as well. Avoid fire colors (reds, purples, pinks, or oranges) in the artwork, rugs, bedding, or wall color. These precautions will ensure harmony in the household.

Home Office

To enhance harmony, prosperity, and romance, face a good direction. While sitting at your desk, face to north (1, 3, 4, or 9 Guas only), east, west, or southwest (all Guas) as these are all good facing stars that will support many opportunities. Choose one of these directions that is also your +70; for example if you are an 8 Gua, choose west as it has romance/writing energy and it's your relationship direction (+70). If you are a 4 Gua, face east—this arrangement indicates recognition at work, a promotion, or meeting a partner through work or at the workplace.

Kitchen/Stove/Firemouth + Toilets

The best directions for the stove knobs to face are to the north, west, southwest, or east, as these directions will activate household harmony, romance, and prosperity. You will have difficulties in relationships if there is a stove or toilet located in your +70 sector of the house. Select a toilet located in one of your negative sectors of the house (-90, -80, -70, or -60).

Best Doors in the House

For great relationships, opportunities, and prosperity—always use and activate good doors; the best ones for this chart are facing to the north, east, west, and southwest. If one of these directions is also your +70, you will be very lucky with relationships! A northwest-facing door, in this chart, is the worst of the worst; avoid if at all possible. It has the evil 5 facing star and its energy attracts all types of disasters. If this is your only door coming and going, you will need to cure it with lots of metal next to or directly on the door itself. Brass, bronze, copper, pewter, and stainless steel are some high-vibrating metals to use.

PERIOD 8

East 2 (82.6° to 97.5°)

Facing Names: **Mao** and the **Rabbit**

East 3 (97.6° to 112.5°)

Facing Name: **Yi**

Chart: **Double Stars Meet at Sitting**
(Shuang Xing Dao Zuo)

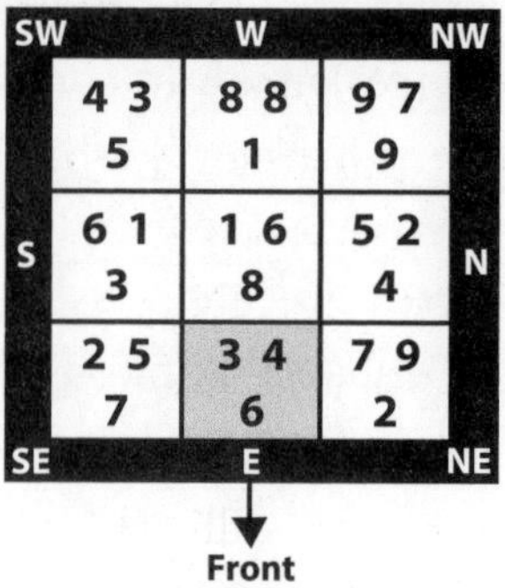

SW		W		NW
	4 3	**8 8**	**9 7**	
	5	**1**	**9**	
S	**6 1**	**1 6**	**5 2**	**N**
	3	**8**	**4**	
	2 5	**3 4**	**7 9**	
	7	**6**	**2**	
SE		E		NE

↓

Front

Figure 34: East 2 & 3

Romancing the Chart

This chart has two areas to enhance romance, sexual energy, relationships, and love-luck.

They are the south (6, 1 Peach Blossom combo) and the east (4 facing star). These areas become intensified when strong romance energy visits the east and northwest in 2015, the west in 2016, and the south in 2018. Wealth, prosperity, and relationship harmony are energies automatically invoked by placing water and a mountain in the west.

Activating the Exterior Environment
Needs Mountain and Water in Back

This chart has the two 8s at the back of the site called **Double Stars Meet at Sitting**. To fully activate the great energy there, you will need a mountain and water in the west (backyard). You should ensure that you have solid and substantial backing such as a solid fence made of brick, stucco, wood, or any combination thereof. You may create tiered or terraced garden beds in front of the solid fencing to increase the effect. If you have a natural mountain, hill, or mound located at the back, you are blessed indeed! Install a beautiful water feature such as a pool, small lake, koi pond, or stream. If you have a pool with a large rock waterfall, the criteria for activating this chart are met.

If you are unable to activate these features to the exterior of your home, install a water fountain inside near the back door. Place two heavy statues or planters inside near the back door or outside if you have a balcony or patio. East-facing properties produce charismatic and loyal professionals such as philosophers, lawyers, judges, and physicians who can become noble and wealthy. For homes facing East 2 there is a possible Eight Killings formation if there is a mountain in the southwest. A possible Peach Blossom Sha haunts this facing if there is a road or real water coming from the north direction and will activate sexual scandals, bad romance, illicit affairs, unrequited love, and extramarital liaisons.

For homes that face East 3, there is a possible Eight Roads of Destruction if there is a road/driveway coming from and exiting from the southeast; they are notorious for bringing extramarital/scandalous affairs, bankruptcy, and divorce. This house also has a potential Goat Blade Water formation if there is a road/driveway or real water coming from or exiting certain areas of the northeast. You will know if you have this formation as it will indicate affairs and excessive behavior such as drug use, alcoholism, and gambling.

Activating the Interior Environment

Master Bedroom

There are two ways to enhance relationships, harmony, and prosperity in the bedroom—location and direction; the *direction* of the bed will give you the most powerful results. To enhance relationship/romance-luck, locate your bedroom in the south, northwest, or west as these areas have good mountain stars with great energy. **Bed Directions:** For more potent relationship luck and for homes that face East 2, place your headboard/bed to the west (2, 6, 7, or 8 Guas only) or south (1, 3, 4, or 9 Guas only). For homes that face East 3, place your headboard/bed to the west, east, or south (all Guas); these directions have good facing and mountain star combinations that will enhance relationships, prosperity, and harmony in the house. If you choose east, be warned that it is a strong Peach Blossom combination, especially for men who may find themselves hounded by women which could produce undesirable results if your Feng Shui is not good. If possible, choose one of the above directions in combination with your +70. For example, if you are a 1 Gua, choose south. It has good Peach Blossom energy and it's your +70.

Take special caution regarding the north and southeast; do not use if at all possible. If the master bedroom is already located there, make sure that the bed direction is not also north or southeast. If so, reposition immediately; activating this direction indicates cancer, bankruptcy, divorce, death, and all types of mishaps and disasters. Additionally, use a soft neutral color palette—whites, creams, taupes, and metal colors such as silver and bronze are good as well. Do not use fire colors (reds, purples, pinks, or oranges) in the artwork, rugs, bedding, or wall color. These precautions will ensure harmony in the household.

Home Office
To enhance harmony, prosperity, and great relationships, activate good directions. For homes that face East 2, place your desk/face west or northeast (2, 6, 7, or 8 Guas only) or to the east or south (1, 3, 4, or 9 Guas only). For homes that face East 3, place your desk/face east, west, northeast, or south; these directions support all Guas.

Kitchen/Stove/Firemouth + Toilets
The best directions for the stove knobs are east, west, south, or northeast; these directions support and activate household harmony, prosperity, and romance. You will have difficulties in relationships if there is a stove or toilet located in your +70 sector of the house. Select a toilet located in one of your negative sectors of the house (-90, -80, -70, or -60).

Best Doors in the House
For great relationships, opportunities, and prosperity—always use and activate good doors; the best ones for this chart are facing west, northeast, east, and south. If one of these directions is also your +70, you will be very lucky with relationships! In this chart, a southeast-facing door

is the worst of the worst; avoid if at all possible. It has the evil 5 facing star and its energy attracts all types of disasters. If this is your only door coming and going you will need to cure it with lots of metal near or directly on the door itself. Brass, bronze, copper, pewter, and stainless steel are some high-vibrating metals to use.

PERIOD 8

Southeast 1 (112.6° to 127.5°)

Facing names: **Chen** and the **Dragon**

Very Special Chart: **Pearl String**
(Lin Cu San Poon Gua)

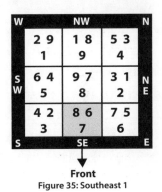

Figure 35: Southeast 1

Romancing the Chart

This chart has two areas to enhance romance, sexual energy, relationships, and love-luck. They are the south (4 mountain star) and the southwest (4 facing star). These areas become intensified when strong romance energy visits the northwest in 2015, the west in 2016, and the northeast in 2017. Wealth, prosperity, and relationship harmony are energies automatically invoked by placing water in the northwest and a mountain in the southeast.

Activating the Exterior Environment
Needs Mountain in Front, Water in Back

This facing has a very special chart called a **Pearl String** that is said to bring triple good luck and opportunities to the occupants. This chart must be activated by a mountain in front and water at the back to be fully realized. The mountain can be high ground, landscape mounds, massive boulders (no jagged or pointed edges) or courtyard walls. Keep the mountain as centered as possible in the front yard without blocking the front door. At the back, install a koi pond, swimming pool, waterfall, or large fountain.

If you are unable to activate the exterior of your site, install a fountain near the back door inside or outside on the balcony or patio if you have one. Place two stone statues or planters on either side of the front door; tall bookcases or armoires also work well as an internal mountain.

An Eight Killings formation is possible if there is a mountain bringing energy to the house from the north. This facing also has a possible Peach Blossom Sha if there is a road or real water coming from the west; they are famous for bringing sex scandals, bad romance, illicit affairs, and unrequited love.

Activating the Interior Environment
Master Bedroom
There are two ways to enhance relationships, harmony, and prosperity in the bedroom—location and direction; the direction of the bed will give you the most powerful results. To enhance wealth-luck, locate your bedroom in the southwest, northwest, or southeast (second floor) as these areas have good mountain stars with wealth energy. **Bed Directions**: For even more potent relationship-luck, place your headboard/bed to the northwest, southwest (all Guas), or southeast (1, 3, 4, or 9 Guas only). These directions have good mountain and facing star combinations that have auspicious energy for relationship and wealth harmony. If you choose your relationship direction (+70), things will speed up; for instance, if you are a 6 Gua, place your bed on the southwest wall for the best results. This direction has good Peach Blossom energy, and it is your +70.

Home Office
To enhance harmony, prosperity, and romance, face one of these great directions. While sitting at your desk, face northwest, southwest, or west (all Guas), northeast (2, 6, 7, or 8 Guas only), southeast (1, 3, 4, or 9 Guas only). If possible, choose one that is also your +70; for example if you are a 6 Gua, face southwest—it has good romance/writing energy and it's your

+70. If you are a 2 Gua, face northwest; this arrangement indicates recognition at work, a promotion, or meeting a partner through work or at the workplace.

Kitchen/Stove/Firemouth + Toilets

The best directions for the stove knobs are northwest, northeast, or west; these directions have energy that supports harmony, prosperity, and romance. You will have difficulties if there is a stove or toilet located in your +70 sector of the house. Select a toilet located in one of your negative sectors of the house (-90, -80, -70, or -60).

Best Doors in the House

For great relationships, opportunities, and prosperity, always use and activate good doors; the best doors in the house are facing northwest, west, northeast, southeast, and southwest. If one of these directions is also your +70, you will be very lucky with relationships. In this chart, an east-facing door is the worst of the worst; avoid if at all possible. It has the evil 5 facing star and its energy attracts all types of disasters. If this is your only door—coming and going—you will need to cure it with lots of metal near or directly on the door itself. Brass, bronze, copper, pewter, and stainless steel are some high-vibrating metals to use.

PERIOD 8

Southeast 2 (127.6° to 142.5°)
    Facing Name: **Xun**

Southeast 3 (142.6° to 157.5°)
    Facing Names: **Su** and the **Snake**

Chart: **Prosperous Sitting and Facing**
    (Wang Shan Wang Shui)

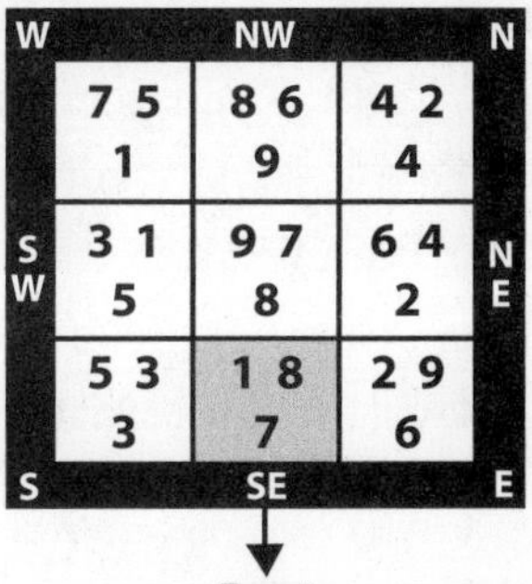

W		NW		N
	7 5	**8 6**	**4 2**	
	1	9	4	
S W	**3 1**	**9 7**	**6 4**	N E
	5	8	2	
	5 3	**1 8**	**2 9**	
	3	7	6	
S		SE		E

Front
Figure 36: Southeast 2 & 3

Romancing the Chart

This chart has two areas to enhance romance, sexual energy, relationships, and love-luck. They are the northeast (4 facing star) and the north (4 mountain star). These areas become intensified when strong romance energy combines together in the northwest in 2015 and the northeast in 2017. Wealth, prosperity, and relationship harmony are energies automatically invoked by placing water in the southeast and a mountain in the northwest.

Activating the Exterior Environment
Needs Water in Front, Mountain in Back

This facing has the very prestigious **Prosperous Sitting and Facing**; this means that it has extremely auspicious energy that is "lucky for people, lucky for money." To properly activate this chart, make sure that you have significant backing with a solid fence made of stone, stucco, bricks, wood, or any combination thereof. If there is a natural mountain, hill or mound behind the property, this is very auspicious! Place a beautiful water feature in the front such as a fountain, stream, koi pond, or waterfall.

If you are unable to activate the exterior of your site, install a fountain near the front door (inside or out). Place two stone planters or statues near the back door (inside or out). You may also use a tall armoire or bookcases near the back door; they work very well as an internal mountain.

There is a possible Eight Roads of Destruction if the house faces Southeast 2 and if a road/driveway comes from or exits the south or east; they will activate extramarital/scandalous affairs, bankruptcy, and divorce. An Eight Killings formation is possible for homes facing Southeast 3 if there is a mountain bringing energy to the house from the west; this formation will unsettle relationships in the house. There is also a possible Peach Blossom Sha if there is a road or real water coming from the south, and will activate sexual scandals, bad romance, illicit affairs, unrequited love, and extramarital liaisons.

Activating the Interior Environment
Master Bedroom

There are two ways to enhance relationships, harmony, and prosperity in the bedroom—location and direction; the direction of the bed will give you the most powerful results. To enhance wealth-luck, locate your bedroom in the northwest, northeast, or southeast (second floor) as these have good mountain stars with wealth energy. **Bed Directions**: For more potent relationship-luck and for homes that face Southeast 2, place your headboard/bed to the northwest or northeast (2, 6, 7, or 8 Guas only) or southeast (1, 3, 4 or 9 Guas only). For homes that face to Southeast 3, place your headboard/bed to the southeast, northwest, or northeast direction (all Guas); these directions have good facing and mountain star combinations that will enhance relationships, prosperity and harmony in the house. Choose a direction in conjunction with your +70 to speed things up; for instance 7 Guas should place their bed on the northeast wall for the best results. This direction is your +70, and it has a good mountain and facing stars to enhance relationships.

Home Office

To enhance harmony, prosperity and romance, face one of these great directions. For homes that face Southeast 2, place your desk/face southeast or east (1, 3, 4, or 9 Guas only), northwest, southwest, or northeast (2, 6, 7, or 8 Guas only) directions. For homes that face Southeast 3, place your desk/face to the southeast, northwest, northeast, southwest, or east (all Guas). Choose one of the directions that is also your +70; for example if you are a 3 Gua, face southeast—this arrangement indicates recognition at work, a promotion, or meeting a partner through work or at the workplace.

Kitchen/Stove/Firemouth + Toilets

The best directions for the stove knobs are southeast, east, northeast, or southwest; these directions support harmony, prosperity, and romance. You will have difficulties if there is a stove or toilet located in your +70 sector of the house. Select a toilet located in one of your negative sectors of the house (-90, -80, -70, or -60).

Best Doors in the House

For great relationships, opportunities and prosperity—always use and activate good doors; the best ones for this chart are facing southeast, northeast, east, or southwest. If one of these directions is also your +70, you will be very lucky with relationships! In this chart, a west-facing door is the worst of the worst; avoid if at all possible. It has the evil 5 facing star and its energy attracts all types of disasters. If this is your only door—coming and going—you will need to cure it with lots of metal near or directly on the door itself. Brass, bronze, copper, pewter, and stainless steel are some high-vibrating metals to use.

Nine

·····················

Period 7 Charts: How to Extract Love, Prosperity, and Harmony

·····················

Better to have never met you in my dream than to
wake and reach for hands that are not there.
Otomo No Yakamochi

The Period 7 homes fell out of luck and lost much of their vitality on February 4, 2004, and are not as auspicious as the Period 8 charts. Period 7 homes may experience "robbery" energy, attract lawsuits, violence, and conflict. However, luck can be extracted depending on the landforms, where the current prosperity is located, and how well-suited the Eight Mansions are for the occupants. The following information will guide you how to activate the exterior and interior to do just that. Please be diligent in correcting any bad formations discussed in chapter 3 or otherwise your great chart and its energy cannot be realized. Have your floor plan in front of you, and take a look at Figure 17 for how to divide up your floor plan and overlay the information.

PERIOD 7

South 1 (157.6° to 172.5°)

Facing Name: **Bing**

Chart: **Double Stars Meet at**
Facing *(Shuang Xing Dao Xiang)*

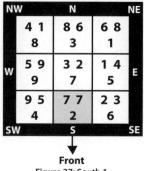

NW	N	NE
4 1 8	8 6 3	6 8 1
5 9 9	3 2 7	1 4 5
9 5 4	7 7 2	2 3 6

W (left) · E (right) · SW · S · SE

↓ **Front**

Figure 37: South 1

Romancing the Chart

This chart has two areas to enhance romance, sexual energy, relationships, and love-luck. They are the east (1, 4 Peach Blossom combo) and the northwest (4, 1 Peach Blossom combo). These areas become intensified when strong romance energy combines together in the northwest and east in 2015, the west in 2016, and in 2018 the south and northwest. Wealth, prosperity, and relationship harmony are energies automatically invoked by placing water in the northeast and a mountain in the north.

Activating the Exterior Environment

Needs Water in Northeast, Mountain in North

This chart has the two 7s in the front of the property known as **Double Stars Meet at Facing** and was quite lucky until February 4, 2004; now the 8s are king. To capture the power of this chart, make sure you have substantial backing with a solid fence comprised of stucco, brick, wood, or any combination thereof. You could also incorporate tiered or terraced garden beds in front of the fence to increase the effect. Water located anywhere at the back of this property works; the northeast is the most desirable. Water at the front is highly disadvantageous, as it will incite disharmony, divorce, lawsuits, and money loss.

If you are unable to activate this chart exterior to your site, then place two stone statues or planters near the back door. Install a tall floor fountain in the northeast corner; this will activate the current, benevolent energy. The south-facing homes support relationships and connections, writing, entrepreneurs, and success in scholarly pursuits.

This house also has a potential Eight Roads of Destruction if there is a road/driveway coming from or exiting the southeast direction which will activate extramarital/scandalous affairs, bankruptcy, and divorce. This house also has a potential Goat Blade Water formation if there is a road/driveway or real water coming from or exiting certain areas of the south. You will know if you have this formation as it will indicate affairs and excessive behavior such as drug use, alcoholism, and gambling. South-facing homes are known for producing charismatic, intelligent, and skillful entrepreneurs.

Activating the Interior Environment
Master Bedroom
There are two ways to enhance relationships, harmony, and prosperity in the bedroom—location and direction; the direction of the bed will give you the most powerful results. To enhance wealth-luck, locate your bedroom in the north, northeast, east, or northwest as these areas have good mountain stars with auspicious energy. **Bed Directions:** For even more potent relationship-luck, place your headboard/bed to the north (1, 3, 4, or 9 Guas only), northeast (2, 6, 7, or 8 Guas only), or east or northwest directions (all Guas); these directions have good facing and mountain star combinations that will enhance relationships, prosperity, and harmony in the house. Using the recommended directions in conjunction with your +70 will give you very powerful, quick results. For example, 4 Guas should place their bed on the east wall, it has good Peach Blossom energy and it's your +70 direction. For 2 Guas, place your bed angled to the northwest, it has good Peach Blossom energy and it's your relationship direction.

Take special caution regarding the west and southwest; do not use if at all possible. If the master bedroom is already located there, make sure that the bed direction is not also west or southwest. If so, reposition immediately; activating this direction indicates cancer, bankruptcy, divorce, sex disease, lawsuits, fires, and all types of mishaps and disasters. Additionally, use a soft neutral color palette—whites and metallic colors such as silver and bronze are good as well. Avoid fire colors (reds, pinks, purples, or oranges) in the artwork, rugs, bedding, or wall color. These precautions will ensure harmony in the household.

Home Office

To enhance harmony, prosperity, and relationship-luck, place your desk/face to the north (1, 3, 4, or 9 Guas only), northeast (2, 6, 7, or 8 Guas only), west, east, or northwest directions (all Guas). Choose one of these great directions that is also your +70; for example if you are a 2 Gua face northwest. This direction has good Peach Blossom energy and it's your relationship direction (+70). If you are a 4 Gua, face east as it is your +70 and has good Peach Blossom energy that supports romance, writing, publishing, and a public persona.

Kitchen/Stove/Firemouth + Toilets

To activate harmony, prosperity and great relationships, the stove knobs (firemouth) should face northeast, northwest, or west. You will have difficulties with relationships if there is a stove or toilet located in your +70 sector of the house. Select a toilet located in one of your negative sectors of the house (-90, -80, -70, or -60).

Best Doors in the House

For great relationships, opportunities, and prosperity—always use and activate good doors; the best ones for this chart are facing north, northeast, west, and northwest. If one of these directions is also your +90, you will be very lucky with relationships. In this chart, a southwest-facing door is the worst of the worst; avoid if at all possible. It has the evil 5 facing star, and it's quite powerful in the southwest. If this is your only door coming and going you will need to cure it with lots of metal near or directly on the door itself. Brass, bronze, copper, pewter, and stainless steel are some high-vibrating metals to use.

PERIOD 7

South 2 (172.6° to 187.5°)

Facing Names: **Wu** and the **Horse**

South 3 (187.6° to 202.5°)

Facing Name: **Ting**

Chart: **Combination of Ten** *(He Shih Chu)*and **Double Stars Meet at Sitting** *(Shuang Xing Dao Zuo)*

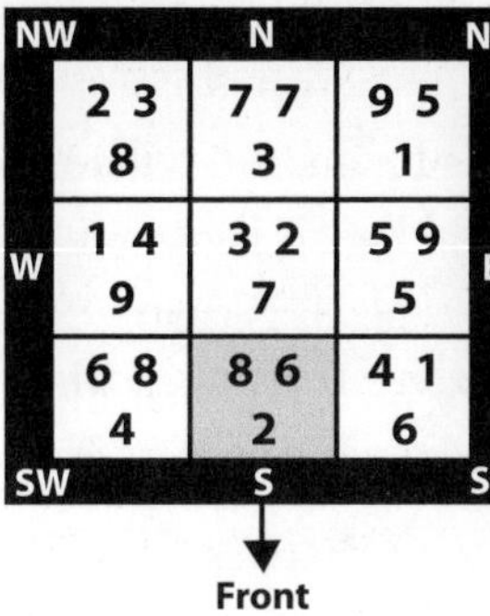

NW	N	NE
2 3 8	7 7 3	9 5 1
1 4 9 (W)	3 2 7	5 9 5 (E)
6 8 4 (SW)	8 6 2 (S)	4 1 6 (SE)

↓

Front

Figure 38: South 2 & 3

Romancing the Chart

This chart has two areas to enhance romance, sexual energy, relationships, and love-luck. They are the west (1, 4 Peach Blossom combo) and the southeast (4, 1 Peach Blossom combo). These areas become intensified when strong romance energy combines together in the west in 2016 and the south in 2018. Wealth, prosperity, and relationship harmony are energies automatically invoked by placing water in the southwest and a mountain in the south.

Activating the Exterior Environment
Needs Water in Southwest, Mountain in South

This chart has the two 7s at the back of the property known as **Double Stars Meet at Sitting** and a **Combination of Ten**; which was extremely auspicious until February 4, 2004, when it fell out of luck. In order to tap the best energy in Period 8, you will need to install a water feature in the front (southwest) and simulate a mountain near the front door but not blocking it. The mountain can be courtyard walls, boulders (no sharp, jagged edges), or landscaping mounds.

If you are unable to activate the chart exterior to your site, place a water fountain in the southwest corner inside. Install two stone statues or planters on either side of the front door (inside or outside). The south-facing homes support relationships/connections, writing, entrepreneurs, and success in scholarly pursuits.

For homes that face South 2, there is a possible Eight Killing Forces formation if there is a mountain coming from the northwest direction; this formation will unsettle relationships in the house. There is also a possible Peach Blossom Sha if there is a road or water coming from the east. The Peach Blossom Sha formations are famous for bringing sexual scandals, bad romance, illicit affairs, unrequited love, and extramarital liaisons.

For homes that face South 3, there is a possible Eight Roads of Destruction if there is a road/driveway coming from and exiting the southwest; this formation will activate extramarital/scandalous affairs, bankruptcy, and divorce. This house also has a potential Goat Blade Water formation if there is a road/driveway or real water coming from or exiting certain areas of the southeast direction. You will know if you have this formation as it will indicate affairs, drug use, alcoholism, and gambling.

Activating the Interior Environment
Master Bedroom

There are two ways to enhance relationships, harmony, and prosperity in the bedroom—location and direction; the direction of the bed will give you the most powerful results. To enhance wealth-luck, locate your bedroom in the west, south, southeast, or southwest, as these sectors have good mountain stars with wealth energy. **Bed Directions**: For even more potent relationship-luck, and for homes that face South 2, place your headboard/bed to the south or southeast (1, 3, 4, or 9 Guas only), west, or southwest (2, 6, 7, or 8 Guas only). For homes that face South 3, place your headboard/bed to the south, southeast, west, or southwest (all Guas only); these directions have good facing and mountain star combinations that will enhance relationships, prosperity, and harmony in the house. Choose one of these facing directions coupled with your +70 (relationship) direction if possible. For example, if you are an 8 Gua, choose west; it has strong romance energy and it's your +70! If you are a 3 Gua, choose southeast direction as it has sexy romance energy and it's your +70 (relationship direction).

Take special caution regarding the east and northeast; do not use if at all possible. If the master bedroom is already located there, make sure that the bed direction is not also east or northeast. If so, reposition immediately; activating this direction indicates cancer, bankruptcy, divorce, sex disease, lawsuits, fires, and all types of mishaps and disasters. Additionally, use a soft neutral color palette—whites, creams, taupes, and metallic colors such as silver and bronze are good as well. Avoid fire colors (reds, purples, pinks, or oranges) in the artwork, rugs, bedding, or wall color. These precautions will ensure harmony in the household.

Home Office
For the best relationship harmony, business opportunities, and romance luck use these great directions; for homes that face South 2, place your desk/face to the south, east, or southeast (1, 3, 4, or 9 Guas only), west or southwest (2, 6, 7, or 8 Guas only). For homes that face South 3, place your desk/face south, southwest, west, east, or southeast (all Guas). Choose one of these directions that is also your +70; for example if you are a 3 Gua, face southeast; this direction has great romance energy and it's your relationship direction(+70). If you are a 6 Gua, face southwest. This arrangement indicates recognition at work, a promotion, or meeting a partner through work or at the workplace.

Kitchen/Stove/Firemouth + Toilets
To activate harmony, prosperity, and great relationships, the best directions for the stove knobs (firemouth) are southwest, southeast, west, or east. You will have difficulties with relationships if there is a stove or toilet located in your +70 sector of the house. Select a toilet located in one of your negative sectors of the house (-90, -80, -70, or -60).

Best Doors in the House
For great relationships, opportunities, and prosperity—always use and activate good doors; the best ones for this chart are facing south, east, southeast,

west, and southwest. If one of these directions is also your +90, you will be very lucky with relationships. In this chart, a northeast-facing door is the worst of the worst; avoid if at all possible. It has the evil 5 facing star, and it's quite powerful in the northeast. If this is your only door coming and going, you will need to cure it with lots of metal near or directly on the door itself. Brass, bronze, copper, pewter, and stainless steel are some high-vibrating metals to use.

PERIOD 7

Southwest 1 (202.6° to 217.5°)

   Facing Names: **Wei** and the **Goat**

Chart: **Double Stars Meet at Facing**
   (Shuang Xing Dao Xiang)

Romancing the Chart

This chart has one area to enhance romance, sexual energy, relationships, and love-luck. It is the northeast (4, 1, Peach Blossom combo). However, strong romance energy combines together in the east in 2015 and the south in 2018. Wealth, prosperity, and relationship harmony are energies automatically invoked by placing water in the north and a mountain in the east.

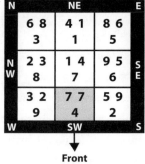

Figure 39: Southwest 1

Activating the Exterior Environment

Needs Water in North or Northeast, Mountain in East

This chart is known as **Double Stars Meeting at Facing** and it has two 7s at the front of the property; this was very auspicious until February 4, 2004, when it fell out of luck. Now in Period 8, you will need to create a mountain in the east corner of your back garden. A mountain could be boulders (no sharp or jagged edges), basalt pillars, or landscape mounds. Install a water feature in the north corner of your back yard; however it should not touch between 352–357 degrees as this will create a Peach Blossom Sha. Water is better placed at the back center in the northeast. This can be a waterfall, koi pond, swimming pool, or fountain. If you are unable to activate the exterior of your site, place a water fountain on the northeast wall inside your home. Place a tall, heavy armoire or bookcases angled in the east corner of your interior space.

The house may have a Peach Blossom Sha formation if there is water or a road coming from the north direction. The Peach Blossom Sha Road formations are famous for bringing sexual scandals, bad romance, illicit affairs, unrequited love, and extramarital liaisons.

Activating the Interior Environment
Master Bedroom

There are two ways to enhance relationships, harmony, and prosperity in the bedroom—location and direction; the direction of the bed will give you the most powerful results. To enhance wealth-luck, locate your bedroom in the north, east, or southeast as these areas have good mountain stars with great energy. **Bed Directions:** For the most potent relationship-luck, place your headboard/bed to the north (1, 3, 4, or 9 Guas only), northeast (2, 6, 7, or 8 Guas only), or east (all Guas); these directions have good facing and mountain star combinations with very auspicious energy that will enhance prosperity, relationship harmony, or romance. Choose one of these facing directions coupled with your +70 (relationship) direction if possible. For example, if you are a 7 Gua, choose the northeast; this has strong romance energy and it's your +70.

Take special caution regarding the southeast and south; do not use if at all possible. If the master bedroom is already located there, make sure that the bed direction is not also southeast or south. If so, reposition immediately; activating this direction indicates cancer, bankruptcy, divorce, sex disease, lawsuits, fires, and all types of mishaps and disasters. Additionally, use a soft neutral color palette—whites, creams, taupes and metallic colors such as silver or bronze are good as well. Avoid fire colors (reds, purples, pinks, or oranges) in the artwork, rugs, bedding, or wall color. These precautions will ensure harmony in the household.

Home Office

For the best relationship harmony, business opportunities, and romance-luck use these great directions; place your desk/face to the north (1, 3, 4, or 9 Guas only), northeast (2, 6, 7, or 8 Guas only), east, or south (all Guas). Choose one of these great directions that is also your +70; for example if you are a 9 Gua, face north. This arrangement indicates recognition at work, a promotion, or meeting a partner through work or at the workplace. If you are a 7 Gua, face northeast. This direction has strong romance energy, and it's your relationship direction (+70).

Kitchen/Stove/Firemouth + Toilets

To activate harmony, prosperity, and great relationships, stove knobs (firemouth) should face north, northeast, or south. You will have difficulties with relationships if there is a stove or toilet located in your +70 sector of the house. Select a toilet located in one of your negative sectors of the house (-90, -80, -70, or -60).

Best Doors in the House

For great relationships, opportunities, and prosperity, always use and activate good doors. The best ones for this chart are facing to the north, northeast, east, and south. If one of these directions is also your +70, you will be very lucky with relationships. In this chart, a southeast-facing door is the worst of the worst; avoid if at all possible. It has the evil 5 facing star and its energy attracts all types of disasters. If this is your only door—coming and going—you will need to cure it with lots of metal near or directly on the door itself. Brass, bronze, copper, pewter, and stainless steel are some high-vibrating metals to use.

PERIOD 7

Southwest 2 (217.6° to 232.5°)
  Facing Name: **Kun**

Southwest 3 (232.6° to 247.5°)
  Facing names: **Shen** and the **Monkey**

Chart: **Double Stars Meet at Sitting**
  (Shuang Xing Dao Zuo)

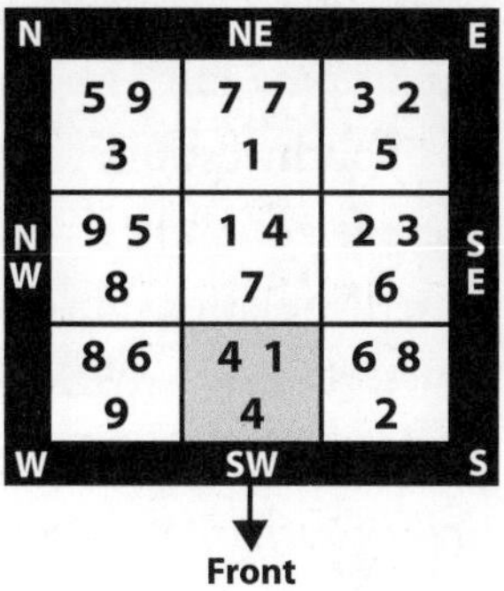

N		NE		E
	5 9	7 7	3 2	
	3	1	5	
N W	9 5	1 4	2 3	S E
	8	7	6	
	8 6	4 1	6 8	
	9	4	2	
W		SW		S

↓
Front
Figure 40: Southwest 2 & 3

Romancing the Chart

This chart has one area to enhance romance, sexual energy, relationships, and love-luck. It is the southwest (4, 1 Peach Blossom combo). Other areas become intensified when strong romance energy combines together in the west in 2016, northeast in 2017, and the south in 2018. Wealth, prosperity, and relationship harmony are energies automatically invoked by placing water in the south and a mountain in the west.

Activating the Exterior Environment
Needs Water in South, Mountain in West

This chart has the two 7s at the back of the property called **Double Stars Meet at Sitting**; this was auspicious until February 4, 2004, when it fell out of luck. Now in Period 8, you will need to place a water feature such as a fountain in the south of your front garden. Simulate a mountain in the west of your front yard by installing a landscape mound, boulders, basalt pillars, or courtyard walls to activate this energy. Southwest, near the front door, is an alternative placement for a water feature. If you are unable to activate the exterior of your site, then place a water fountain angled in the south corner inside your home. Place a tall, heavy armoire or bookcases angled in the west corner of your interior space.

Homes facing Southwest 2 could have an Eight Roads of Destruction formation if a road/driveway comes from or exits the south or west directions; they are notorious for bringing extramarital/scandalous affairs, bankruptcy, killing good business deals/relationships, and divorce.

Southwest 3 facing homes may have an Eight Killings formation if there is a mountain coming from the east direction; this formation will unsettle relationships in the house. There is also a possible Peach Blossom Sha if there is a road or real water coming from the west; they are famous for bringing sexual scandals, bad romance, illicit affairs, unrequited love, and extramarital liaisons.

Activating the Interior Environment
Master Bedroom

There are two ways to enhance relationships, harmony, and prosperity in the bedroom—location and direction; the direction of the bed will give you the most powerful results. To enhance relationship-luck, locate your bedroom in the southwest, south, or west; these sectors of the house have good mountain stars. **Bed Directions**: For the most potent relationship-luck, and for homes that face Southwest 2, place your headboard/bed to the south (1, 3, 4, or 9 Guas only), southwest, or west (2, 6, 7, or 8 Guas only). For homes that face Southwest 3, place your headboard/bed to the south, southwest, or west (all Guas); these directions have good facing and mountain star combinations that will enhance relationships, prosperity, and harmony in the house. Choose one of these facing directions coupled with your +70 (relationship) direction if possible. For example, if you are a 6 Gua, choose the southwest; this has strong romance energy and it's your +70!

Take special caution regarding the north and northwest; do not use if at all possible. If the master bedroom is already located there, make sure that the bed direction is not also north and northwest. If so, reposition immediately; activating this direction indicates cancer, bankruptcy, divorce, sex disease, lawsuits, fires, and all types of mishaps and disasters. Additionally, use a soft neutral color palette—whites, creams, taupes, and metal colors such as silver or bronze are good as well. Avoid fire colors (reds, purples, pinks, or oranges) in the artwork, rugs, bedding, or wall color. These precautions will ensure harmony in the household.

Home Office

For the best relationship harmony, business opportunities and romance luck, face one of these great directions. For homes facing Southwest 2, place your desk/face north or south (1, 3, 4, or 9 Guas only), southwest, or west (2, 6, 7, or 8 Guas only). For homes that face Southwest 3, place your desk/face north (1, 3, 4, or 9 Guas only), south, southwest, or west (all Guas). Choose one of these directions that is also your +70; for example if you are a 1 Gua, face south. This arrangement indicates recognition at work, a promotion, or meeting a partner through work or at the workplace. If you are a 6 Gua, face the southwest as this is your +70 and it has good Peach Blossom energy.

Kitchen/Stove/Firemouth + Toilets

To activate harmony, prosperity, and great relationships, the best directions for the stove knobs (firemouth) are south, southwest, or north. You will have difficulties with relationships if there is a stove or toilet located in your +70 sector of the house. Select a toilet located in one of your negative sectors of the house (-90, -80, -70, or -60).

Best Doors in the House

For great relationships, opportunities and prosperity—always use and activate good doors; the best ones for this chart are facing to the north, south, southwest, and west. If one of these directions is also your +90, you will be very lucky with relationships! A northwest-facing door, in this chart, is the worst of the worst; avoid if at all possible. It has the evil 5 facing star and its energy attracts all types of disasters. If this is your only door coming and going, you will need to cure it with lots of metal near or directly on the door itself. Brass, bronze, copper, pewter, and stainless steel are some high-vibrating metals to use.

PERIOD 7

West 1 (247.6° to 262.5°)

　　Facing Name: **Geng**

Chart: **Reverse Formation**

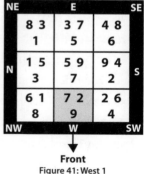

Figure 41: West 1

Romancing the Chart

This chart has two areas to enhance romance, sexual energy, relationships and love-luck. They are the northwest (6, 1 Peach Blossom combo) and the south (4 facing star). These areas become intensified when strong romance energy visits the northwest and east in 2015, and the south in 2018. Wealth, prosperity, and relationship harmony are energies automatically invoked by placing water in the southeast and a mountain in the northeast.

Activating the Exterior Environment
Needs Water in Southeast, Mountain in Northeast

This chart is known as a **Reverse Formation,** and even in Period 7 was not particularly auspicious. Create a mountain in the northeast of your back garden; this can be accomplished by using boulders (no sharp or jagged edges), landscape mounds, tiered or terraced garden beds, basalt pillars, or high ground. Install a gorgeous water feature in the southeast corner of your back yard. This can be a waterfall, koi pond, swimming pool, or large fountain. If you are unable to activate this chart exterior to your site, install a water fountain in the southeast corner indoors. Place a tall armoire or bookcases in the northeast corner at the back of your space.

West-facing properties produce well-educated, intelligent, polite, and charming people who can become very wealthy in good business management or getting involved in politics. The house does have a possible Eight Roads of Destruction formation if there is a road/driveway coming from or exiting southwest. Eight Roads of Destruction are notorious for bringing extramarital/scandalous affairs, bankruptcy, and divorce. This house also has a potential Goat Blade Water formation if there is a road/driveway or real water coming from or exiting certain areas of the west direction. You will know if you have this formation as it will indicate affairs, drug use, alcoholism, and gambling.

Activating the Interior Environment
Master Bedroom

There are two ways to enhance relationships, harmony, and prosperity in the bedroom—location and direction; the direction of the bed will give you the most powerful results. To enhance relationship-luck, locate your bedroom in the northeast, south, or northwest as these sectors have good mountain stars. **Bed Directions:** For the most potent relationship-luck, place your headboard/bed to the northwest and south (all Guas), and southeast (1, 3, 4, or 9 Guas only) directions; these directions have good facing and mountain star combinations that will enhance relationships, prosperity, and harmony in the house. Choose one of these facing directions coupled with your +70 (relationship) direction if possible. For example, if you are a 2 Gua, choose the northwest; this has strong romance energy and it's your +70.

Home Office

For the best relationship harmony, business opportunities, and romance-luck, face your desk/body to the northwest, south, or southwest (all Guas), and southeast (1, 3, 4, or 9 Guas only). Choose one of these directions that is also your +70; for example if you are a 3 Gua, face southeast. This arrangement indicates recognition at work, a promotion, or meeting a partner through work or at the workplace. If you are a 2 Gua, face the northwest as this is your +70 and it has good Peach Blossom energy.

Kitchen/Stove/Firemouth + Toilets

To activate harmony, prosperity, and great relationships, stove knobs (fire-mouth) should face southeast, south, or northwest. You will have difficulties with relationships if there is a stove or toilet located in your +70 sector of the house. Select a toilet located in one of your negative sectors of the house (-90, -80, -70, or -60).

Best Doors in the House

For great relationships, opportunities, and prosperity—always use and activate good doors; the best ones for this chart are facing northwest, south, southwest, and southeast. If one of these directions is also your +70, you will be very lucky with relationships! A north-facing door in this chart is the worst of the worst; avoid if at all possible. It has the evil 5 facing star and its energy attracts all types of disasters. If this is your only door—coming and going—you will need to cure it with lots of metal next to or directly on the door itself. Brass, bronze, copper, pewter, and stainless steel are some high-vibrating metals to use.

PERIOD 7

West 2 (262.6° to 277.5°)
   Facing Names: **You** and the **Rooster**

West 3 (277.6° to 292.5°)
   Facing Name: **Xin**

Chart: **Prosperous Sitting and Facing**
   (Wang Shan Wang Shui)

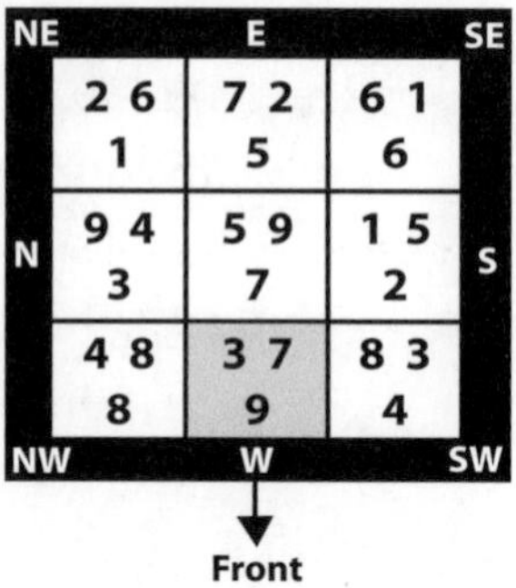

NE	E	SE
2 6	7 2	6 1
1	5	6
9 4	5 9	1 5
3	7	2
4 8	3 7	8 3
8	9	4
NW	W	SW

N (left) / S (right)

↓
Front
Figure 42: West 2 & 3

Romancing the Chart

This chart has two areas to enhance romance, sexual energy, relationships, and love-luck. They are the southeast (6, 1 Peach Blossom combo) and the north (4 facing star). These areas become intensified when strong romance energy visits the west and southeast in 2016 and the southeast again in 2017. Wealth, prosperity, and relationship harmony are energies automatically invoked by placing water in the northwest and a mountain in the southwest.

Activating the Exterior Environment
Needs Water in Northwest, Mountain in Southwest, Alternate or Extra Water in Southeast

This house had the two 7s perfectly placed in Period 7 known as **Prosperous Sitting and Facing** that was very auspicious until February 4, 2004 when it fell out of luck. Now the 8s are the ruling energy. To extract the auspicious energy of this chart, install a gorgeous water feature in your front garden in the northwest. This can be a fountain, koi pond, or waterfall, but it must flow toward the house. Create a mountain in the southwest area of your front garden using boulders (no sharp or jagged edges), basalt pillars, or landscaping mounds. If you are unable to activate this chart exterior to your site, then place a water fountain in the northwest corner indoors. Place a heavy armoire or tall bookcases in the southwest corner inside. West-facing properties produce and support people who can be powerful in the politics, super athletes, and those very accomplished in academia.

The West 2 homes have a possible Eight Killing Forces if there is mountain chi coming from the southeast. West 2 homes may have a Peach Blossom Sha formation if there is a road or real water coming from the south direction; this formation will activate sexual scandals, bad romance, illicit affairs, unrequited love, and extramarital liaisons.

The West 3 facing homes have a possible Eight Roads of Destruction formation if there is a road/driveway coming from or exiting the northwest; they are notorious for bringing extramarital/scandalous affairs, bankruptcy, and divorce. This house also has a potential Goat Blade Water formation if there is a road/driveway or real water coming from or exiting certain areas of the southwest. You will know if you have this formation as it will indicate affairs, drug use, alcoholism, and gambling.

Activating the Interior Environment
Master Bedroom

There are two ways to enhance relationships, harmony, and prosperity in the bedroom—location and direction; the direction of the bed will give you the most powerful results. To enhance relationship-luck, locate your bedroom in the north, southwest, northwest, or southeast as these sectors have good mountain stars with great energy. **Bed Directions:** For the most potent relationship-luck for West 2 homes, place your headboard/bed to the northwest (2, 6, 7, or 8 Guas only), north, or southeast (1, 3, 4, or 9 Guas only). For homes that face West 3, place your headboard/bed to the northwest, southeast (all Guas), or north (1, 3, 4 or 9 Guas); these directions have good facing and mountain star combinations that will enhance relationships, prosperity, and harmony in the house. Choose one of these facing directions coupled with your +70 (relationship) direction if possible. For example, if you are a 3 Gua, choose southeast; this has strong romance energy and it's your +70! If you are a 1 Gua, choose north, as it has sexy romance energy and is your +70 (relationship direction).

Home Office

For the best relationship-harmony, business opportunities and romance luck, face your desk to one of these great directions. For homes that face West 2, place your desk/face northwest or northeast (2, 6, 7, or 8 Guas only), north or southeast (1, 3, 4, or 9 Guas only). For homes that face West 3, place your desk/face northwest, northeast, or southeast (all Guas), or north (1, 3, 4, or 9 Guas only). Southeast is especially good for 3 Guas as this is their unique relationship direction (+70) and it has romance energy. For the 2 Life Gua, northwest is their +70 and has extremely prosperous energy—activating this direction indicates a partner with wealth or meeting a partner through work or at the workplace.

Kitchen/Stove/Firemouth + Toilets

To activate harmony, prosperity and great relationships, the stove knobs (firemouth) should face north, northwest, or southeast. You will have difficulties with relationships if there is a stove or toilet located in your +70 sector of the house. Select a toilet located in one of your negative sectors of the house (-90, -80, -70, or -60).

Best Doors in the House

For great relationships, opportunities, and prosperity—always use and activate good doors; the best ones for this chart are facing north, northwest, northeast, and southeast. If one of these directions is also your +70, you will be very lucky with relationships! A south-facing door in this chart is the worst of the worst; avoid if at all possible. It has the evil 5 facing star and it's quite powerful in the south. If this is your only door—coming and going—you will need to cure it with lots of metal near or directly on the door itself. Brass, bronze, copper, pewter, and stainless steel are some high-vibrating metals to use.

PERIOD 7

Northwest 1 (292.6° to 307.5°)
   Facing Names: **Xu** and the **Dog**

Chart: **Prosperous Sitting and**
   Facing *(Wang Shan Wang Shui)*

Romancing the Chart

This chart has two areas to enhance romance, sexual energy, relationships and love-luck. They are the south (4 facing star) and the west (4 mountain star). These areas become intensified when strong romance energy combines together in the east and northwest in 2015; the west and southeast in 2016; the south and

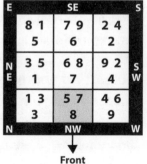

Figure 43: Northwest 1

northwest in 2018. Wealth, prosperity, and relationship harmony are energies automatically invoked by placing water and a mountain in the east.

Activating the Exterior Environment
Needs Water and Mountain in East

This house had the two 7s perfectly placed in Period 7 known as **Prosperous Sitting and Facing**; it was very auspicious until February 4, 2004, when it fell out of luck. Now the 8s are the ruling energy; to extract the auspicious vitality of this chart—install a gorgeous tall, stone water fountain in the east. The water should not touch between 82° and 97°, as this can create a Peach Blossom Sha; the water may be better placed in the southeast (center of your back garden). Alternatively, creating a rock waterfall with a collection pool in the east corner of your back garden would also fulfill the criteria of activating the most benevolent energy of the chart. If you are unable to activate this chart exterior to your site, place a tall, heavy water fountain indoors in the east corner or on the back wall inside which is southeast. Place a heavy armoire or tall bookcases on the southwest wall or in the north corner for additional supporting energy.

There is a possible Peach Blossom Sha Road if there is water or a road from the east. The Peach Blossom Sha Road formations are famous for bringing sexual scandals, bad romance, illicit affairs, unrequited love, and extramarital liaisons.

Activating the Interior Environment
Master Bedroom

There are two ways to enhance relationships, harmony, and prosperity in the bedroom—location and direction; the direction of the bed will give you the most powerful results. To enhance household harmony, locate your bedroom in the north, southwest, or east as these sectors have good mountain stars. **Bed Directions:** For the most potent relationship-luck, place your headboard to the east or west (all Guas) as these directions have good facing and mountain star combinations that will enhance relationships, prosperity, and harmony. Choose one of these facing directions coupled with your +70 (relationship) direction if possible. For example, if you are an 8 Gua, choose the west, as it has strong romance energy and it's your +70!

Home Office

For the best relationship harmony, business opportunities, and romance-luck, face your desk/body to the south, east, or west (all Guas), or south-east (1, 3, 4, or 9 Guas only). South is especially good for 1 Guas as this is their unique relationship direction (+70) and the 4 facing star known for its romance energy. For 4 Life Guas, east is their +70 and it has very prosperous energy; activating this direction indicates a partner with wealth or meeting a partner through work or at the workplace.

Kitchen/Stove/Firemouth + Toilets

To activate harmony, prosperity, and great relationships, the best direction for the stove knobs (firemouth) is east, south, or southeast. You will have difficulties with relationships if there is a stove or toilet located in your +70 sector of the house. Select a toilet located in one of your negative sectors of the house (-90, -80, -70, or -60).

Best Doors in the House

For great relationships, opportunities and prosperity—always use and activate good doors; the best ones for this chart are facing south, east, west, and southeast. If one of these directions is also your +70, you will be very lucky with relationships! A northeast-facing door in this chart is the worst of the worst; avoid if at all possible. It has the evil 5 facing star and it's quite powerful in the northeast. If this is your only door—coming and going—you will need to cure it with lots of metal next to or directly on the door itself. Brass, bronze, copper, pewter, and stainless steel are some high-vibrating metals to use.

PERIOD 7

Northwest 2 (307.6° to 322.5°)

Facing Name: **Chien**

Northwest 3 (322.6° to 337.5°)

Facing Names: **Hai** and the **Pig**

Chart: **Pearl String Formation**

(Lin Cu San Poon Gua)

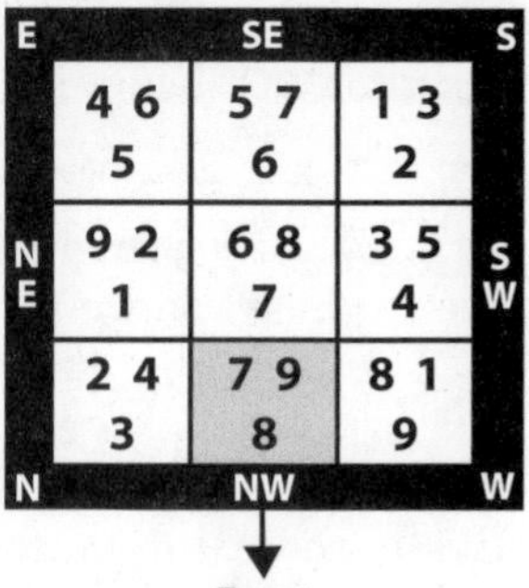

	E	SE		S
	4 6 5	**5 7** 6	**1 3** 2	
NE	**9 2** 1	**6 8** 7	**3 5** 4	**SW**
	2 4 3	**7 9** 8	**8 1** 9	
N		**NW**		**W**

↓

Front

Figure 44: Northwest 2 & 3

Romancing the Chart

This chart has two areas to enhance romance, sexual energy, relationships, and love-luck. They are the north (4 facing star) and the east (4 mountain star). These areas become intensified when strong romance energy combines together in the northwest and east in 2015; southeast and west in 2016; and northwest again in 2018. Wealth, prosperity, and relationship harmony are energies automatically invoked by placing water in the northwest and a mountain in the west.

Activating the Exterior Environment
Water in Northwest, Mountain in West

This was one of the best charts in Period 7, known as a **Pearl String**; as of February 4, 2004, however, it lost much of its vitality. In order to extract the benevolent energy, you will need water in the northwest and a mountain in the west. This can be accomplished by installing a rock waterfall (water must flow towards the house), or placing a tall stone fountain. An alternative water feature may be located in the front of the property (northwest). However, you will still need to create a mountain in the west with high ground, landscape mounds, or boulders (no sharp or jagged edges).

For homes that face Northwest 2, there is a possible Eight Roads of Destruction if you have a road coming to the house from either the west or north directions; they will activate extramarital/scandalous affairs, kill good business deals/relationships, bankruptcy, and divorce.

For Northwest 3 facing homes if mountain energy/chi comes to the home from the South direction you could have an Eight Killing Forces formation; this formation will unsettle relationships in the house. Northwest 3 facing homes may also have a Peach Blossom Sha formation if water or a road comes from the north direction; these formations are famous for bringing sexual scandals, bad romance, illicit affairs, unrequited love, and extramarital liaisons.

Activating the Interior Environment
Master Bedroom
There are two ways to enhance relationships, harmony, and prosperity in the bedroom—location and direction; the direction of the bed will give you the most powerful results. To enhance household harmony, locate your bedroom in the south, west, or northeast as these sectors have good mountain stars. **Bed Directions:** For the most potent relationship-luck, and for homes that face Northwest 2, place your headboard/bed to the to the west (2, 6, 7, or 8 Guas only), or east (1, 3, 4, or 9 Guas only); these directions have good facing and mountain star combinations with auspicious energy. For homes that face Northwest 3, place your headboard/bed to the west or east (all Guas). Choose one of these facing directions coupled with your +70 (relationship) direction if possible. For example, if you are a 4 Gua, choose east; this has strong romance energy and it's your +70!

Home Office
For the best relationship harmony, business opportunities, and romance-luck, face your desk/body to one of these great directions. For homes that face Northwest 2, place your desk/face northwest or west (2, 6, 7, or 8 Guas only), or east or north (1, 3, 4, or 9 Guas only). For homes that face Northwest 3, place your desk/face north (1, 3, 4, or 9 Guas only), northwest, west, or east (all Guas). North is especially good for 9 Guas as this is their unique relationship direction (+70) and the 4 facing star known for its romance energy. For the 8 Life Guas, west is their +70 and

extremely prosperous energy; activating this direction indicates a partner with wealth or meeting a partner through work or at the workplace.

Kitchen/Stove/Firemouth + Toilets

To activate harmony, prosperity, and great relationships, stove knobs (firemouth) should face west, north, or northwest. You will have difficulties with relationships if there is a stove or toilet located in your +70 sector of the house. Select a toilet located in one of your negative sectors of the house (-90, -80, -70, or -60).

Best Doors in the House

For great relationships, opportunities, and prosperity—always use and activate good doors; the best ones for this chart are facing northwest, north, west, and east. If one of these directions is also your +70, you will be very lucky with relationships! In this chart, a southwest-facing door is the worst of the worst; avoid if at all possible. It has the evil 5 facing star and it's quite powerful in the southwest. If this is your only door coming and going, you will need to cure it with lots of metal next to or directly on the door itself. Brass, bronze, copper, pewter, and stainless steel are some high-vibrating metals to use.

PERIOD 7

North 1 (337.6° to 352.5°)

   Facing Name: **Ren**

Chart: **Double Stars Meet at Sitting**

   (Shuang Xing Dao Zuo)

Romancing the Chart

This chart has two areas to enhance romance, sexual energy, relationships, and love-luck. They are the northwest (1, 4 Peach Blossom

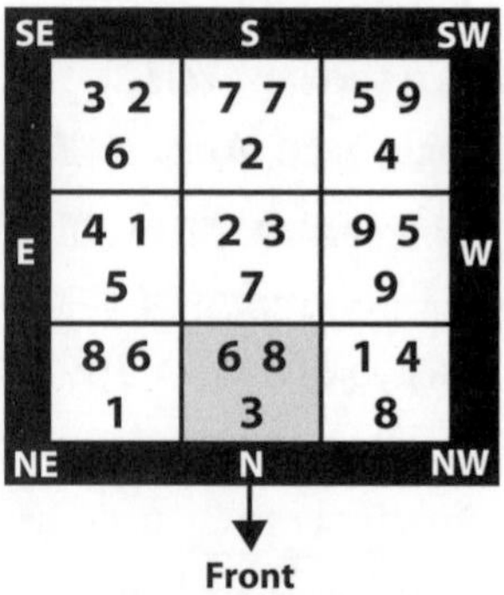

SE	S	SW
3 2 6	7 7 2	5 9 4
4 1 5	2 3 7	9 5 9
8 6 1	6 8 3	1 4 8
NE	N	NW

E (left side), W (right side)

↓
Front
Figure 45: North 1

combo) and the east (4, 1 Peach Blossom combo). These areas become intensified when strong romance energy combines together in the northwest and east in 2015; northeast and northwest in 2017; and northwest again in 2018. Wealth, prosperity, and relationship harmony are energies automatically invoked by placing water in the north and a mountain in the northeast.

Activating the Exterior Environment
Water in North, Mountain in Northeast

This property has the two 7s at the back, called **Double Stars Meet at Sitting** that was quite auspicious for relationships and people until February 4, 2004, when it fell out of luck. Now that we are in a new period, it needs to be activated differently. However, this is the only Period 7 chart with the 8 facing star in the front; very auspicious indeed! You will need to place a mountain in the northeast area of your front garden. This can be done with landscape mounds, basalt pillars, or large boulders (no sharp or jagged edges). Install a gorgeous water feature in the front (north). This can be a koi pond, tall stone fountain, a stream, or waterfall (the water must flow toward the house). If you are unable to activate this chart exterior to your site, place a fountain inside near your front door. Also place a tall armoire or bookcases in the northeast corner indoors. Alternative or additional water may be placed in the east (indoors or outdoors).

There is a possible Eight Roads of Destruction if you have a road/driveway coming from or exiting the northwest direction; this formation will activate extramarital/scandalous affairs, bankruptcy, and divorce. This house also has a potential Goat Blade Water formation if there is a road/driveway or real water coming from or exiting certain areas of the northwest direction. You will know if you have this formation as it will indicate affairs, drug use, alcoholism, and gambling.

Activating the Interior Environment
Master Bedroom

There are two ways to enhance relationships, harmony, and prosperity in the bedroom—location and direction; the direction of the bed will give you the most powerful results. To enhance relationship/romance-luck, locate your bedroom in the east, northwest, north (second floor) or northeast; these sectors have good mountain stars with great energy. **Bed Directions:** For the most potent relationship-luck, place your headboard/bed to the northwest or east (all Guas), northeast (2, 6, 7, or 8 Guas only), or north (1, 3, 4, or 9 Guas only); these directions have good facing and mountain star combinations that will enhance relationships, prosperity, and harmony in the house. Choose one of these facing directions coupled with your +70 (relationship) direction if possible. For example, if you are a 4 Gua, choose east; this has strong romance energy and it's your +70! If you are a 2 Gua, choose the northwest direction as it has sexy romance energy and it's your +70 (relationship direction).

Take special caution regarding the southwest and west; do not use either direction if at all possible. If the master bedroom is already located there, make sure that the bed direction is not also southwest or west. If so, reposition immediately; activating this direction indicates cancer, bankruptcy, divorce, sex disease, lawsuits, fires, and all types of disasters. Additionally, use a soft neutral color palette—whites, creams, taupes, and metal colors such as silver or bronze are good as well. Avoid fire colors (reds, purples, pinks, or oranges) in the artwork, rugs, bedding, or wall color. These precautions will ensure harmony in the household.

Home Office

For the best relationship harmony, business opportunities, and romance-luck, face your desk/body to northwest, southwest, or east (all Guas), northeast (2, 6, 7, or 8 Guas only), or north (1, 3, 4, or 9 Guas only). The northwest direction is especially good for 2 Guas as this is their unique relationship direction (+70) and the 4 facing star known for its romance energy. For the 9 Life Gua, the north is their +70 and extremely prosperous energy—activating this direction indicates a partner with wealth or meeting a partner through work or at the workplace.

Kitchen/Stove/Firemouth + Toilets

To activate harmony, prosperity and great relationships, the stove knobs (firemouth) should face north, northwest, east, or southwest. You will have difficulties in relationships if there is a stove or toilet located in your +70 sector of the house. Select a toilet located in one of your negative sectors of the house (-90, -80, -70, or -60).

Best Doors in the House

For great relationships, opportunities, and prosperity—always use and activate good doors; the best ones for this chart are facing southwest, north, northwest, east, and northeast. If one of these directions is also your +70, you will be very lucky with relationships! A west-facing door, in this chart, is the worst of the worst; avoid if at all possible. It has the evil 5 facing star and its energy attracts all types of disasters. If this is your only door in and out, you will need to cure it with lots of metal next to or directly on the door. Brass, bronze, copper, pewter, and stainless steel are some high-vibrating metals.

PERIOD 7

North 2 (352.6° to 7.5°)

   Facing Names: **Tzi** and the **Rat**

North 3 (7.6° to 22.5)

   Facing Name: **Kwei**

Chart: **Combination of Ten** (*He Shih Chu*)

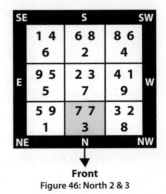

Front

Figure 46: North 2 & 3

Romancing the Chart

This chart has two areas to enhance romance, sexual energy, relationships, and love-luck. They are the southeast (1, 4 Peach Blossom combo) and the west (4, 1 Peach Blossom combo). These areas become intensified when strong romance energy combines together in the southeast and west in 2016, and the northeast in 2017. Wealth, prosperity, and relationship harmony are energies automatically invoked by placing water in the south and a mountain in the southwest.

Activating the Exterior Environment
Water in South, Mountain in Southwest

This chart, known as a **Combination of Ten,** was very auspicious until February 4, 2004, when much of its vitality and luck expired. This property must be extracted with a mountain in the southwest corner of the back yard; a mountain could be created with large boulders (no sharp or jagged edges), basalt pillars, landscape mounds, or tiered/terraced garden beds. Install a lovely water feature in the south of your garden. This can be a swimming pool, koi pond, waterfall, or large stone fountain. If you are unable to activate the exterior of your site, then install an indoor fountain near your back door (south). Place a tall armoire or bookcases in the southwest corner; these are good representations of an internal mountain.

The North 2 homes may have a Peach Blossom Sha formation if there is water or a road coming from the west; this direction also has a strong Peach Blossom combination of stars. While normally this combination of stars can handle water very well, in this case you would get a negative result by creating the dreaded Peach Blossom Sha formation which is famous for bringing sexual scandals, bad romance, illicit affairs, unrequited love, and extramarital liaisons.

For homes that face North 3, there is a possible Eight Roads of Destruction if you have a road/driveway coming from or exiting the northeast and will activate extramarital/scandalous affairs, bankruptcy, and divorce. The

North 3 homes also have a potential Goat Blade Water formation if there is a road/driveway or real water coming from or exiting certain areas of the north. You will know if you have this formation as it will indicate affairs, drug use, alcoholism, and gambling.

Activating the Interior Environment
Master Bedroom

There are two ways to enhance relationships, harmony, and prosperity in the bedroom—location and direction; the direction of the bed will give you the most powerful results. To enhance relationship/romance-luck, locate your bedroom in the west, southeast, south, or southwest as these sectors have good mountain stars. **Bed Directions:** For the most potent relationship-luck, and for homes that face North 2, place your headboard/bed to the west, or southwest (2, 6, 7, or 8 Guas only), southeast, or south (1, 3, 4, or 9 Guas only). For homes that face North 3, place your headboard/bed to the southeast, west, southwest, or south (all Guas); these directions have good facing and mountain star combinations that will enhance relationships, prosperity, and harmony in the house. Choose one of these facing directions coupled with your +70 (relationship) direction if possible. For example, if you are an 8 Gua, choose west, as this has strong romance energy and it's your +70! If you are a 3 Gua, choose the southeast direction as it has sexy romance energy and it's your +70 (relationship direction).

Take special caution regarding the east and northeast; do not use if at all possible. If the master bedroom is already located there, make sure that the bed direction is not also east or northeast. If so, reposition immediately; activating this direction indicates cancer, bankruptcy, divorce, sex disease, lawsuits, fires, and all types of mishaps and disasters. Additionally, use a soft neutral color palette—whites, creams, taupes, and metal colors such as silver or bronze are good as well. Avoid fire colors (reds, purples, pinks, or oranges) in the artwork, rugs, bedding, or wall color. These precautions will ensure harmony in the household.

Home Office

For the best relationship harmony, business opportunities, and romance-luck, face your desk/body to one of these great directions. For homes that face North 2, place your desk/face northeast, west, or southwest (2, 6, 7, or 8 Guas only), south, or southeast (1, 3, 4, or 9 Guas only). For homes that face North 3, place your desk/face to the northeast, west, southwest, southeast, and south (all Guas). Southeast is especially good for 3 Guas as this is their unique relationship direction (+70) and the 4 facing star known for its romance energy. For 1 Life Guas, south is their +70 and extremely prosperous energy—activating this direction indicates a partner with wealth or meeting a partner through work or at the workplace.

Kitchen/Stove/Firemouth + Toilets

To activate harmony, prosperity and great relationships, the stove knobs (firemouth) should face southeast, south, west, or northeast. You will have difficulties with relationships if there is a stove or toilet located in your +70 sector of the house. Select a toilet located in one of your negative sectors of the house (-90, -80, -70, or -60).

Best Doors in the House

For great relationships, opportunities, and prosperity—always use and activate good doors; the best ones for this chart are facing southeast, northeast, west, southwest, and south. If one of these directions is also your +70, you will be very lucky with relationships! An east-facing door, in this chart, is the worst of the worst; avoid if at all possible. It has the evil 5 facing star and its energy attracts all types of disasters. If this is your only door—in and out—you will need to cure it with lots of metal next to or directly on the door. Brass, bronze, copper, pewter, and stainless steel are some high-vibrating metals.

PERIOD 7

Northeast 1 (22.6° to 37.5°)

    Facing name: **Chou**

Chart: **Double Stars Meet at Sitting**

    (Shuang Xing Dao Zuo)

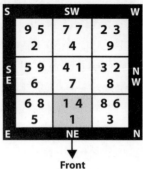

Front

Figure 47: Northeast 1

Romancing the Chart

This chart has one area to enhance romance, sexual energy, relationships and love-luck; that area is the northeast (1, 4 Peach Blossom combo). This area becomes intensified when strong romance energy combines together in the southeast in 2016, and the northeast in 2017. Wealth, prosperity, and relationship harmony are energies automatically invoked by placing water in the east and a mountain in the north.

Activating the Exterior Environment
Needs Water in East, Mountain in North

This chart has the two 7s at the back of the site known as **Double Stars Meet at Sitting** and was very lucky for relationships and people-luck until February 4, 2004, when this energy expired. Now in Period 8, the energy must be extracted creatively by simulating a mountain in the north which will enhance relationships. A mountain could be created with large boulders (no sharp or jagged edges), basalt pillars, courtyard walls, or landscape mounds. Install a beautiful water feature in the east, such as a fountain, waterfall (must flow toward the house), or koi pond. This will activate the most benevolent energy in Period 8. If you are unable to activate this chart exterior on your site, then install a fountain indoors in the east corner. Place a tall armoire or bookcases in the north corner inside your home.

This house may have a Peach Blossom Sha formation if there is a road or real water coming from the direction of the south; they are notorious for bringing sexual scandals, bad romance, illicit affairs, unrequited love, and extramarital liaisons.

Activating the Interior Environment
Master Bedroom

There are two ways to enhance relationships, harmony, and prosperity in the bedroom—location and direction; the direction of the bed will give you the most powerful results. To enhance relationship/romance-luck, locate your bedroom in the north, northeast, or east as these sectors have good mountain stars with great energy. **Bed Directions**: For the most potent relationship-luck, place your headboard/bed to the north (1, 3, 4, or 9 Guas only), east (all Guas), or northeast (2, 6, 7, or 8 Guas only); these directions have good facing and mountain star combinations that will enhance prosperity and harmony in the house. Choose one of these facing directions coupled with your +70 (relationship) direction if possible. For example, if you are a 7 Gua, choose northeast; this has strong romance energy and it's your +70!

Take special caution regarding the southeast and south; do not use if at all possible. If the master bedroom is already located there, make sure that the bed direction is not either southeast or south. If so, reposition immediately; activating this direction indicates cancer, bankruptcy, divorce, sex disease, lawsuits, fires, and all types of disasters. Additionally, use a soft neutral color palette—whites, creams, taupes, and metal colors such as silver or bronze are good as well. Avoid fire colors (reds, purples, pinks, or oranges) in the artwork, rugs, bedding, or wall color. These precautions will ensure harmony in the household.

Home Office

For the best relationship harmony, business opportunities, and romance luck, face your desk/body to the north or southeast (1, 3, 4, or 9 Guas only), northeast (2, 6, 7, or 8 Guas only), or east (all Guas). The northeast direction is especially good for 7 Guas as this is their unique relationship direction (+70) and the 4 facing star known for its romance energy. For the 4 Life Gua, east is their +70 and extremely prosperous energy—activating this direction indicates a partner with wealth or meeting a partner through work or at the workplace.

Kitchen/Stove/Firemouth + Toilets

To activate harmony, prosperity, and great relationships, the best directions for the stove knobs (firemouth) are east, southeast, or northeast. You will have difficulties with relationships if there is a stove or toilet located in your +70 sector of the house. Select a toilet located in one of your negative sectors of the house (-90, -80, -70, or -60).

Best Doors in the House

For great relationships, opportunities, and prosperity—always use and activate good doors; the best ones for this chart are facing north, northeast, southeast, and east. If one of these directions is also your +70, you will be very lucky with relationships! A south-facing door, in this chart, is the worst of the worst; avoid if at all possible. It has the evil 5 facing star and it is quite powerful in the south. If this is your only door—in and out—you will need to cure it with lots of metal next to or directly on the door. Brass, bronze, copper, pewter, and stainless steel are some high-vibrating metals.

PERIOD 7

Northeast 2 (37.6° to 52.5°)

  Facing Name: **Gen**

Northeast 3 (52.6° to 67.5°)

  Facing Names: **Yin** and the **Tiger**

Chart: **Double Stars Meet at Facing**

  (Shuang Xing Dao Xiang)

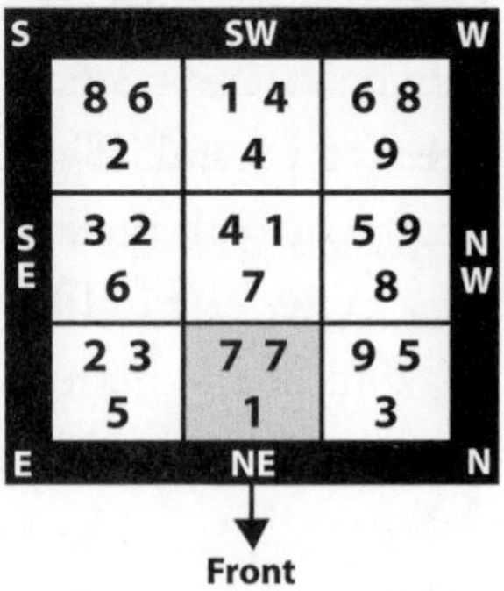

S		SW		W
	8 6 **2**	**1 4** **4**	**6 8** **9**	
S **E**	**3 2** **6**	**4 1** **7**	**5 9** **8**	**N** **W**
	2 3 **5**	**7 7** **1**	**9 5** **3**	
E		**NE**		**N**

↓

Front

Figure 48: Northeast 2 & 3

Romancing the Chart

This chart has one area to enhance romance, sexual energy, relationships, and love-luck; the southwest (1, 4 Peach Blossom combo). Additional romance energy combines together in the northwest in 2015; northeast in 2017; and the northwest again in 2018. Wealth, prosperity, and relationship harmony are energies automatically invoked by placing water in the west and a mountain in the south.

Activating the Exterior Environment

Needs Water in West, Mountain in South

This chart has two 7s at the front of the property known as the **Double Stars Meet at Facing** and was very auspicious until February 4, 2004, when it went from good to bad. Now, in the new Period 8, the chart must be extracted with a mountain in the south corner of your backyard. Emulate the energy of a real mountain by using large boulders (no sharp or jagged edges), basalt pillars, landscape mounds, or tiered/terraced garden beds. Install a gorgeous water feature in the west corner of your garden. This can be a swimming pool, koi pond, waterfall, or large stone fountain. If you are unable to activate this chart exterior on your site, then install a large indoor water fountain in the west corner. Place a tall armoire or bookcases in the south corner; these are good representations of an internal mountain.

For homes facing Northeast 2 there is a possible Eight Roads of Destruction formation if you have a road/driveway coming from or exiting the north and east directions and will activate extramarital/scandalous affairs, bankruptcy, and divorce. For Northeast 3 facing properties there is a possible Eight Killing Forces if there is a mountain in front of the property on the left-hand side; this formation will unsettle relationships in the house. The Northeast 3 facing homes may also have a Peach Blossom Sha formation if there a road or real water coming from the east direction; these formations are famous for bringing sexual scandals, bad romance, illicit affairs, unrequited love, and extramarital liaisons.

Activating the Interior Environment
Master Bedroom

There are two ways to enhance relationships, harmony, and prosperity in the bedroom—location and direction; the direction of the bed will give you the most powerful results. To enhance relationship/romance-luck, locate your bedroom in the south, southwest, or west as these sectors of the house have good mountain stars with great energy. **Bed Directions:** For the most potent relationship-luck, and for homes that face Northeast 2, place your headboard/bed to the south (1, 3, 4, or 9 Guas only), southwest, or west (2, 6, 7, or 8 Guas only). For homes that face Northeast 3, place your headboard/bed to the south, west, or southwest (all Guas). These directions have good facing and mountain star combinations that will enhance relationships, prosperity, and harmony in the house. Choose one of these facing directions coupled with your +70 (relationship) direction if possible. For example, if you are a 6 Gua, choose the northwest; this has strong romance energy and it's your +70.

Take special caution regarding the north and northwest; do not use if at all possible. If the master bedroom is already located there, make sure that the bed direction is not also north or northwest. If so, reposition immediately; activating this direction indicates cancer, bankruptcy, divorce, sex disease, lawsuits, fires, and all types of disasters. Additionally, use a soft neutral color palette—whites, creams, taupes, and metal colors such as silver or bronze are good as well. Avoid fire colors (reds, purples, pinks, or oranges) in the artwork, rugs, bedding, or wall color. These precautions will ensure harmony in the household.

Home Office

For the best relationship harmony, business opportunities, and romance-luck, face your desk/body to one of these great directions. For homes that face Northeast 2, place your desk/face to the south, (1, 3, 4, or 9 Guas only), southwest, west, or northwest (2, 6, 7, or 8 Guas only). For homes that face Northeast 3, place your desk/face to the south, southwest, west, or northwest (all Guas). The southwest direction is especially good for 6 Guas as this is their unique relationship direction (+70) and the 4 facing star known for its romance energy. For 8 Life Guas, the west is their +70 and extremely prosperous energy—activating this direction indicates a partner with wealth or meeting a partner through work or at the workplace.

Kitchen/Stove/Firemouth + Toilets

To activate harmony, prosperity, and great relationships, stove knobs (firemouth) should face southwest, west, or northwest. You will have difficulties with relationships if there is a stove or toilet located in your +70 sector of the house. Select a toilet located in one of your negative sectors of the house (-90, -80, -70, or -60).

Best Doors in the House

For great relationships, opportunities, and prosperity—always use and activate good doors; the best ones for this chart are facing to the south, southwest, west, and northwest. If one of these directions is also your +70, you will be very lucky with relationships! A north-facing door, in this chart, is the worst of the worst; avoid if at all possible. It has the evil 5 facing star and its energy attracts all types of disasters. If this is your only door—in and out—you will need to cure it with lots of metal next or directly on the door. Brass, bronze, copper, pewter, and stainless steel are some high-vibrating metals.

PERIOD 7

East 1 (67.6° to 82.5°)

   Facing Name: **Jia**

Chart: **Reverse Formation**

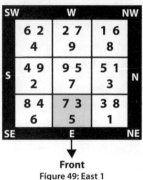

Figure 49: East 1

Romancing the Chart

This chart has three areas to enhance romance, sexual energy, relationships and love-luck. They are the south (4 mountain star), northwest (1, 6 Peach Blossom combo), and southeast (4 facing star). These areas become intensified when strong romance energy combines together in the northwest in 2015; west and southeast in 2016; and the northwest again in 2018. Wealth, prosperity, and relationship harmony are energies automatically invoked by placing water in the northeast and a mountain in the southeast.

Activating the Exterior Environment
Needs Water in Northeast, Mountain in Southeast

This property has an unusual chart called **Reverse Formation** that required specific activation to be considered auspicious. Any good energy of the chart expired as of February 4, 2004, when we entered into a new period/age. In order to extract the best energy of this chart, you will need to create a mountain in the southeast area of your front garden. A mountain can be large boulders (no sharp or jagged edges), landscape mounds, or courtyard walls. Any of these features will emulate the energy of a real mountain. Install a gorgeous water feature in the northeast area of your front garden. It can be a koi pond, fountain, or waterfall (the water must flow toward the house). If you are unable to activate the exterior of your site, then install a water fountain indoors in the northeast corner. Place a tall armoire or bookcases in the southeast corner. Generally speaking, east-facing properties produce those who excel in the world of academia.

There is a possible Eight Roads of Destruction formation if you have a road/driveway coming from or exiting the northeast direction. This formation will attract extramarital/scandalous affairs, bankruptcy, and divorce. This house also has a potential Goat Blade Water formation if there is a road/driveway or real water coming from or exiting certain areas of the east direction. You will know if you have this formation as it will indicate affairs, drug use, alcoholism, and gambling.

Activating the Interior Environment
Master Bedroom

There are two ways to enhance relationships, harmony, and prosperity in the bedroom—location and direction; the direction of the bed will give you the most powerful results. To enhance relationship/romance-luck, locate your bedroom in the northwest, south, or southeast as these sectors have good mountain stars with great energy. **Bed Directions:** For the most potent relationship-luck, place your headboard/bed to the northwest or south (all Guas), or southeast (1, 3, 4, or 9 Guas only). Choose one of these facing directions coupled with your +70 (relationship) direction if possible. For example, if you are a 2 Gua, choose the northwest direction as it has sexy romance energy and it's your +70 (relationship direction). If you are a 1 Gua, choose the south direction as it has sexy romance energy and it's your +70 (relationship direction).

Home Office

For the best relationship harmony, business opportunities, and romance-luck, face your desk/body to the northwest or south (all Guas), north or southeast (1, 3, 4, or 9 Guas only), or northeast (2, 6, 7, or 8 Guas only). The southeast direction is especially good for 3 Guas as this is their unique relationship direction (+70) and the 4 facing star known for its romance energy. For the 7 Life Guas, the northeast is their +70 and extremely prosperous energy—activating this direction indicates a partner with wealth or meeting a partner through work or at the workplace.

Kitchen/Stove/Firemouth + Toilet

To activate harmony, prosperity, and great relationships, the stove knobs (firemouth) should face northeast, south, southeast, or north. You will have difficulties with money if there is a stove or toilet located in your +90 sector of the house. Select a toilet located in one of your negative sectors of the house (-90, -80, -70, or -60).

Best Doors in the House

For great relationships, opportunities, and prosperity—always use and activate good doors; the best ones for this chart are facing to the north-west, south, southeast, north, and northeast. If one of these directions is also your +70, you will be very lucky with relationships.

PERIOD 7

East 2 (82.6° to 97.5°)

　　Facing Names: **Mao** and the **Rabbit**

East 3 (97.6° to 112.5°)

　　Facing Name: **Yi**

Chart: **Prosperous Sitting and Facing**
　　(Wang Shan Wang Shui)

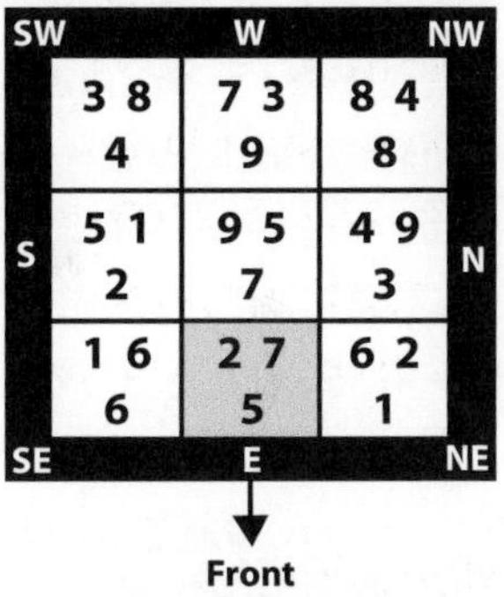

SW	W	NW
3 8 **4**	**7 3** **9**	**8 4** **8**
5 1 **2**	**9 5** **7**	**4 9** **3**
1 6 **6**	**2 7** **5**	**6 2** **1**

S (left) · N (right)

SE　　　　E　　　　NE

↓

Front
Figure 50: East 2 & 3

Romancing the Chart

This chart has two areas to enhance romance, sexual energy, relationships, and love-luck.

They are the southeast (1, 6 Peach Blossom combo) and the northwest (4 facing star). These areas become intensified when strong romance energy combines together in the northwest and east in 2015, the south-east in 2016, and the south and northwest in 2018. Wealth, prosperity, and relationship harmony are energies automatically invoked by placing water in the southwest and a mountain in the northwest.

Activating the Exterior Environment
Needs Water in Southwest, Mountain in Northwest

This house had the two 7s perfectly placed in Period 7 known as **Prosperous Sitting and Facing;** it was very auspicious until February 4, 2004, when it lost much of its vitality. Now the 8s are the ruling energy; to extract the auspicious energy of this chart—install a stunning water feature in the southwest corner of your backyard. This can be a fountain, koi pond, or waterfall. Create a mountain in the northwest corner of your back garden using boulders (no sharp or jagged edges), tiered or terraced beds, basalt pillars, or landscaping mounds. If you are unable to activate the exterior of your site, put a water fountain in the southwest corner indoors. Place a heavy armoire or tall bookcases in the northwest corner inside.

For homes facing East 2 there is a possible Eight Killings formation if there is a mountain in the southwest direction; this formation will unsettle relationships in the house. The East 2 facing homes may also have a Peach Blossom Sha formation if there is a road or real water coming from the north. The Peach Blossom Sha Road formations are famous for bringing sexual scandals, bad romance, illicit affairs, unrequited love, and extramarital liaisons.

For homes that face East 3, there is a possible Eight Roads of Destruction if there is a road/driveway coming from or exiting from the southeast direction; these formations will attract extramarital/scandalous affairs, bankruptcy, and divorce. This house also has a potential Goat Blade Water formation if there is a road/driveway or real water coming from or exiting certain areas of the northeast. You will know if you have this formation as it will indicate affairs, drug use, alcoholism, and gambling.

Activating the Interior Environment
Master Bedroom

There are two ways to enhance relationships, harmony, and prosperity in the bedroom—location and direction; the direction of the bed will give you the most powerful results. To enhance relationship-luck, locate your bedroom in the northwest or southeast as these locations have good mountain stars. **Bed Directions:** For the most potent relationship-luck, and for homes that face East 2, place your headboard/bed to the north or southeast (1, 3, 4, or 9 Guas only), or northwest (2, 6, 7, or 8 Guas only). For homes that face East 3, place your headboard/bed to the northwest, southeast (all Guas), or north (1, 3, 4, or 9 Guas only)—these directions all have good facing and mountain star combinations that will enhance prosperity, harmony, and great relationships. Choose one of these facing directions coupled with your +70 (relationship) direction if possible. For example, if you are a 3 Gua, choose the southeast; this has strong romance energy and it's your +70! If you are a 2 Gua, choose the northwest direction as it has sexy romance energy and it's your +70 (relationship direction).

Home Office

For the best relationship harmony, business opportunities, and romance-luck, face your desk/body to one of these great directions. For homes that face East 2, face to the northwest or southwest (2, 6, 7, or 8 Guas only), north, southeast, or south (1, 3, 4, or 9 Guas only). For homes that face East 3, face northwest, southwest, southeast, or south (all Guas), or north (1, 3, 4, or 9 Guas only) as they all have good facing stars. The northwest direction is especially good for 2 Guas as this is their unique relationship direction (+70) and the 4 facing star known for its romance energy. For the 6 Life Guas, southwest is their +70 and extremely prosperous energy—activating this direction indicates a partner with wealth or meeting a partner through work or at the workplace.

Kitchen/Stove/Firemouth + Toilets

To activate harmony, prosperity and great relationships, the best direction for the stove knobs (firemouth) should face to the south, north, northwest, or southwest. You will have difficulties with relationships if there is a stove or toilet located in your +70 sector of the house. Select a toilet located in one of your negative sectors of the house (-90, -80, -70, or -60).

Best Doors in the House

For great relationships, opportunities, and prosperity—always use and activate good doors; the best ones for this chart are facing to the southwest, north, northwest, southeast, and south. If one of these directions is also your +70, you will be very lucky with relationships!

PERIOD 7

Southeast 1 (112.6° to 127.5°)

Facing Names: **Chen** and the **Dragon**

Chart: **Prosperous Sitting and Facing**
(Wang Shan Wang Shui)

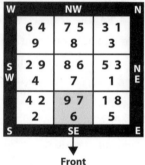

Front

Figure 51: Southeast 1

Romancing the Chart

This chart has two areas to enhance romance, sexual energy, relationships, and love-luck. They are the west (4 facing star) and the south (4 mountain star). Certain areas become intensified when strong romance energy combines together in the north, west, and southeast in 2016. Wealth, prosperity, and relationship harmony are energies automatically invoked by placing water in the east or north and a mountain in the east or southeast.

Activating the Exterior Environment

Needs Water in East or North, Mountain in Southeast

This house had the two 7s perfectly placed in Period 7 known as **Prosperous Sitting and Facing**; it was very auspicious until February 4, 2004, when it fell out of luck. Now the 8s are the ruling energy. To extract the auspicious energy of this chart, install a striking water feature in the east area of the front garden such as a fountain, koi pond, or waterfall (it must flow toward the house). An alternate location for water is north. Create a mountain in front by placing two stone statues of planters on either side of the front door. You may also create a mountain in the front yard by using boulders (no sharp or jagged edges), basalt pillars, or landscaping mounds—don't block or perfectly align it to the front door. If you are unable to activate the exterior of your site, then put a water fountain in the east corner indoors. Place two heavy stone statues on either side of the door indoors.

An Eight Killings formation is possible if there is a mountain bringing energy to the house from the north direction; this formation will unsettle relationships in the house. The house may also have a Peach Blossom Sha formation if there is road or real water coming from the West direction; these formations are famous for bringing sexual scandals, bad romance, illicit affairs, unrequited love, and extramarital liaisons.

Activating the Interior Environment
Master Bedroom

There are two ways to enhance relationships, harmony, and prosperity in the bedroom—location and direction; the direction of the bed will give you the most powerful results. To enhance romance, wealth, and relationships, place your headboard/bed to the west, east, or southeast (upstairs) as these sectors all have good mountain stars. **Bed Directions:** For the most potent relationship-luck and harmony, place your headboard/bed to the east or west (all Guas), or north (1, 3, 4, or 9 Guas only and those who are lawyers, judges, or litigators), as these directions have good facing and mountain star combinations that will enhance prosperity, harmony, and great relationships. Choose one of these facing directions coupled with your +70 (relationship) direction if possible. For example, if you are an 8 Gua, choose the west; this has strong romance energy and it's your +70! If you are a 4 Gua, choose the east direction as it has sexy romance energy and it's your +70 (relationship) direction.

Home Office

For the best relationship harmony, business opportunities, and romance-luck, face your desk/body the east, west, or southwest (all Guas), north (1, 3, 4, or 9 Guas only). The west direction is especially good for 8 Guas as this is their unique relationship direction (+70) and the 4 facing star known for its romance energy. For the 4 Life Guas, the east is their +70 and has extremely prosperous energy—activating this direction indicates a partner with wealth or meeting a partner through work or at the workplace.

Kitchen/Stove/Firemouth + Toilets

To activate harmony, prosperity, and great relationships, the stove knobs (firemouth) should face to the east, southwest, west, or north. You will have difficulties with relationships if there is a stove or toilet located in your +70 sector of the house. Select a toilet located in one of your negative sectors of the house (-90, -80, -70, or -60).

Best Doors in the House

For great relationships, opportunities and prosperity—always use and activate good doors; the best ones for this chart are facing to the east, west, north, and southwest. If one of these directions is also your +70, you will be very lucky with relationships! A northwest-facing door, in this chart, is the worst of the worst; avoid if at all possible. It has the evil 5 facing star and its energy attracts all types of disasters. If this is your only door—in and out—you will need to cure it with lots of metal next to or directly on the door. Brass, bronze, copper, pewter, and stainless steel are some high-vibrating metals.

PERIOD 7

Southeast 2 (127.6° to 142.5°)
    Facing Name: **Xun**

Southeast 3 (142.6° to 157.5°)
    Facing Names: **Su** and the **Snake**

Chart: **Pearl String** *(Lin Cu San Poon Gua)*

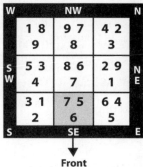

Figure 52: Southeast 2 & 3

Romancing the Chart

This chart has two areas to enhance romance, sexual energy, relationships and love-luck. They are the north (4 mountain star) and the east (4 facing star). Certain areas become intensified when strong romance energy combines together in the south, northwest, and east in 2015; south and east in 2018. Wealth, prosperity, and relationship harmony are energies automatically invoked by placing water in the west or south and a mountain in the northwest or west.

Activating the Exterior Environment

Needs Water in West or South, Mountain in Northwest or West

This was one of the best charts in Period 7, known as a **Pearl String**; as of February 4, 2004, however much of the energy and vitality has been greatly diminished. In order to extract the benevolent energy, you will need a mountain in the northwest or west. This can be accomplished by using boulders (no sharp or jagged edges), landscape mounds, or significant, solid fencing comprised of stucco, stone, or brick at the back. To increase the effect, add tiered or terraced garden beds against the fence. Install a lovely water feature in the west or south corner of your backyard such as a water-fall, swimming pool, or tall, heavy stone fountain. If you are unable to activate the exterior, then put an indoor fountain in the west or south corner of your space. Place heavy stone statues or planters on either side of your back door.

There is a possible Eight Roads of Destruction if the house faces Southeast 2 and if a road/driveway enters/exits the south or east; they are notorious for bringing extramarital/scandalous affairs, bankruptcy, and divorce.

An Eight Killings formation is possible for homes facing Southeast 3 if there is a mountain bringing energy to the house from the west direction; this formation will unsettle relationships in the house. Southeast 3 facing homes may also have a Peach Blossom Sha formation if there is road or real water coming from the south. This energy brings sexual scandals, bad romance, illicit affairs, unrequited love, and extramarital liaisons.

Activating the Interior Environment
Master Bedroom
There are two ways to enhance relationships, harmony, and prosperity in the bedroom—location and direction; the direction of the bed will give you the most powerful results. To enhance wealth-luck, locate your bedroom in the west, northwest, or east; these sectors all have good mountain stars. **Bed Directions:** For the most potent relationship-luck, and for homes that face Southeast 2, place your headboard/bed to the west (2, 6, 7, or 8 Guas only), or east (1, 3, 4, or 9 Guas only) as these directions have good facing and mountain star combinations. For homes that face Southeast 3, place your headboard/bed to the east or west, (all Guas) as these directions have good facing and mountain star combinations that will enhance relationships, prosperity, and harmony in the house. Choose one of these facing directions coupled with your +70 (relationship) direction if possible. For example, if you are an 8 Gua, choose west; this has strong romance energy and it's your +70! If you are a 4 Gua, choose the east direction as it has sexy romance energy and it's your +70 (relationship direction).

Home Office
For the best relationship harmony, business opportunities, and romance luck, face your desk/body to one of these great directions. For homes that face Southeast 2, place your desk/face to the west or northeast (2,

6, 7, or 8 Guas only), east or south (1, 3, 4, or 9 Guas only). For homes that face Southeast 3, place your desk/face to the east, west, northeast, or south (all Guas). East is especially good for 4 Guas as this is their unique relationship direction (+70) and the 4 facing star known for its romance energy. For the 8 Life Guas, south is their +70 and extremely prosperous energy—activating this direction indicates a partner with wealth or meeting a partner through work or at the workplace.

Kitchen/Stove/Firemouth + Toilets

To activate harmony, prosperity, and great relationships, stove knobs (fire-mouth) should face east, west, northeast, or south. You will have difficulties with relationships if there is a stove or toilet located in your +70 sector of the house. Select a toilet located in one of your negative sectors of the house (-90, -80, -70, or -60).

Best Doors in the House

For great relationships, opportunities and prosperity—always use and activate good doors; the best ones for this chart are facing to the west, northeast, east, and south. If one of these directions is also your +70, you will be very lucky with relationships! Unfortunately, the southeast-facing front door in this chart is the worst of the worst; avoid if at all possible. It has the evil 5 facing star and its energy attracts all types of disasters. If this is your only door—in and out—you will need to cure it with lots of metal next to or directly on the door. Brass, bronze, copper, pewter, and stainless steel are some high-vibrating metals.

Glossary of Terms

This book includes Feng Shui terms using both Wade-Giles and Pinyin; in several instances the glossary gives both spellings. The Chinese-to-English translations also include some in Mandarin and others in Cantonese.

24 Mountains: This is the single most important ring on the Chinese Luo Pan/compass; all homes and buildings will be one of these facing directions. Each of the eight directions has three divisions comprising a total of 24.

Age of 8: Also known as Period 8; a 20-year period of time that affects the luck of man and influences the world with its energy. These 20-year periods were first tracked and recorded by the ancient Chinese in about 2500 BCE. They observed that every 180 years, the planets in our solar system line up. It was further noted that every 20 years the Milky Way shifts and influences the events of humanity. These periods run from 1 to 9 every 20 years and then start all over again. The current Age of 8 began February 4, 2004. This is part of the Flying Star system (Xuan Kong Fei Xing).

Auspicious: The Chinese favor the term "auspicious," meaning something is lucky, and good events will ensue.

Ba Gua: Also spelled as Pa Kua. An octagonal arrangement of the eight trigrams or Guas of Taoist mysticism; used as a basic tool of energy assessment in Feng Shui.

Ba Gua Mirror: This mirror (flat, concave, or convex) is surrounded by the eight trigrams and used to deflect negative energy or something in view that is not desirable. This Ba Gua is identified as having three solid lines at the top known as the Chien/Qian trigram or Gua.

Bankruptcy: The inability to pay debts; insolvency; losing all your wealth or property.

Big Dipper Casting Golden Light: Known as *Jin Guang Dou Lin Jing* in Chinese and also spelled as *Kam Kwong Dou Lam King*. This style of Eight Mansions is used in this book; it is also called *Golden Star Classic*.

Black Hat Sect: A new school of Feng Shui created in the 1980s. It was brought to the Western world by Professor Thomas Lin Yun, a Buddhist monk of the Black Hat Order of Tibetan Buddhism. Although not considered an authentic system of Feng Shui, Black Hat is the most recognized style in the world except in Asian countries, which are most familiar with traditional schools of Feng Shui.

Black Turtle: The back of your property, one of the Celestial Animals.

Bright Hall: This area is an open space near the front door (interior and exterior) where chi can collect; in Chinese known as the Ming Tang.

Broken Mountain: This is a term used in Feng Shui to depict a mountain that has been excavated, scarred, or destroyed in any fashion. If such a mountain is in view of a home site or business, it is considered extremely inauspicious.

Canal: An artificial waterway for boats or irrigation. In Feng Shui, canals are considered rivers; they can be particularly ruinous if they run behind your home.

Cardinal Directions: Points of geographic orientation—north, south, east, and west. The specific and exact points of these directions are 0/360, north; 90 degrees, east; 180 degrees, south; and 270 degrees, west.

Chai: House, also spelled *Zhai*.

Chen: One of the eight trigrams of the Ba Gua. It represents the eldest son, thunder, and spring. In the Later Heaven arrangement of the Ba Gua, the Chen trigram is located in the east.

Chueh Ming: In the Eight Mansions system, this represents total loss, divorce, and bankruptcy. According to Master Yap's numeric representation, it is -90.

Chi: The vital life-force energy of the universe and everything in it; sometimes chi is referred to as "cosmic breath." It is also spelled *ch'i* or *qi* and is pronounced *chee*.

Chien: One of the eight trigrams of the Ba Gua, also spelled as *Qian*. It represents the father, the heavens, and late autumn. In the Later Heaven arrangement of the Ba Gua, the Chien trigram is located in the northwest.

Chinese Lunar Calendar: A calendar based on the moon cycles.

Chinese Solar Calendar: A calendar based on the rotation of the earth around the sun.

Chinese Zodiac: A system that relates each year to an animal and its reputed attributes, according to a 12-year mathematical cycle. It remains popular in several East Asian countries, such as China, Vietnam, Korea, and Japan.

Ching Dynasty: The last ruling dynasty of China; lasted between 1644 and 1912.

Classical Feng Shui: Also known as traditional Feng Shui. It is the authentic, genuine Feng Shui that has been developed and applied for hundreds, even thousands, of years in Asia. Sophisticated forms are practiced in Hong Kong, Taiwan, Malaysia, and Singapore. Classical Feng Shui is just being introduced and practiced in Western countries, and has not reached mainstream status. The traditional systems of Feng Shui are the *San He*, meaning "three combinations," and *San Yuan* or "three cycles." All techniques, methods, and formulas will be under one or the other. Feng Shui Masters and practitioners will use both systems as one comprehensive body of knowledge.

Combination of 10: A wealth-producing chart in the Flying Star system where the stars add to ten in all nine palaces. In Chinese it is translated as *He Shih Chu*.

Compass, Chinese: *See* Luo Pan.

Cosmic Trinity: Known in Chinese as *Tien-Di-Ren*; this is the three categories of luck, specifically Heaven Luck, Man Luck, and Earth Luck. The Chinese believe Heaven Luck is fixed, however, humans have control over Feng Shui (Earth Luck), and personal effort (Man Luck).

Double Stars Meet at Facing: *Shuang Xing Dao Xiang* in Chinese means that two stars in the Flying Star system are in the front of the house or building.

Double Stars Meet at Sitting: *Shuang Xing Dao Zuo* in Chinese means that two stars in the Flying Star system are at the back of the house or building.

Direction: One of the most important aspects of determining the energy of a site or structure is it's directional orientation.

Dragon: In Feng Shui, a dragon is a mountain. Dragon is a term also used for something powerful or curving, as in the mythical body of a dragon. It can apply to land and water. The Chinese so revere the dragon that it is used in multiple applications and meanings.

Drain: An opening in the ground, usually covered with a grate, which takes water away from an area. Uncovered drains are rectangular and sometimes seen in subdivisions. In Feng Shui, these are considered *water exits* and can bring wealth or disaster. A drain near a main door of a home or business is always bad. Only exposed drains are important in Feng Shui; underground and invisible formations do not count.

Early Heaven Ba Gua: This is the first arrangement of the eight trigrams; known as the *Ho Tien* or *Fu Xi* Ba Gua in Chinese. It can be easily recognized as the Chien trigram (three solid lines) and is always placed on the top. This is the arrangement used in Ba Gua mirrors to deter Sha Chi.

Earth Luck: One of the three categories of luck that humans can experience; your luck will increase by using Feng Shui, also known as Earth Luck. The Chinese word for "earth" is *Di*.

East Life Group: In the Eight Mansions system, people are divided into the East or West group. The 1, 3, 4, and 9 Life Guas are part of the East Life Group.

Eight House: This is another name for the Eight Mansions; in Chinese it is *Pa Chai* or *Ba Zhai*.

Eight House Bright Mirror: In Chinese *Pa Chai Ming Jing*, is one of the eight different styles of the Eight Mansions system. This style uses the sitting direction of the house instead of the facing.

Eight Life Aspirations: Also known as the *Eight Life Stations*, these stations correspond to a point on the Ba Gua and an aspect of life—south, fame; southwest, marriage; southeast, wealth; north, career; and so forth. This is the work of Black Hat Sect founder Lin Yun. Eight Life Stations is not found in classic texts or part of the genuine Feng Shui of ancient practice and principles. It is neither an aspect of the Eight Mansions system nor even a derivative of that system. Some popular Feng Shui books that promote Classical Feng Shui also include the Eight Life Aspirations, which only adds to the confusion.

Eight Killing Forces: A formation where the door direction and the energy of a nearby mountain are out of harmony; they are serious and will bring disaster to the household.

Eight Roads of Destruction: Also known as the Eight Roads to Hell, this formation is based on the egress of a road or driveway from a property in correlation to the front door. Even though the road or driveway is considered virtual water, the direction it exits is called a "water exit." This unlucky formation can have disastrous results, so remedial measures must be taken.

Energy: The Chinese call energy *chi* (also spelled *qi*) and pronounced *chee*. Our entire universe is energy; there are many types of chi—human, environmental, and heaven (the solar system).

Esoteric: Knowledge that is available only to a narrow circle of enlightened or initiated people or a specially educated group. Feng Shui is part of Chinese metaphysics and is considered esoteric.

External Environment: This covers the terrain and topography, including mountains, water, and other natural formations. It also encompasses man-made features, such as roads, pools, retaining walls, highways, poles, drains, washes, tall buildings, stop signs, fire hydrants, and other structures.

Facing Direction: The front side of the home or building, generally where the front or main door is located and faces the street.

Facing Star: Also known as the water star, this star is located in the upper right-hand corner of a Flying Star chart in all nine palaces or sectors. The facing star is in charge of wealth-luck.

Feng: The Chinese word for wind; pronounced "fung," although "foong" is a more accurate sound.

Feng Shui: Known as *Kan Yu* (translated as "the way of heaven and earth") until about a hundred years ago, the Chinese system of maximizing the accumulation of beneficial chi improves the quality of life and luck of the occupants of a particular building or location. The literal translation is "wind and water"; however, in Classical Feng Shui wind means "direction" and water means "energy." Pronounced "fung shway."

Feng Shui Master: One who has mastered the skills of Classical Feng Shui and/or has been declared as such by his or her teacher, or both. It is also said that a practitioner becomes a Master when his or her clients refer to them as master. Most Feng Shui Masters from classic traditions will belong to a lineage of their teachers. This is also known as a "lineage carrier," meaning the Master carries on the teachings and practices of his or her education. A Feng Shui Master generally oversees his or her own school and students, too.

Feng Shui Schools: There are two major schools (not physical locations, rather they are systems) of Classical Feng Shui; San He and San Yuan; hundreds of formulas, techniques, and systems serve as subsets of either school. If you practice Classical Feng Shui, you use the San He and the San Yuan systems as one extensive body of knowledge.

Flying Stars: Known as *Xuan Kong Fei Xing* in Chinese, which means "mysterious void" or "the subtle mysteries of time and space." It is a popular Feng Shui system that is superior in addressing the time aspect of energy. Refer to chapter 6 for additional information on this vast system.

Fu Wie: The direction and location for stability as it applies to the Eight Mansions system. According to Master Yap's numeric representation, it is the +60.

Fu Xi: A sage, king, and shaman who was responsible for discovering and arranging the Early Heaven Ba Gua.

Gen: One of the eight trigrams of the Ba Gua also spelled as *Ken*. It represents the youngest son, the mountain, and early spring. In the Later Heaven arrangement of the Ba Gua, the Gen trigram is located in the northeast.

Goat Blade: These formations relate to the door direction being in conflict with water placement or road direction. It will activate affairs, drug use, gambling, and adultery.

Golden Star Classic: Translates as *Kam Kwong Dou Lam King* in Chinese—also spelled as *Jin Guang Dou Lin Jing*. It is also known as the Big Dipper Casting Golden Light, the style of Eight Mansions used in this book.

Great Cycle: Lasts for 180 years; *see* Age of 8.

Green Dragon: A Celestial Animal that represents the left side of your property as you look out the front door.

Gua: Alternatively spelled *Kua* and also known as a trigram. It represents one of eight Guas of the Ba Gua, defined by a combination of three solid or broken lines.

Gua Number: Also referred to as *Ming Gua* (nothing to do with the Ming Dynasty). To determine your personal Life Gua number, use your birthday. See chapter 3 for specific instructions.

Heaven Luck: One of the three categories of luck that humans can experience. The Chinese believe every human has a destiny and a fate determined by the heavens (tien). This category cannot be changed and is considered *fixed*. *See* Tien-Di-Ren.

High-Rise Building: In the external environment, high-rise buildings and skyscrapers function as *virtual* or *urban mountains*.

Ho Hai: Also known as *Wo Hai*. Part of the Eight Mansions system and can bring mishaps—nothing goes smoothly. According to Master Yap's numeric representation, this is the -60.

Huo: Chinese for "fire." Also sometimes romanized as *ho*.

I Ching: A philosophical and divinatory book based on the 64 hexagrams of Taoist mysticism. It is also known as the *Classic of Changes* or *Book of Changes*.

Incoming Dragon: The energy of a mountain that comes directly to your home or building. If a mountain range is nearby, the highest peak is measured with a Luo Pan because it has the most powerful energy. An entire science is based on determining the effects of mountain energy on any given site. In Feng Shui, mountains and dragons are used interchangeably.

Interior Environment: The interior environment encompasses anything that falls within the walls of a structure, including kitchen, staircase, master bedroom, fireplaces, bathrooms, hallways, dining room, bedrooms, appliances, furniture, and so on.

Intercardinal Directions: Northwest, southwest, northeast, and southeast.

Kan: One of the eight trigrams. It represents the middle son, the moon, and mid-winter. In the Later Heaven Arrangement of the Ba Gua, it is located in the north.

Kun: One of the eight trigrams. It represents the mother, the earth, and late summer. In the Later Heaven Arrangement of the Ba Gua, it is located in the southwest.

Later Heaven Ba Gua: The second arrangement of the trigrams known as the *Wen Wang* or *Xien Tien* Ba Gua. This is used extensively in the application of Classical Feng Shui.

Li: One of the eight trigrams. It represents the middle daughter, fire, and full summer. In the Later Heaven Arrangement of the Ba Gua, it is located in the south.

Life Gua Number: A number assigned to people, based on birthday and gender, in the Eight Mansions system (Ba Zhai).

Life Gua Personalities™: A description of personality types based on the Life Gua number in the Eight Mansion system expanded on and trademarked by the author and first seen in *Classical Feng Shui for Wealth and Abundance.*

The Life Gua-Zodiac Personalities™: A combination of the Life Gua and the animal year of birth or the Chinese Zodiac, trademarked by the author.

Liu Sha: In the Eight Mansions system, it also known as the *Six Killings* direction and can bring backstabbing, affairs, and lawsuits. According to Master Yap's numeric representation, it is the -80.

Location: A particular place or position, differing from the concept of *direction*. For example, your living room might be located on the south side of your home (location), but your desk faces north (direction).

Lunar Calendar: A calendar based on the cycles of the moon.

Lung: The Chinese word for "dragon."

Luo Pan: The Luo Pan is the quintessential tool of a Feng Shui practitioner. It is a compass that contains four to 40 concentric rings of information. The most popular model is approximately ten inches across, square, and often constructed of fine woods. The circle part of the Luo Pan is made of brass and rotates to align with the compass itself, which is located in the center. There are three major types of Luo Pans—the *San Yuan* Luo Pan, the *San He* Luo Pan, and the *Chung He* Luo Pan (also known as *Zong He* or *Zhung He*), which is a combination of the first two. Though Luo Pans have similar basic components, Feng Shui Masters do customize their own with secret information for them and their students.

Luo Shu: A square that contains nine palaces or cells with a number in each; it adds to 15 in any direction. The Luo Shu is also known as the "Magic Square of 15."

Main Door: This is usually the front door of the home or business. If the occupants always enter the residence from the garage, this may also be considered a main door.

Man Luck: One of the three categories of luck a person can experience. This area of fortune is mutable and defined by individual effort, such as hard work, study, education, experience, and good deeds. The Chinese word for person is *ren*. *See* Tien-Di-Ren.

Metal Cures: The best metals are bronze, copper, brass, pewter, stainless steel and wrought iron to weaken the 2 or 5 star.

Mountains: Includes real mountains and virtual mountains, such as tall buildings, landscape mounds, retaining walls, huge boulders, or any object of mass in the environment. *See* Dragon.

Nien Yen: This is the incorrect spelling of the *Yen Nien* (+70) in the Eight Mansions system; you will see this mistake in many Feng Shui books.

Online Dating: Also called Internet dating, a dating system that allows individuals to make contact and communicate with each other over the Internet, usually with the objective of developing a friendly, romantic, or sexual relationship.

Pa Sha Hwang Chuen: The Chinese translation of the Eight Killing Forces.

Parent String Formation: Known in Chinese as *Fu Mu San Poon Gua* and sometimes referred to as the *Three Combinations*, these are special wealth-producing Flying Star charts. This formation of energy applies to certain structures—which are activated by a mountain in the front of the property and water in the back—on intercardinal directions. They only last for 20 years and are unlucky if not activated properly.

Pearl String Formation: Known in Chinese as *Lin Cu San Poon Gua* and sometimes referred to as the *Continuous Bead Formations,* these are special wealth-producing Flying Star charts that only show up in homes that face an intercardinal direction. Though excellent energy for prosperity, this formation only lasts for 20 years and is unlucky if not activated properly.

Peach Blossom Sha: This is where there is improperly placed water in relation to the main door; it will ignite affairs, sex scandals, and adultery.

Peach Blossom Technique: This is a technique in which flowers in a vase are placed in a specific direction (based on your animal year of birth) to invite a new lover, a marriage proposal, or increase attractiveness.

Peach Blossom Combinations: These are special combination of stars that indicate romance, love, and sexual activity—the strongest is the 4, 1 combination.

Period: The 20-year increment of the Flying Star system; currently the world is in Period 8. Nine periods comprise a megacycle of 180 years.

Period 7: Part of the Flying Star system; Period 7 began February 4, 1984 and ended February 3, 2004. Each period is 20 years in duration.

Period 8: Part of the Flying Star system; Period 8 began February 4, 2004, and will end on February 3, 2024. Each period is 20 years in duration.

Precious and Jewel Line (PJL): Also known as "Gold Dragons," these are specific degrees that brings precious assets and jewels, wealth-luck, and nobility to your life. There are only 48 of these degrees out of 360.

Prosperous Sitting and Facing: Known in Chinese as *Wang Shan Wang Shui*; a Flying Star chart that means "good for people, good for money." These charts have the perfect placement of the current prosperous stars—the facing star is at the facing (good for money), and the mountain star is at the sitting (good for people).

Red Phoenix: A Celestial Animal that represents the front edge of your property; also known as "Vermillion Bird."

Retaining Walls: High walls, at least three to six feet in height, which can be used to secure a site and prevent loss of energy. The more dynamic the landscape, the more walls are needed to protect sloping areas or sharp drop-offs.

Road: A route, path, or open way for vehicles. In Feng Shui, roads are "rivers" of energy, or chi, and play a huge part in analyzing a site because energy is powerful. These virtual or urban rivers are calculated when assessing, designing, enhancing, or implementing countermeasures or enhancements for a site.

San He: Also known as *San Hup*. One of the two major schools of study in Classical Feng Shui—the other is San Yuan. The San He system, excellent for tapping natural landforms, primarily addresses large-scale projects, land plots, urban developments, city planning, and master-planned communities. The system is extensive and has several practical techniques for new and existing residential spaces as well. When assessing and altering a site or a structure, San He and San Yuan can be blended for maximum results.

San Yuan: One of the two major schools of Classical Feng Shui. The Flying Stars is part of this system; it excels in techniques of timing.

Sector: An area inside or outside a building: south sector, north sector, and so on.

Sha Chi: Also known as *Shar Chi*. Extremely negative energy; killing chi.

Shan: The Chinese word for "mountain."

Sheng Chi: Part of the Eight Mansions system. It can bring life-generating energy, wealth, and opportunities. Using Master Yap's numeric representation, this is the +90.

Shui: The Chinese word for "water"; pronounced "shway."

Sitting: In Feng Shui it refers to the back of the house, as if the structure is sitting in a chair on the land or property. It is the heavy part of the house; also consider a mountain.

Sitting Star: Also known as the Mountain Star in the Flying Star system. It influences people-luck, such as fertility, employees, and health.

Solar Calendar: A calendar based on the movements of the sun.

Tantric Sex: Neotantra, or tantric sex, is the modern, Western variation of tantra. This includes both the New Age and modern Western interpretations of traditional Indian and Buddhist tantra. Some of its proponents refer to ancient and traditional texts and principles; many others use tantra as a catch-all phrase for "sacred sexuality," and may incorporate unorthodox practices. In addition, not all of the elements of Indian tantra are used in neotantric practices.

Tai Chi: The black and white symbol of Taoist philosophy; a sphere with two semi-circles intertwined showing the division of yin and yang energy. An alternate spelling is *Taiji*.

Tao: Also known as "The Way," it is the core of Taoism (pronounced with a D sound).

Tapping the Energy or Chi: A technique that invites the available energy from the external environment to support the occupants of a structure.

Thin Slicing: A term used in psychology and philosophy to describe the ability to find patterns in events based only on "thin slices," or narrow windows, of experience. The term seems to have been coined in 1992 by Nalini Ambady and Robert Rosenthal in a paper in the *Psychological Bulletin*. The term and concept is also featured in *Blink* by Malcolm Gladwell.

Three Harmony Doorways: A technique that uses door direction and a pathway or driveway to bring harmony and wealth to a house.

Tien Yi: Part of the Eight Mansion system. It can bring excellent health and wealth. In Chinese it means "heavenly doctor" or the "doctor from heaven watches over you." Using Master Yap's numeric representation, it is the +80.

Tilting a Door: A time-honored tradition used by Feng Shui Masters and practitioners to change the degree of a door and the energy of a space. The doorframe and threshold are re-angled toward the desired degree. When the door is re-hung, it is tilted on a different degree.

Time Star: Also known as the Base Star in the Flying Star system; it is the single star below the mountain and facing star of the chart.

Tipping Point: The moment a product or idea spreads like wildfire. A phrase coined by Malcolm Gladwell in his book *The Tipping Point: How Little Things Can Make a Big Difference.*

T-Juncture: When two roads meet perpendicularly to create a T. The formation is toxic when a home or business sits at the top and center of that T.

Three-Door Harmony: A San He formula that brings nobility and harmony to a household. The energy (both yin and yang) is tapped by bringing the door and a pathway, driveway, or road into perfect harmony.

Traditional Feng Shui: Another term for Classical Chinese Feng Shui.

Tui: Also spelled *Dui*. One of the eight trigrams that represents the youngest daughter, the lake, and mid-fall. In the Later Heaven Ba Gua it is located in the west.

Twelve Animals: Rat, Ox, Tiger, Rabbit, Dragon, Snake, Horse, Goat, Monkey, Rooster, Dog, and Pig; part of the Chinese Zodiac and used extensively in Classical Feng Shui and Chinese Astrology.

Virtual Mountains: High-rise structures, such as apartments, office buildings, and skyscrapers, are considered virtual or urban mountains and will influence the energy of nearby structures accordingly.

Virtual Water: Roads, sidewalks, driveways, low ground, highways, and other similar formations that are purveyors of chi.

Water: In Feng Shui, water is the secret to enhancing wealth, prosperity, longevity, nobility, and relationships. The Chinese word, *shui*, represents energy and life force. Water, according to Feng Shui, is the most powerful element on the planet.

Water Exits: The location or direction where water leaves a site. Water exits are used in Feng Shui to bring good results, but if they are not placed well, disaster can ensue.

Water Star: Also called the Facing Star in the Flying Star system; it is in charge of wealth-luck.

West Life Group: In the Eight Mansions system, people are divided into the East or West group. The 2, 6, 7, and 8 Life Guas are part of the West Life Group.

Western Feng Shui: In addition to the Black Hat Sect, other schools cropped up that incorporated the principles, but not the rituals, associated with Lin-Yun's followers. As the Masters of Classical Feng Shui started to teach around the world, some of the most well-acclaimed instructors and authors of Western Feng Shui began to learn Classical Feng Shui. Unwilling to give up the Western-style Feng Shui that made them famous, they mixed the old with the new, thereby adding to the confusion over authentic Feng Shui. More than half of the Feng Shui books written about the subject include a hodgepodge of both theories.

White Tiger: The celestial animal that represents the right-hand side of your property as you look out your front door.

Wu Gwei: Part of the Eight Mansions system that can attract lawsuits, bad romance, and betrayals. Using Master Yap's numeric representation, it is the -70. This is also known as the Five Ghosts direction.

Wu Xing: Also known as the five elements of Feng Shui: Wood, Fire, Earth, Metal, and Water.

Yang: Alive, active and moving energy; considered the male energy of the Yin-Yang symbol.

Yang Feng Shui: Feng Shui was first practiced for the selection of a perfect gravesite, or what is commonly known by the Chinese as Yin Feng Shui—Feng Shui for the dead. Later, techniques were developed to increase luck and opportunities for houses of the living.

Yellow Spring: A term used by the Chinese to describe hell or the underworld.

Yen Nien: Part of the Eight Mansions system that can bring longevity, good relationships, and love. Using Master Yap's numeric representation, it is the +70. It is a common mistake to spell this term as Nen Yien.

Yin: Female energy, passive, and dead; the perfect complement is yang energy.

Xun: One of the eight trigrams of the Ba Gua, also spelled *Sun*. It represents the eldest daughter, the wind, and early summer. In the Later Heaven arrangement of the Ba Gua, the Xun trigram is located in the southeast.

Appendix

See chart on next page.

Life Gua Determination if You Were Born on February 3, 4, or 5
Using dates/times based on Universal Time—the time at the Greenwich Meridian—to avoid the confusion that can be caused by different time zones and the International Date Line.

Animal	Year	Feb.	Time	Animal	Year	Feb.	Time	Animal	Year	Feb.	Time
Rooster	1933	4	2:10 p	Dragon	1964	5	3:05 a	Pig	1995	4	3:14 p
Dog	1934	4	8:04 p	Snake	1965	4	8:46 a	Rat	1996	4	9:08 p
Pig	1935	5	1:49 a	Horse	1966	4	2:38 p	Ox	1997	4	3:04 a
Rat	1936	5	7:30 a	Goat	1967	4	8:31 p	Tiger	1998	4	8:53 a
Ox	1937	4	1:26 p	Monkey	1968	5	2:08 a	Rabbit	1999	4	2:42 p
Tiger	1938	4	7:15 p	Rooster	1969	4	7:59 a	Dragon	2000	4	8:32 p
Rabbit	1939	5	1:11 a	Dog	1970	4	1:46 p	Snake	2001	4	2:20 a
Dragon	1940	5	7:08 a	Pig	1971	4	7:26 p	Horse	2002	4	8:08 a
Snake	1941	4	12:50 p	Rat	1972	5	1:20 a	Goat	2003	4	1:57 p
Horse	1942	4	6:49 p	Ox	1973	4	7:04 a	Monkey	2004	4	7:46 p
Goat	1943	5	12:41 a	Tiger	1974	4	1:00 p	Rooster	2005	4	1:34 a
Monkey	1944	5	6:23 a	Rabbit	1975	4	6:59 p	Dog	2006	4	7:25 a
Rooster	1945	4	12:20 p	Dragon	1976	5	12:40 a	Pig	2007	4	1:14 p
Dog	1946	4	6:05 p	Snake	1977	4	6:34 a	Rat	2008	4	7:03 p
Pig	1947	4	11:55 p	Horse	1978	4	12:27 p	Ox	2009	4	12:52 a
Rat	1948	5	5:43 a	Goat	1979	4	6:13 p	Tiger	2010	4	6:42 a
Ox	1949	4	11:23 a	Monkey	1980	5	12:10 a	Rabbit	2011	4	12:32 p
Tiger	1950	4	5:21 p	Rooster	1981	4	5:56 a	Dragon	2012	4	6:40 p
Rabbit	1951	4	11:14 p	Dog	1982	4	11:46 a	Snake	2013	4	12:24 a
Dragon	1952	5	4:54 a	Pig	1983	4	5:40 p	Horse	2014	4	6:21 a
Snake	1953	4	10:46 a	Rat	1984	4	11:19 p	Goat	2015	4	12:09 p
Horse	1954	4	4:31 p	Ox	1985	4	5:12 a	Monkey	2016	4	6:00 p
Goat	1955	4	10:18 p	Tiger	1986	4	11:09 a	Rooster	2017	3	11:49 p
Monkey	1956	5	4:13 a	Rabbit	1987	4	4:52 p	Dog	2018	4	5:38 a
Rooster	1957	4	9:55 a	Dragon	1988	4	10:43 p	Pig	2019	4	11:28 a
Dog	1958	4	3:50 p	Snake	1989	4	4:27 a	Rat	2020	4	5:18 p
Pig	1959	4	9:43 p	Horse	1990	4	10:15 a	Ox	2021	3	11:08 p
Rat	1960	5	3:23 a	Goat	1991	4	4:08 p	Tiger	2022	4	4:58 a
Ox	1961	4	9:23 a	Monkey	1992	4	9:48 p	Rabbit	2023	4	10:47 a
Tiger	1962	4	3:18 p	Rooster	1993	4	3:38 a	Dragon	2024	4	4:37 p
Rabbit	1963	4	9:08 p	Dog	1994	4	9:31 a	Snake	2025	3	10:27 p

....

Appendix Chart: Life Gua Determination.

Bibliography

(no author). "Census Bureau Reports 55 Percent Have Married One Time" from www.census.gov/newsroom/releases/archives/marital _status_living_arrangements/cb11-90.html.

Carter, Niyaso. "What is Tantra?" from www.sacredloving.net.

Chia, Mantak. "Integrating Immortality: Sexual Essence, Inner Child and the Immortal Spirit Body" from mantakchia.com /immortal-selfs-9-secrets-of-taoist-inner-alchemy.

Gladwell, Malcolm. *Blink: The Power of Thinking Without Thinking*. New York: Little, Brown and Company, 2005.

Huang, Alfred. *The Numerology of the I Ching: A Sourcebook of Symbols, Structures, and Traditional Wisdom*. Rochester, VT: Inner Traditions, 2000.

Too, Lillian. *Chinese Astrology for Romance and Relationships*. Kuala Lumpur: Konsep Books, 1996.

Feng Shui Resources

Recommended Reading

Allen, Patricia, and Sandra Harmon. *Getting to "I Do": The Secret to Doing Relationships Right.* New York: Avon Books, 1995.

Argoy, Sherry. *Why Men Love Bitches: From Doormat to Dreamgirl—A Woman's Guide to Holding Her Own in a Relationship.* Avon, MA: Adams Media, 2002.

———. *Why Men Marry Bitches: A Woman's Guide to Winning Her Man's Heart.* New York: Simon and Schuster, 2006.

Dennis, Denise Liotta. *Classical Feng Shui for Wealth and Abundance: Activating Ancient Wisdom for a Rich and Prosperous Life.* Woodbury, MN: Llewellyn Worldwide, 2013.

Fein, Ellen, and Sherrie Schneidee. *All the Rules: Time-Tested Secrets for Capturing the Heart of Mr. Right.* New York: Grand Central Publishing, 2007.

Fein, Ellen, and Sherrie Schneidee. *Not Your Mother's Rules: The New Secrets for Dating (The Rules)*. New York: Grand Central Publishing, 2013.

———. *The New Rules: the Dating Do's and Don'ts for the Digital Generation*. London: Piatkus Books, 2013.

———. *The Rules for Online Dating: Capturing the Heart of Mr. Right in Cyberspace*. New York: Gallery Books, 2002.

———. *The Rules I*. New York: Grand Central Publishing, 1997.

Gray, John. *Men Are from Mars, Women Are from Venus: The Classic Guide to Understanding the Opposite Sex*. New York: Harper, 2012.

———. *Venus on Fire, Mars on Ice: Hormonal Balance—The Key to Life, Love and Energy*. Salt Lake City: Mind Publishing, May, 2010.

Pease, Barbara, and Allan Pease. *Why Men Don't Have a Clue and Women Always Need More Shoes: The Ultimate Guide to the Opposite Sex*. New York: Harmony, 2004.

Sterling, A. Justin. *What Really Works with Men: Solve 95% of Your Relationship Problems (And Cope With the Rest)*. New York: Time Warner International, 1992.

Classical Feng Shui Classes

If you're interested in learning Classical Feng Shui, there are a number of excellent Feng Shui Masters around the world that offer classes on one or more of the Five Chinese metaphysical arts. You can receive training on Classical Feng Shui (*San He* and *San Yuan*), Face Reading (*Mian Xiang*) and Chinese Astrology (*Ba Zi* also known as *Four Pillars of Destiny* and *Zi Wei Dou Shu*). For an extensive list refer to *Classical Feng Shui for Wealth and Abundance: Activating Ancient Wisdom for a Rich and Prosperous Life.*

The American College of Classical Feng Shui [13]
Dragon Gate Feng Shui, LLC Consulting

Master Denise Liotta Dennis

Scottsdale, Arizona USA

Phone: 480-241-5211

email: denise@dragongatefengshui.com

Web: www.dragongatefengshui.com

Dragon Gate Feng Shui, LLC offers books, consulting services (residential and commercial), specializes in master-planned communities, mixed-use developments, new-home builds and urban/village development; free presentations and training classes. ACCFS has 36 different modules that compromise the Foundation Series, Professional Series, and Mastery Series. Live classes are conducted every month by Feng Shui Masters in Scottsdale, Arizona (Master Denise Liotta Dennis), Phoenix, Arizona and Denver, Colorado (Katherine Gould), Los Angeles (Jennifer Bonetto), Chicago, Phoenix (Peg Burton), and New York (Kelsey Groetken).

---

13. The American College of Classical Feng Shui (ACCFS) is the "training arm" of Dragon Gate Feng Shui, LLC.

Index

24 Mountain Ring, 30

180-year cycle, 159

A

Advanced Eight Mansions, 63, 64, 166

B

Ba Gua, 2, 15, 16, 19, 23, 26–28, 30, 282–286, 288–290, 297, 299

Ba Zhai, 56, 286, 290

Beams, 48

Black Hat Sect Feng Shui, 31

C

Chinese Metaphysics, 16, 24, 287

Combination of Ten, 3, 178, 179, 190, 191, 215, 216, 237, 259, 260

Compass, 2, 8, 28–31, 61, 158, 160, 161, 167, 168, 176, 281, 285, 291

Cosmic Trinity, 21, 179, 285

D

Determine the Facing, 160, 161

Divorce, 2, 9, 11, 12, 33–36,
   38–43, 45–48, 55, 56, 60, 158,
   170, 171, 185, 186, 188–190,
   195, 199, 201, 203, 207, 210,
   211, 213, 214, 222, 223, 225,
   226, 230, 234, 235, 238, 239,
   241, 244, 247, 249, 254, 257,
   258, 260, 261, 264, 267, 270,
   272, 278, 283

E

Eight Guas, 19, 20, 27, 289
Eight Killing Forces, 170, 188,
   201, 207, 219, 238, 249, 255,
   267, 286, 292
Eight Mansions, 2, 45, 46, 50,
   51, 53, 55, 56, 61–67, 153,
   158, 166, 167, 172, 175, 233,
   282, 283, 286, 288–292, 295,
   297, 298
Eight Roads of Destruction, 36,
   170, 185, 188, 195, 198, 202,
   207, 210, 213, 219, 222, 225,
   230, 235, 238, 244, 246, 247,
   249, 254, 257, 260, 267, 270,
   272, 278, 286

F

Five Elements, 2, 22, 24, 25, 298
Five Yellow, 170, 171

G

Goat Blade Water, 40, 170, 185,
   188, 198, 202, 210, 213, 222,
   225, 235, 238, 247, 249, 257,
   261, 270, 272
Grand Duke, 170, 171
Gua, 2, 15, 16, 19, 23, 26–28, 30,
   45, 56, 58–60, 63–153, 159,
   167, 177, 179, 185, 189, 190,
   193, 194, 196, 197, 199, 200,
   202–205, 208, 211, 214, 217,
   218, 220, 222, 223, 226–229,
   231, 236, 238, 239, 241, 242,
   244, 245, 247, 250, 253–255,
   258, 259, 261, 264, 265, 267,
   270, 273, 275, 277, 278, 282–
   286, 288–293, 297, 299, 302

H

He Tu, 22–24

L

Life Gua Zodiac Personalities
   1 Gua as a Rat, 68
   1 Gua as a Tiger, 69
   1 Gua as a Rabbit, 71
   1 Gua as a Snake, 73
   1 Gua as a Horse, 74

1 Gua as a Monkey, 76

1 Gua as a Rooster, 77

1 Gua as a Pig, 79

2 Gua as a Rat, 80

2 Gua as a Tiger, 82

2 Gua as a Rabbit, 83

2 Gua as a Snake, 85

2 Gua as a Horse, 86

2 Gua as a Monkey, 88

2 Gua as a Rooster, 89

2 Gua as a Pig, 91

3 Gua as an Ox, 93

3 Gua as a Dragon, 94

3 Gua as a Goat, 96

3 Gua as a Dog, 98

4 Gua as a Rat, 99

4 Gua as a Tiger, 101

4 Gua as a Rabbit, 102

4 Gua as a Snake, 104

4 Gua as a Horse, 105

4 Gua as a Monkey, 107

4 Gua as a Rooster, 109

4 Gua as a Pig, 110

6 Gua as an Ox, 112

6 Gua as a Dragon, 113

6 Gua as a Goat, 115

6 Gua as a Dog, 117

7 Gua as a Rat, 119

7 Gua as a Tiger, 121

7 Gua as a Rabbit, 122

7 Gua as a Snake, 124

7 Gua as a Horse, 125

7 Gua as a Monkey, 127

7 Gua as a Rooster, 128

7 Gua as a Pig, 130

8 Gua as a Rat, 132

8 Gua as a Tiger, 133

8 Gua as a Rabbit, 135

8 Gua as a Snake, 136

8 Gua as a Horse, 138

8 Gua as a Monkey, 139

8 Gua as a Rooster, 141

8 Gua as a Pig, 143

9 Gua as an Ox, 145

9 Gua as a Dragon, 147

9 Gua as a Goat, 149

9 Gua as a Dog, 150

Luo Shu, 2, 22–24, 27, 291

Luo Pan, 28–31, 281, 285, 290, 291

M

Mirrors, 47, 48, 172, 285

Move-in Date, 3, 160, 162, 165

P

Parent String Formation, 180, 195, 292

Peach Blossom Direction, 175, 176

Peach Blossom Technique, 3, 175, 181, 293

Peach Blossom Sha, 37, 38, 40, 42, 170, 174, 175, 181, 188, 192, 195, 201, 205, 207, 213, 216, 219, 225, 228, 230, 238, 241, 244, 249, 252, 255, 260, 264, 267, 272, 275, 278, 293

Pearl String Formation, 178, 254, 293

Period 7, 162, 166, 167, 178–180, 233, 234, 237, 240, 243, 246, 248, 249, 251, 252, 254, 256, 257, 259, 263, 266, 269, 271, 272, 274, 277, 293

Period 8, 159, 162, 164–167, 169, 178–180, 183, 184, 187, 190, 191, 194, 197, 200, 204, 206, 209, 212, 215, 216, 218, 221, 224, 227, 229, 233, 237, 240, 243, 263, 266, 282, 293

Physiognomy, 16, 17

Precious and Jewel Line, 293

R

Renovation Taboos, 172

T

Tantric Sex, 9, 10, 295

Tao Hua, 174

Three Harmony Doorways, 3, 172, 180, 181, 296

Three Killings, 170, 171

T-Juncture, 38, 39, 42, 185, 296

Trigram, 23, 159, 282–285, 288, 289, 299

W

Western Feng Shui, 173, 174, 298

Y

Yap, Cheng Hai, 11, 17, 58

GET MORE AT LLEWELLYN.COM

Visit us online to browse hundreds of our books and decks, plus sign up to receive our e-newsletters and exclusive online offers.

- **Free tarot readings • Spell-a-Day • Moon phases**
- **Recipes, spells, and tips • Blogs • Encyclopedia**
- **Author interviews, articles, and upcoming events**

GET SOCIAL WITH LLEWELLYN

Find us on

www.Facebook.com/LlewellynBooks

Follow us on

www.Twitter.com/Llewellynbooks

GET BOOKS AT LLEWELLYN

LLEWELLYN ORDERING INFORMATION

Order online: Visit our website at www.llewellyn.com to select your books and place an order on our secure server.

Order by phone:
- Call toll free within the U.S. at 1-877-NEW-WRLD (1-877-639-9753)
- Call toll free within Canada at 1-866-NEW-WRLD (1-866-639-9753)
- We accept VISA, MasterCard, and American Express

Order by mail:
Send the full price of your order (MN residents add 6.875% sales tax) in U.S. funds, plus postage and handling to: Llewellyn Worldwide, 2143 Wooddale Drive, Woodbury, MN 55125-2989

POSTAGE AND HANDLING:

STANDARD: (U.S. & Canada)
(Please allow 12 business days)
$25.00 and under, add $4.00.
$25.01 and over, FREE SHIPPING.

INTERNATIONAL ORDERS (airmail only):
$16.00 for one book, plus $3.00 for each additional book.

Visit us online for more shipping options. Prices subject to change.

FREE CATALOG!

To order, call
1-877-
NEW-WRLD
ext. 8236
or visit our
website

Classical

Feng Shui

for

Wealth &
Abundance

Activating Ancient Wisdom
for a Rich & Prosperous Life

MASTER DENISE LIOTTA DENNIS

Classical Feng Shui for Wealth & Abundance
Activating Ancient Wisdom for a Rich & Prosperous Life
MASTER DENISE LIOTTA DENNIS

Unlock your full wealth potential using the ancient wisdom of classical Feng Shui. Written by a Feng Shui master, this book delivers authentic techniques and closely held secrets for leveraging success with money, careers, relationships, health, and all aspects of life.

Unlike the over-simplified Western school of Feng Shui, you'll find genuine, wealth-building formulas practiced by highly-trained masters, as well as today's successful business moguls, like Donald Trump. These easy-to-follow, powerful techniques and tips apply to everything from choosing a site to designing your space inside and out. Discover how to work with your personal Gua number and your building's natal chart. Use get-rich keys and avoid causes of money depletion. Whether you're designing or building an apartment, house, or high-rise, these practical guidelines apply to any home or business.

978-0-7387-3353-1, 336 pp., 6 x 9   **$17.99**

Feng Shui for Beginners
Successful Living by Design
RICHARD WEBSTER

Not advancing fast enough in your career? Maybe your desk is located in a "negative position." Wish you had a more peaceful family life? Hang a mirror in your dining room and watch what happens. Is money flowing out of your life rather than into it? You may want to look to the construction of your staircase!

For thousands of years, the ancient art of feng shui has helped people harness universal forces and lead lives rich in good health, wealth, and happiness. The basic techniques in *Feng Shui for Beginners* are very simple, and you can put them into place immediately in your home and work environments. Gain peace of mind, a quiet confidence, and turn adversity to your advantage with feng shui remedies.

978-1-56718-803-5, 224 pp., 5³⁄₁₆ x 8   **$13.95**

101 Feng Shui Tips For Your Home
Book 1 of the "Feng Shui Series"
RICHARD WEBSTER

Shape your home for harmony. From deep contentment to financial and romantic success, you will feel the difference feng shui can make in your life. If you are in the market for a house, learn what to look for in room design, single level versus split level, staircases, front door location, and more. To improve your existing home, find out how its current design may be creating negative energy and uncover simple ways to remedy the situation without the cost of major renovations or remodeling. Put feng shui to work in your own home today and discover the harmonious future that awaits you.

978-1-56718-809-7, 192 pp., 5³⁄₁₆ x 8   **$11.95**

FENG SHUI
FOR YOUR
APARTMENT

R I C H A R D   W E B S T E R

Feng Shui For Your Apartment
Book 2 of the "Feng Shui Series"
RICHARD WEBSTER

Make the most of your condo, studio apartment, or dorm room. No matter what the size of your living space is, you can turn it into a magnet for good luck, prosperity, and peace—at little or no expense. This book will show you the subtle changes you can make to improve the harmony and balance in your apartment.

Learn what to look for when selecting an apartment and how to protect yourself from energy-zapping "shars" that might be directed at your apartment or building. Discover the single most important piece of furniture in a studio apartment and how repositioning it will improve the quality of your life. You will also learn how to conduct a feng shui evaluation for others.

978-1-56718-794-6, 160 pp., 5³⁄₁₆ x 8   **$9.95**

FENG SHUI
in
5 MINUTES

SELENA SUMMERS

Feng Shui in Five Minutes
Selena Summers

The world's most easy-to-use guide to feng shui!

To prosper, is it better to live in a small house in a wealthy area or a large house in a less expensive area? How can a radio, television set, or computer be a feng shui cure? What are the luckiest shapes for blocks of land?

These are just three of the many questions you'll find answered in *Feng Shui in Five Minutes*. Learn intriguing no-cost methods to improve your luck, a mystic way to hurry house sales, ancient techniques to win more dates, the Nine Celestial Cures, common feng shui faults, and much more.

978-0-7387-0291-9, 216 pp., 5³⁄₁₆ x 8   **$12.95**
